Collected Poems

Alan Stephens

COLLECTED POEMS

1958–1998

Edited by A.A. Stephens

Dowitcher Press
Santa Barbara, California

Acknowledgments are given to the original publishers.

Copyright 2012 by A.A. Stephens

alanstephenspoems.com

All rights reserved
Printed in the United States of America

Cover art: Tom Stephens
Book design and composition:
Valerie Brewster, Scribe Typography

ISBN 978-0-9857812-1-7 (hardback)
ISBN 978-0-9857812-0-0 (paper)

3 5 7 9 8 6 4 2
FIRST PRINTING

Dowitcher Press
www.dowitcherpress.com

For Fran

Contents

The White Boat

(1995)

───────

I

LONG SHADOW TIME

II

SOME MOUNTAIN POEMS

III

OVER AT THE ACADEMY

IV

FAR FROM YOSHITOSHI

V

TWO WOMEN IN THE MIDDLE DISTANCE

VI

ODD PAIR

Water Among the Stones

ALONG THE MATILIJA

(1987)

In Plain Air

(1982)

TOAD SWEAT

RUNNING AT HENDRY'S

from *Tree Meditation and Others*

(1970)

———————

The Heat Lightning

(1967)

from *Between Matter and Principle*

(1963)

from *The Sum*

(1958)

White River Poems

(1976)

Collected Poems

Away from the Road

(1998)

FRAGMENT ON A THEME BY AUSONIUS

Remembering early fall evenings on the Upper North Fork, Matilija

… now that the evening star is bringing on
earlier the day's last light and its shadows,
how many minutes more will that calm reach
hold the bright tan hillside? and the dark bay leaves
make dark bay leaves on the surface along the bank
of a pool there? and toyon berries, dead ripe by now and
hanging by the fistful, put their redness in your riffles …?

THE TEACHER

Don't be a fool, leave the important things,
Always, unsaid: you owe this courtesy
To all the good ones—give them the chance to hear them
Not being said (they are the ones that see
The swift elated bold activity
    Of the angels as tall as the letters
Of the words in the poems you're reading—shine of wings
    Banking through O's, past A's…).

As for the one whose brain's not seated right,
And all the rest—keep them well off from their betters
With a poker face, that none may be aware
(All souls must loom the same size in your sight).
What will you give the rest for occupation?
    Shovel them information
(Which for the good ones spills out here and there
    A gem-stone in a blaze).

Item in the paper:
'In people over sixty the
sweat glands have begun
to deteriorate.' It is
yet another touch
on the hair-trigger
of this horror at what
has been happening
to him.
       How quietly
the small disasters arrive
and form up in this
irreversible disaster
old age. Every change
now, is for the worse.
'There's no future in it,'
he jokes to a smooth-faced
young friend, knowing they belong
to different species now.

He'd been thinking
about the young waiter in
the Hemingway tale,
who declares, 'An old man
is a nasty thing.' The kid's
exasperated: it's closing
time, his girlfriend
is waiting for him. The old
man, the one remaining
patron, quite drunk, has,
with his dignity
intact, just ordered
another brandy. The older

of the two waiters defends
the old man, quietly
and well. The other, not
disputing him, serving
the old man his one more
brandy, sticks to
his own opinion.

He folds up the newspaper.
Nothing to be done
but make 'Spinoza's
laconic agreement to
conspire with necessity,'
phrasing he had copied
(from whom? he's forgotten)
years ago into a notebook.
As for the knowledge and
wisdom of old age, such as
they may be, their basis
and most of their substance
he had built up, well
before he was old, back
when thoughts and perceptions
came at propitious times
unsought-for, quick and clear.…

Mid-July, down the back-country
streamside trail
he loved most, the stream
slow and low, mid-day
air quivering
above the scrub, how
he'd pour sweat, soak
his heavy belt clear through.

July 21, 1994

WATCHING THE SHOREBIRDS THAT WINTER HERE

... the limits and the lack
Set in their finished features.
—W.H. AUDEN

They are exactly
as intelligent as

they need to be, to
be what they are: having

limits, but no lack,
in their physical

perfection, each is, in
each detail, on close

inspection a wonder and
matter-of-fact. *Clear-*

ly clearly clearly cry
some curlews flying by

us assorted humans here.

BACK IN 1946–47

We'd turn first to those poems by him,
when the new issue came out, though knowing
they would just be studies of flowers—
brief, accurate, vivid—different
individual flowers, their shapes, their
positions and balancings on their stems,
small movements special to them, the varying

gradations of light and shadow
to be watched for in their interiors—
quick-moving, elegant poems, though.

He was one of the crowd of us vets
on campuses right after the war.
He kept to the edges, was of us
but not among us. His laconic
observations—offered quietly with
his hands in his pockets as always
(we never saw him with a book)—were admired,
not least for their genial and ever-
inventive use of the meager stock
of the stale obscenities in soldier talk.

None of us could say just when
he left that campus, on its hill
above the then pleasant city,
across which we could see, through
the then clear air, the blue Rockies
looking near. You could find his poems
back there, in the library basement files—
that is, if the files still exist.

May, 1994

UNTITLED

Han Shan, old, in three poems
has written my own life for me
and left me with nothing to do.

TWO PIECES OUT OF A WINTER MORNING

I. UP CLOSE

On the far side of the crossing
Where the stream swung under a cliff
There was a big boulder, roughly the shape
Of a bull bison lying down.

A low-leaning oak shades it in the heat
Of summers up there. Winter sunlight (often subtle,
As there, in its treatment of what it crosses)
Reached in and warmed it a bit on the south end.

It was a stopping-place. That day he only paused
And keeping his pack on leaned with a bare hand
On the shoulder of stone at the north end. The cold
Stored inside it from last night went into his palm.

He saw for the first time that the stone
With its dark iron tones, deep in chill shadow,
Bore a crop of lichens, round patches, with edgings,
Flower-like in many shades of subdued

Yet luminous grays. Among them grew irregular plots
Of moss, some olive-green and very bright, even
In that shade, some a fresh brownish green, in velvety
Low mounds: a sort of park for the eye to wander in

For a moment or so. He let be, those days, the enigma
He'd studied for years—the attraction that all
The boulders up here have exerted on him, in all
Their shapes and sizes: say, showing their backs
In the rapids and slow runs of the streams,
Or flood-crammed onto canyon floors, or poised,
Huge and single on the slopes (one over a pool
He used to fish), or choking the side-gulches,

Or standing here and there in the open grassy places,
Or paired and flanking the trail at one bend he knew.

2. OVER THE FENCE

You went in between big orange groves
On the way up there. The trees,
Standing in long straight rows
Each row and each tree in it
Spaced the same, were once
Skillfully tended. Neglected later,
Yellowing, some of them
Already dead, they were some more
Speculative real estate, though that morning
As he drove through they were still
Sending equidistant shadows
Aslant over the black-top, between which
The low-going sun had laid flush a row
Of wide palings, pure light: they hurt his eyes,
One after another flashing an instant
Before vanishing smoothly under the tires.

Mid-December, 1993

HIGH SUMMER

She moved so fast
sometimes—in the house
and out and back in
in one rush—but unruffled—
just from her usual
abounding energy
that one time
the dog sat up
and began barking
from sheer excitement.

UNDER CRICKET MUSIC

A fragment

1

Crickets from where the hill is steep
And dark under the oaks across the street
Keep up a clear and brilliant *threep—threep—threep,*
   A little harsh, with a quick beat,
Filtering through trees the jounce of harness bells,
These late fall nights, somehow, from some place else—

2

Some time else. I remember, though,
Mainly the sound, with much else fallen away,
Leaving nostalgia with no place to go.
   A team heading home, end of the day.
Would the small bright bells chink from tugs, or hames,
   Or bridles—I don't know.
I cannot even recall the horses' names....

3

At a small hour I again awake;
In the live silence one cricket's creaking on
Slowly, now, muted, but without a break.
   He's quiet when I wake at dawn:
Trim bit of reality for in between
   Dreams, and oblivion,
That take their turns all night on the inner scene.

4

Oblivion that slides in, recedes,
Slides in, all the while floating all that is,
Is best of all—'Come, sleep,' come dark that feeds
   Into the veins cool nothingness—

The old poets, broken, wrote their loveliest
        That the god might dip misdeeds,
Fears, all, in the deep sleep of the old psychopannychist—

5

        And yet just yesterday I fought
Afternoon drowsiness off to watch how each
        Curt stroke of Nicholas of Cusa's thought
        Bore him on, into a bright reach
Where Infinite and Finite co-inhered
        And the mere world on a taut
And shining gossamer of wisdom reappeared....

6

        A rocks-crawling-with-rattlers dream,
Dream where each act, as Clausewitz said of war,
Is simple, and very difficult; trout stream
        I know I've visited before
(But where?) flowing opaque with sewage; gray
        Steep vacant street, dark store
And office in a strange, vast city where I stray

7

        Dread-filled, and what am I doing there—
And my son is a puny baby, putting by
His pitiful few possessions with great care
        Next to him, on the rug. As I
Laugh hard, he crawls off, thin-limbed, spirited,
        On his own, to disappear
Through a dark opening, sloping below his bed—

[left unfinished]

ca. 1979; August 23, 1996

Last night I lay awake
From some sound in the night
And pictured I could take
(Knowing that I could not)
The firm and quiet way
Of the gentle monk Gensei,
Who watched from his Grass Hill
(Three hundred years away)
Beneath a favorite tree,
Or from his leaky hut,
Travels of crow, cloud, sail;
With some food and wine
Welcomed the always rare
Visit from old friends; wrote
His poems, though unwell
Much of the time; read; gave
Lessons, again while sick,
Kept clear of pedantry
(And all he wrote of it
Rings true of it today),
With his goose-foot walking stick
To keep him company
Took walks, kept his mind free
And agile as the air,
Transcending tragedy,
Under his bent old pine
With writing brush in hand
Quiet at close of day
Saw out the evening sun
Across the shadowy land.

~

Slight rustlings in a tree
And a slow car going by
Returned me to what's mine,
What it had all come to,
What I still had to do
With my own dwindling days.

HERDERS MOVING A FLOCK DOWN HIGHWAY 395

A thousand sheep crowding the mountain road
Make it look like a dirty-foam-capped river
In this dim light. They've blocked the truck ahead.
His double chrome exhaust pipes snort and quiver.

He needs to be getting on, and so do I,
And all those headlights behind us, stopped at dawn.
The road is narrow, the mountain stops the eye
Rightward, thin air on the left goes on and on.

Sleepy, hatless, uncombed, after a night on the ground
In the clothes they're wearing, two herders amble
Behind the flock, and the three dogs in sight
Keep the flanks neat—make a rare laggard scramble.

What leads the flock is a burro, while a third
Man wades along in their midst—now and then waves
A bough torn from a bay tree over the herd.
Dew soaks their wool and the dark, fresh bay leaves.

Across the blat and clatter, through the daze
Of recent sleep he sees us apparitions
With a wide, flashing, and incurious gaze
Now that we creep past in our own conditions.

Now that we creep past in our own conditions
And catch in the dawn, along with the ancient moral
Of simple sheep, and shepherds, and our ambitions,
Reek of damp wool, pungency of torn laurel.

Early summer, 1982; August, 1996

A MEMORIAL IN THE NEIGHBORHOOD

It is a young oak tree and a stone
with a bronze plaque in it, for
a boy who lived all his life
in a house up the street from ours,
near the park entrance-road. He died in
his room over the garage, a suicide.

His mother had her memorial for him
placed on a piece of ground scraped bare
and packed hard, in the weedy area
at the upper end of the park,
between the creek and a trailhead
where you start out for the back-country.

We never knew, but knew of
the family. I glimpsed the father once—
handsome, dark-haired. Took off when the boy
was small, and the brothers grown
and gone; among the cousins and uncles
were artists and actors; some widely known.

The boy himself was a painter,
quiet and shyly friendly
the one time when I met him. After
his death we would see his mother
now and then, for a year or so,
then she sold the house and left.

In her grief (I'm supposing) she left the choice
of a stone and the placement of the plaque
to the stonemason. It's a puzzle
that the man should botch that simple job: why choose
an unshapely, lopsided stone? and then set
the plaque in violently askew?

Later, somebody in the mix
of the people using a public park—some one
of those whose furtive doings make for
that slight, pervading taint of evil
in the air of a park: as here, over the boulders, the creek,
and trees and grassy open places—someone

took the trouble to batter a big chunk
off that poor specimen of a stone.
So it stands there now, in a place where boulders
of all sizes abound in a variety of fine
rounded shapes, tablet shapes, shapes of mountains
in miniature with ledges, hollows, cliffs; and then,

a back-country peak stands over us all
down here, in our houses deep in trees, and for
situation, and shape, this peak is a match
for Fuji, I swear; and mornings, ocean air,
evenings, canyon air, moves in the trees here, it's all
a garden here, violated variously, but a garden.

~

The words the mother chose for
the plaque could not be more plain.

*This tree was planted
in memory of*

then the name and the two dates—one morning
I stood there and did the subtraction
in my head, getting the number of years,
months, and days that the boy lived.

The young oak has grown tall now, straight-stemmed,
well above the thick stakes it is held between,
its crown shapely, its leaves rich dark green
with the special shine all living things have in
their youth. Around it its elders lean, in their contortions
from crowding, as is their nature; fallen limbs under them.

~

This Christmas, as on every Christmas,
now, for fourteen years, decorations have appeared
on the tree. I went up there early
one weekday morning, when nobody
would be around. I wanted the time
to study them and not get stared at.

A huge bow of shiny red plastic is tied
on the trunk this time. Globes covered with some
shiny synthetic fiber hang from the branches:
twenty-three red ones, two blue, and in no
discernible arrangement, have hung there weeks, now,
past the holiday season, fraying and fading, in

this winter's rainstorms. They'll be taken down,
always have been. They don't get forgotten about:
the choice, arrangement, and handling of them do not
matter, Taste doesn't matter, behind them being
the grief that stays on, alive, under whatever
the rest may be by which living gets done.
There to be visited, on its occasions.

December 18, 1994

THREE STUDIES FROM TWO DAYS

The Upper North Fork, Matilija, 1986

1. LATE IN THE DAY

Part of the thin shadow
    of a weed stem
Cutting the trail solidified
    into a lizard
And ran away, still
    shadow-colored.

2. PHOTOGRAPHING AN UNCOMMON WILDFLOWER

Now it's been found.
Shapely and fresh dark blue,
    Fine-stemmed, neat-leaved,
    On the baked-white ground—
A subject, magnified, swaying there
    In its prime,
    A foot away,
    Difficult still
To catch, on this dry, stony, steep hill
    (That would kill
    Its garden cousins in no time).

You lean, shaken with late-in-the-day
    Fatigue, and with one knee
    Wedged between rocks, one eye
    At the eye-piece, water-blurred
    By the hot breeze,
    The other shut tight, by
    Sweat and two crawling flies
    Whose cohorts whirl above—
    You'll wait till it holds still …

Unlikely place for both flower and you
    To choose (all but absurd
      For you to love).
Still, there you both are, each in your way
    (By reflex) hopeful, too.
    The least breeze shakes your prize,
      In its brief stay,
      As naturally
    As fatigue and more shake you
      At sixty-two....

3. THE LIZARDS OF LIZARD FLAT

Just ahead of us they run, stop, run, stop, their transit
Building a structure light and elegant,
    Jointed with pauses,

Extending itself in segments (with time out
For slewing sidewise to look back at the humans)
    Like shooting bamboo.

A PULL-OUT BY THE SESPE

For years this stream ran clear.
I'd fish it alone, all day.
Then came the long drought. Now
we stand in the familiar
dirt pull-out, drinking coffee.
When the off-and-on breeze hits,
two young cottonwoods begin stirring
on the near bank, half their branches
still green, the others yellow.
We watch their all-over shivery
hard twinkling leaves
throwing off flakes and

sharp flicks of light, at all
angles, continuously: all the while
the leaves send out their sounds
of running water, as if in recollection
of the stream they grew up by; which is
now silent—dusty stones, weeds. Someone
has hung a jumbo empty
Frito bag carefully
on a bush on the far bank.

AWAY FROM THE ROAD

1. FOR A GREAT BASIN BRISTLECONE PINE

For picking a high place,
unsheltered; using shattered rock
to thread roots through to the poor and
shallow soil; strong at extremes: in
relentless winds, only a few
cushion-plants for company
on the last ridge twisting up, up
aslant in thin bright-blue air,
slow swerves in its multiple
twistings, in its grain its warm
colors staying fresh in this dry cold
through the centuries—tree that is one wild contortion
from its sprawled-out clenched-down root system
half-bared by erosion, to the snag
of its tip, single existence in
among existences which sustain
and assail it at the same time: what else
is there to be found—you cannot
imagine the nothingness of the before
and after—you get no further than
the silence of stone, of a standing bristlecone

in the terrific fixity of its achieved exertions.
Still there is a certain casualness in
its leaning into open space, and
in its reach for air and light up here
there's eagerness not anguish. You see it
in the jaunty half-twirl of
the barkless twig at the top.

2. FOR THE ASPENS AND COTTONWOODS
    UP ON BIG PINE CREEK

Just the one branch lifts,
hesitates, and subsides
in small splashings of light.

~

Half-waking in hemlock shade
he lies listening, eyes still shut:
is it the voice of a young woman
that he hears upstream? But it goes on
earnestly, eagerly, the tones
explanatory, never pausing
for a breath, never varying
in volume: they are water-sounds.
He opens his eyes and sees
three aspens full of light,
one of them against the dark
of an old pine, all three quiet
at the moment. Onset of boredom
both with the sounds of the creek
upstream and the aspens alike
involuntarily declaring themselves.
A faint breeze that hasn't yet
reached him strikes the trees, making
a kind of silent clinking

with fine spikes of light from
the leaves in movement....
Fairly good logs can be made
from aspens for barns and sheds,
also a good quality pulp, though
as fenceposts they rot out fast.
What they are best for is
catching light in high air
and sending it uselessly out. When
he walks over to these three,
he leaves the daylight,
and stands inside aspen light.

3. FOR THE UTAH JUNIPER

They find in ruins of the Anasazi
(the name in Navajo: the Vanished
Ones, Old Ones, Old Enemies)
juniper roof-beams, still sound,
juniper-bark torches. Slow growers,
roots fed into sandstone, the junipers
dot the scene to the horizon, holding their dark
over the pale rock; in summer light
lightless; grave green the year round,
stolid; tragic trees, for the long haul,
their coarse black blunt flame-shapes
leaving the sandy canyon bottoms
to the cottonwoods, those gleamers
and glisteners of brief summer,
quickly undone, stripped and stilled—
non-participants in the bitter winters.

There is much that's wondrous, much that awakens dread—
Nothing more so than the human, *Sophocles says,*
In the best description of us ever made:
This creature crosses the gray sea in the winter
With the storm-winds, making his way along
In the troughs of the billows,
And of all goddesses the one greatest, Earth
The undying, the tireless—he wears her down
With his plowing back and forth, year after year.

The light-witted race of the birds he takes,
And the tribes of the wild beasts, and the swimmers
Through sea-deeps, in the meshy folds of his nets,
This busy-thinking human.
With his tactics he masters the field-dwellers,
And the hill-ranging animals; shaggy-maned
Horses he reins in, he yokes the necks
Of the powerful bulls he brings down from the mountains.

And speech, and wind-quick thought, and living
In a city together, he taught himself, and how to avoid
The bolts of storms, and having to sleep out
In cold clear weather. He is all inventiveness.
Never does he go bereft of means into
The future. Death alone he cannot contrive to elude; though
From hopeless diseases he has found escapes.

Cleverness surpassing all hopes he possesses
In his plans and devices; by which sometimes to evil
Sometimes to excellence he creeps. Honoring
Earth and her laws, and the sworn justice
Of the gods, he may thrive in his city.—Shun him
When he harms what's good out of recklessness,
Shun the contagion of an arrogant cast of mind....

A LAST TIME

He still has poems to write
but that region of his mind
which got busy and mobilized
the words, will not budge now.

It's like an old saddle horse
that has stopped on his own.
The rider puts a heel
to the flank. The horse stands there,

then turns his head back around,
rolling an eye at his rider
as if to say, You ought to know
that if I could I'd go on.

THE FOX

In the year 1954 of a bygone era

Fall came and he took a leave
(certain he could not sit through
another graduate class—not
yet), wrote a bit, taught one class—
he liked to teach, they needed
the money he put with what
she earned at her office job.

He'd fish the small stream that ran
below the cliffs at the edge
of town. They ate what he caught;
ate the blackberries, soft-ripe
large ones, that grew at streamside.
They made some blackberry wine,
once, from a small bucketful.

And sometimes he went hunting.
He found a good single-shot
.22 in a cluttered
second-hand store outside town.
It was old but well cared-for—
smelt of gun-oil, and the bore
was bright, clear of corrosion.

Through friends who rented one floor
of a farmhouse out from town
a mile or so, he'd obtained
permission from the owner
to hunt on his land—squirrels,
the man said, had been raiding
the cornfield he'd not yet picked.

He parked in the yard at dawn
on the first day he hunted
and walked up a wagon road
that wound through leafless gray woods.
The trees were unfamiliar.
Once he had edged in among them—
he'd heard a squirrel chatter.

The trunks stood close together.
How the land lay further in,
he could neither see nor guess.
Another squirrel chattered
further in. He retreated
to the road, and felt relieved.
As he went on, the woods thinned.

In a clearing by the road
stood a small persimmon tree,
leafless in the reddish light,
the first one he'd ever seen.

He walked up the grassy slope
for a closer look. In the quiet
the bright fruit hung motionless.

He never saw another person,
nor a sign of one, back here,
nor even any livestock.
He had come out here in part,
he now knew, for the stillness.
There were no noises here—
only sounds, to be listened for.

~

Once his wife had come along
with him and a friend, hunting
at dusk, just outside the town.
The friend brought down a squirrel,
it ran off, he and the friend
lunged after it, stumbling, on
rocks and downed wood in deep leaves.

He recalled her clear laughter—
clear of derision: to her
the chase was pure comedy.…
That night they ate squirrel he
had shot. Like chicken, they said.
But no—an alien tang
which cooking, and seasoning,

could never quite get rid of
caused them an uneasiness
that, though slight, persisted
like the strong scent of the fresh
pelt still in the kitchen. And
bits of the underfur, pale,
hard to see, stuck to the meat.…

On one late November day
he came up the wagon-track
through the stands of long-bare trees,
mild sunlight came slanting in,
the different trunk-shadows
ahead of him were soft gray.
He stepped through shafts of the light.

He heard the far, crashing sounds
of squirrels making long leaps
through the leaves from trunk to trunk.
The persimmon tree stood now
stripped of fruit—the strong, thin twigs
stayed bent. The road left the woods
and turned, to follow the edge

of a bluff that overlooked
the farmer's bottom-land field—
light streaming through the ripe crop
made it buckskin-colored now.
A creek ran past the far edge
of the field, big sycamores
on the near bank caught the light.

The far bank, though, steep and dark,
dense with trees and undergrowth,
looked cold, dank, in its deep shade.
A breeze came up as he watched.
He heard the rattle and rasp
of the dry, sharp-edged, stiff leaves
of the corn. He walked on down

watching for any movement
that was not caused by the breeze,
went past the head of the field
to the creek. The breeze died down.

He'd seen crows, but no squirrels
except one pair that vanished,
high in an old sycamore.

~

He sat under that same tree,
on the stream-bank, his feet
dangling. He could hear water
going past slowly, hidden
under leaves, among the stones.
A clear, crescent-shaped pool lay
along the bank, just upstream.

The bank there was undercut.
The massive trunk of the tree
let down a tangle of roots
over the pool. The water,
motionless, mirrored the roots.
Leaves on the pale bottom-stones
lay draped, their colors still fresh.

For those few moments the place
had magical properties.
This stayed clear and fresh, for him,
from then on—the time of day,
and the season, did their part
no doubt, and that cold, dank slope,
and the bright field at his back.

The air stayed quiet. The day
would soon be cooling, a slow
flow of air would wind downstream,
its chill seep into the folds
of his clothes; but this air still
was mild. As he watched, the light
weakened on the chalky-white

undersides of two big limbs
the tree had sent out, level
and winding, over the creek.
The limbs remained motionless.
He listened to a trickle
of water dripping over
a rock ledge, somewhere below.

He heard a dry, light rustling
far up past the bend upstream.
For all its slightness, the sound
came to him clearly, the air
having been still for so long.
He looked upstream and waited.
What appeared around the bend

was a gray fox. It was tired,
and came on, down the center
of the streambed, at a slow
steady trot with its head low,
its tail level with its back.
It held its eyes straight ahead
as it drew near where he sat.

They were eyes dulled by fatigue.
Mud had soaked its legs, belly,
and flanks, and matted the long,
fine fur of the underside
of its plume. The fox went by
sparing itself the effort
of a glance aside at him,

and rounded the bend downstream.
He listened till the dwindling
rustle of leaves had died out,
and then he kept on listening

in the new stillness around
for some minutes. Well, he thought,
he has built up a good lead.

He pictured the fox moving
through the coming dusk and dark
downstream toward settled country.
He could not convincingly
see where the fox then might go.
He was getting up to leave
when he first heard the foxhounds.

The far-off, varied baying,
oddly melodious, came
drifting in through the stillness.
—Yes, they're a long way upstream.
And this creekbed that the fox
chose for its course, is a choice
course for a pack of foxhounds.

He did not stay on to watch
the pack go by. He gathered
his gun and rucksack and left,
glad he had brought a flashlight.
He knew this breed was tireless.
They'd stream past, wild-eyed, long ears
flapping, tails up and waving....

~

One mild spring evening two years
later, as the dusk thickened
toward darkness in the soft air,
he came back down to his car
as he'd done five or six times
since the day he saw the fox;
but this was for the last time.

He still carried the rifle,
from habit, and his liking
for it. But lately he'd come
just to take the track up there
between the trees, to the bluff,
then down to the creek, to see
how things were out there that day.

He had done all you did for
the degree. They were leaving
that place, for one with no woods
but plenty of cactus; then
on to a place with ocean,
and mountains. They settled there,
knew the mountain trails, the streams,

knew shores after winter storms
left them stony, driftwood-strewn;
knew the salt-marshes, russet
in winter, where shore-birds came
from the far north. Certain days
they've had there stay in his mind,
none more detailed, none clearer,

than the day he saw the fox.

August 11, 1996

Note: The ancient Greeks saw that such places were sacred and had a goddess. You disregarded her at your peril. She was Artemis, and as my *Oxford Classical Dictionary* words it, 'her proper sphere is the earth, and specifically the uncultivated parts, forests, and hills, where wild beasts are plentiful.' Not to have been able to spend sufficient time appropriately in such places would have made me waste away in the other phases of my life.

REFLECTING POOL

Time: the middle hours of a day in late December

*I, who love walking, and who always hated riding, who am fond
of some society, but never had spirits that would endure a great deal,
could not, as you perceive, be better situated.*

—WILLIAM COWPER, *THE LETTERS...*,
(EVERYMAN LIBRARY NO. 774, p. 201)

The sound of a waterfall down below
had made him turn off the trail; now
he was working his way down,
crouching to get under low
branches, shoving aside or
snapping off the smaller stuff,
his boots skidding, his cap
snatched off once, his pack
twice lodging against a limb,
stopping him dead with a jolt,
making him bend even lower
to go on. He was sliding sidewise
when the falls and its big pool
came into sight. He was here
for the first time.
                    Just below him,
a boulder sunk into the slope would do
for a seat with the vantage-point
he wanted, once he'd found stones
to fill a wide cleft in it
and cleared away some intruding
thin branches and twigs.

~

He eased off his pack and sat, still
catching his breath. He'd come out
near the foot of the pool, where the ripples
were pushing upstream in shallow arcs

evenly spaced. The waterfall was bright white,
small and steady. It dropped from the V
formed by a pair of big, clean boulders
up above. *And it can't be improved upon,*
he thought.
           He was out of sight
from the trail above, and from the far bank
where the slope was steep and the trees
and the undergrowth too dense for a hiker
to force. He was alone with the place.

He worked out of his pack the box
he'd squeezed a big sandwich into.
He positioned three river-stones on
the slope, to set the box upon. It was almost
level. He drew out his thermos, steadied it
between his boots, and with the edge
of a piece of flat, thin sandstone
that had broken cleanly, loosened
and levelled the soil between two rocks,
unscrewed the thermos cup, and pressed
the rounded bottom into the ground,
rotating it back and forth, to make a socket
for the cup to stand in; and then slowly
filled the cup with coffee. He replaced
the stopper and laid the thermos on the slope,
its base against a boulder. There was no spot
to stand it on. Then he ate, and watched
the yellow leaves revolving at the lower end
of the pool. They went counterclockwise. Those
in front of him travelled upstream, then swerved
back across the water, rejoining the main current
where it drove against, then along, the far bank. Then,
slowing and swinging on back around, the leaves
came toward him on the quiet water. Alder leaves,
brilliant where sunlit, bright in the shadows.

The whole place lay held in the water-fall noise.

~

He would come up alone to see
what the day here would be like
this time, on this or the other
branch of the little river.
He had been doing so since the days
when few people came up here. He still
liked the hidden edge of danger
here, and the change from the useful
and not so useful routines
at home. As he walked along
taking in things around, his mind
might, on its own, work at some
persisting difficulty in some of
his reading, or in some writing,
and the lacking thing arrive by itself,
he getting it down without delay,
having learned that his memory could
not be trusted with it. The other day
he had read in Aubrey that Hobbes
when at work on *Leviathan*
often took walks and kept a pen
and inkhorn in the head of
his walking-staff, so that when 'a
notion darted,' he could write it
down, on the spot.

—Coming up here
was no escape from any
bad time he was having. He'd learned
that the bad time tagged along.

He liked walking up here
with his wife, with his sons,
with a friend or friends.
When you are here with others,
the place is the occasion and
being with others is the event.
Those were good times.
Memories of them stayed
lively. Always his need
to go up here alone was
for the place itself. In time
it became a physical need.

~

Within the water-noise he was hearing the *buzz-buzz*
of some small bird. He couldn't identify it. Now, still
buzzing, the bird approached in stages, keeping hidden,
causing no movements of the leaves that might
give away its position, but keeping on the move and
both scolding him and sending out the news
of his presence here.
    No voices, no other
sounds from above of people going by
up on the trail. The U.S. Forest Service built
the trail, he reminded himself. Trail that leads on
into these mountains—and then on back
down to the narrow dirt road, that takes
you down to the locked gate, where the blacktop
begins, that takes you winding back
down toward.... His sense of things here today
was temporary. Well, so was any sense of things.
He thought of the phrase 'the lightning flash
of reality' in a van Gogh letter.

~

One soft
spring day many years back, he was on
the trail along the main fork, nearing
a stretch of the stream he considered his.
You reached it by a hard-to-make-out
way through the scrub. He told no one
about it, he'd never seen anyone else
on it. The stream was beautiful, and it had
many trout in it.
Out of view in his pack
was his new pack-rod, and his other tackle,
all of it first rate. It had taken him years
to get it all together, one item
at a time, mostly. The day before,
a dozen trout-flies had been delivered
Air Mail, Special Delivery, just
in time. They rested now in the clear box
they came in, next to his reel, in the pack
(he kept all his tackle out of sight
until he got down to the stream)
and his mind was on them. They had come
from Livingston, Montana. They were tied
by local women, mostly middle-aged,
sitting at long benches. One year
there had been a photograph of them
in the catalog. The flies were packed
and shipped (by another such woman,
maybe) upon the arrival of his order,
check enclosed. The money it was
that brought them. His dozen
Royal Wulffs had come bobbing down
from Dan Bailey's on a rivulet
of money—liquidity, that was
the lingo; cash flow, that his job had
turned into; job he was, well, spending
his life in. He saw the whole

country afloat on money. All things were
soaked in it (including money
itself) so that from them money
could be squeezed. A great convenience,
no doubt. Too bad about its power
to pervert.... *On such a day
as this, in such a place—what a topic,*
he'd thought, his eye alert once again
to any slight change portending
danger to the place: this narrow
road, grassy and weedy down
the middle, dwindling vaguely into
the trail up ahead, was a great threat....

He had turned off and made his way
down toward the stream, easing through
the stiff, abrasive chaparral, clambering
over boulders, crossing several gullies.
He was fifty miles from home. Inventing
the wheel, Ford Madox Ford had written,
was where we had gone wrong. He'd laughed
when he read that. It had come to seem,
some forty years later, his consideration
of it fitfully persisting, plausible.
He tried to recall the title of that book.

~

He was midway through lunch when he saw
the quick indistinct movement, deep in the pool.
Getting out his binoculars he soon found
the two trout: six-inchers, like twins.
The floating leaves made excellent cover for
the pair moving slowly below them. Their bodies,
being the green of the clear green sunny water,
looked translucent, their shadows were inconspicuous
among the shadows of the leaves and of the flat

stones on the sandy bottom. He watched the pair
hover, and then cruise, with an easy flick
of fin shifting direction, assured and
unhurried among the shifting pillars of
the shadows of floating alder leaves.

He no longer fished. His tackle stayed in its cabinet.
One day soon he'd divide it among his sons.
They could cut cards to settle any disputes. Now
he was content with just coming up here.

It was one of those places that has
a radiance of its own. You could see it
when your state of attention was right.

~

The whole pool was lying in one cold shadow.
He replaced the empty thermos and box
in the pack, worked the binoculars back
into their case, and passing the strap over
his head, hung it over his right shoulder so that
the binoculars rested on his left hip. He hoisted
the pack and shrugged into it, buckling
the waist-belt, tightening the shoulder-straps.
The pack had some weight to it. He always carried
what he would need if for any reason
he should have to spend the night up here.
He secured the binoculars to the waist-belt
with a thong, buckled the chest-strap, turned
away from the pool and its waterfall, fought
his way back up to the trail, and once again
headed back down into what lay outspread below.

December 19, 1994

Note: The title of Ford's book is *Great Trade Route.*

A SIP OF THE MANZANA

A long time since he'd been here,
and now, it was against
doctor's orders ('… and stay out
of the heat …'). He had come up
through the deep sand of the trail,
at mid-day, through the dry
fiery air summers bring
up here. Back of him lay
the campground, where he'd parked,
two horse-trailers nearby,
and a single, sagging, small tent.

Now he slogged along, through
sand (loosened by hooves)
hot and white in the white
blaze of over-head sun,
and no movement of air,
his face heating up,
his skin staying dry—
only ten minutes
to the grove of big oak,
digger pine, cottonwood,
and the slow-shifting, black-
shadow shelter they gave.

Near a scatter of boulders
with air tremors above them,
in the dead grasses and weeds
and low, twisting shrubs
drought-stricken and prickly
on the rise he chose,
he sat eating his lunch,
taking drinks of ice-water
from a small thermos.
The plan: he would use

ten minutes to get here,
say twenty to eat
and take in what was here,
then ten more to return,
then drive back to the cool
blue of the coast. He stuck
with the plan.

       From his spot
on the rise, he looked at—no,
watched, a young digger pine,
slender, airy; sunlight slid
up and down its needles
whenever they moved. Nearby
stood its tall forebear, hung
with old, long-opened cones
in heavy, dark clumps,
their scales tipped with claws.
Beside it three sycamores
towered, limbs sprawling out
in the air, and a cottonwood
flickered—its glossy leaves
swivelling on those thin, flat
stems set at right angles
to the leaf surfaces—
they made a light clatter
as a lazy air movement
eased its way through the boughs,
and the digger pines hissed
and the sounds of the river
out of sight from this rise
came in more distinctly.
Now and then a bird crossed
from one tree to another
while keeping the silence
birds observe at mid-day
in the midsummer up here.

At his feet, under grass-stems
low-leaning, or snapped off
cleanly at the base, lying
full length in the dirt,
still sleek and bright-pale
in this shade, lay last year's
weather-discolored
cottonwood leaves, their
high polish ruined, though
some still showed as luminous
where brushed now by light
sifting down through the boughs
of the oak just above him.
The few oak leaves among them
had kept their dull brown—
weather-proof, tough—their
hard, convex surfaces
with clean, scalloped edges
gripping the ground
with the just-visible
sharp hooks at their tips.

Once a doctor, treating
some other affliction, had told him
'No alcohol' and thereupon
at the end of the day,
he would take one swallow
of no substitute, but
absolutely the real thing,
straight from the bottle,
in its full—if transient—
restorative powers
(then he let the ritual
lapse).—What had Saint Ben
said, in his shining iambics,
but the whole truth?—'In small

proportions we just
beauties see: and in
short measures, life
may perfect be....'

On that rise, with the great trees
around and above him
with their sounds and movements
and with them the distant,
fitful sound of the river,
he had entered a state
he'd not gone there to be in
(if he had, he would never
have entered it), and of which
he was not aware—was not able
to be—while in it. It was
something he'd know of,
and be able to visit,
*   only afterward.*

NAMES OF TROUT FLIES

Out of his mail, which was heavy
with catalogs, he pulled the early
spring numbers of the catalogs
of Orvis and Dan Bailey,
and on this gray day of this
bleak February turned to the pages
of splendid photographs in color
of the trout flies. Dan Bailey's
number lined them up in rows
of six, stacked seven high. Inset
on one page was a photograph
of a vast brown meadow backed by
mountains, light blue and with many peaks

tipped and streaked with snow. Barely
showing at the far edge of the meadow
was a thread-thin scratch of light:
the river over there.
                        The front half
of a heavy trout in close-up, speckled
jet-black on light green, loomed
in an inset on one Orvis page of nymphs.
A hand suspended the trout just above
a blur of rapid water. One clear drop
of that water was hanging midway
along the jutting jaw of the trout,
another from one knuckle of the hand.
The fly that the big trout had taken
had been removed. The hand was about
to release the trout.

                        ~

                        Glanced at,
they formed a fine, small spectacle,
the rows of trout flies. On impulse
he made a rough count: three hundred
or so flies across eight pages
in the Orvis. Dan Bailey showed,
across thirteen pages, around four
hundred fifty. The little order form
in the corner of one page was for a book
of patterns and materials for more
than a thousand classic and contemporary
flies.
     Without their names, the trout flies
would just be their exotic materials
tied together and trimmed—feathers
(Guinea, Peacock, Silver Pheasant, Jungle
Cock, etc.), hair (Northern Whitetail,
Coastal Deer, Yearling Elk, Antelope,

Moose Mane, etc.), specimens of fur,
of silk floss, of chenille (Regular,
Tinsel, Short Flash, Long Flash, Ultra),
French Wire (gold, silver, copper, in
Small, Medium, and Large), and so on.
The trout flies have their names, though.
Hard to match them for liveliness and
unexpectedness in certain sequences
or pairings the names come in: bright
miniature assemblages of the language
into not-quite-compositions, with
their fleeting intimations, so that
each fly has its aureole, hovering
just out of reach with just sufficient
resistance to a filled-out meaning
you could take hold of.
                    The names
entranced him when he was a boy,
he remembered. He was pausing here and there
at the name beneath the photograph
of a trout fly in its row. Some names
had their accidental beauty, some
an unaccountable oddity (e.g.
Bead Head Blood Mohair); some
a satisfying plainness (Joe's Hopper,
this with the most recessive of
aureoles). He turned to the first section
of Orvis flies and began sampling.
Pale Evening Dun (his favorite, in
the beauty category), Halfback
Nymph (a combination that can't
be imagined), Rat Face McDougal, Green
Drake, Light Cahill, Hare's Ear, Blue Dun,
Dark Spruce, Royal Wulff, Grizzly
Wulff, Quill Gordon (one of the oldest
of patterns), Yellow Stimulator,
Marabou Muddler, Royal Trude, Elk

Hair Humpy, Blonde Wulff (the family
of Wulffs is large), The Professor,
Green Double Humpy, Renegade,
Female Adams, Adams Dry, Hairwing
Bluewing Olive, Silver Doctor (another
old one), Golden Fluttering Stone,
Cow Dung (he could never reconstruct
pathways by which the mind in search
of a name for a new trout fly might
arrive at Cow Dung; however, Cow Dung
it was, for what is a still serviceable
old trout fly), Blue Quill, Bitch Creek,
Cream Crane Fly, Olive Peeking Nymph
(vivid little almost-picture). He looks up
again, thinking of the light skittering
across fast water, the calm shine
of water full of leaf reflections
at a bend; the sudden cold clamped
into his legs through his waders, the almost
alarming force of this particular current
as he entered some wide water moving
majestically in near-perfect silence
through one mountain meadow; pool
under a single leaning tree, white uproar
in the narrows, and he balancing there
on a boulder.…
   Looking down again:
it was the Irresistible catching his eye,
then Zug Bug, and South Fork Sally,
and Gray Fox, Hare's Ear Flashback,
Parmachene Belle (another of the old
ones, still good), Madame X Rubberlegs,
Grizzly King, Heavy Bitch Creek, Brown
Matuka, Gray Ghost, Black Leech,
Adult Blue Damsel, Royal Stimulator,
Brassie, Spruce Fly, Babine Special,
Jack Scott, and the Royal Coachman

(striking handiwork of the man of
that title who served Queen Victoria).

He got down a brittle, yellowing
1949 paperback and located the page
displaying "The Preferred Flies
in 1892." All but two were listed
in his new catalogs.
                    He himself
in the last eleven of some sixty
years of fishing, used just one fly,
in one size: the Royal Wulff
(a variant, by the master
Lee Wulff, of the Royal Coachman)
barbless, size 14. The other flies
he had chosen over the years—
dry flies, wet flies, in many sizes,
streamers and nymphs and muddlers
and the big stoneflies—flies for various
times of day in every phase of
the trout season, lay shut tight,
each kind in its own compartment
in a clear box, the boxes stacked
in the dark of their cabinet.
Whether the trout took his Royal Wulff
or not, he had been satisfied.
He'd caught enough trout. If, now
and then, he took and let go another,
he admired as always the all-out
startled indignant struggle of a wild
trout, even a small one. (Planted trout—
pellet-fed, soft-bodied from a life of
finning in one place side by side in hatchery
ponds—he shunned.)
                    In the last two seasons
he had left his tackle at home,
content with walking along a stream

by himself, content with a leisurely
survey of things, with the occasional
prolonged observation of this
or that; with sitting still.
                              To do
otherwise now, to take up active
fishing, would be like taking up
years later one of those books
which, as he read it, became
the signal event of that time
in his life. And such a book, once read,
had then become (while his mind
went on to other books and other
concerns) an occupant, vivid and
quiet in him. If one day years later
he took down the book and read
into it a little way, he'd find it was
still alive there in him. There were only
a few such books. The physical
book, the one that got dusty,
he would dust, and put back on its shelf.

                      ~

He became aware, belatedly, that
a long narrow elegant isosceles
triangle of blazing sunlight
had been lengthening across the carpet
from the lower pane in the door
behind him, and had just arrived
at the far edge. The room had filled
with an early dusk of its own. The afternoon
had gone by, and he eased himself
out of his chair, dropping the catalogs
onto the catalogs sprawling in their basket.

                                    Late February, 1995

The White Boat

(1995)

Reality doesn't last very long.
— SIMENON

I

Long Shadow Time

———————

LONG SHADOW INSTANTS AT HENDRY'S BEACH

The sun is going down over the slack
Pale surface of a sea at minus tide.
It is large and its light is rich.

Streaming across the water, it
Picks out in bright jags
The crust-like foam which rims
Low-lapping crests easing shoreward.

Onshore the light is soaking into the white, soft-looking
Fur of the flank of a black-lipped Samoyed
Which is standing there quietly. The light is shaping
Itself to perfection onto the contours of
The strong legs of the girl who owns the dog.

She's in shorts and sweatshirt; idly
Dabbles her toes in the thin ripplings
Of the backwash; head down, mind elsewhere. The light
Smooths itself with a finishing intensity
Over the figure of a crippled girl:
She is laughing politely while she shrinks

(But just perceptibly) from an Irish setter
Which has just come dashing madly up to her
While its owner, a thin little girl
Of perhaps seven, mortified, is frantically
Calling out to her 'She likes you!'

And hurrying forward.... *All of it equally*
In this lovely, momentary light, thinks a bent old man
Taking it in, who just then, with a start
At the unlikeliness of it, separately

Becomes aware that he has been feeling
Like a boy this whole day. *Which has not happened*
Before, he reflects. *Wouldn't expect it to again.*

Late December, 1992

THE CLUBMAN

Happy to find myself among
This crowd of ancient commonplaces,
   White-eyebrowed ruddy faces,
Such company as I shunned when young;
   And now we chat on terms
Experience we've squeaked through confirms,
And watch for the secret glinting in each other's eyes
   (Euripides let it out), that wisdom isn't wise.

THE MORNING OF GLENN GOULD'S FUNERAL

Hearing him now on the car stereo—
   That's as he wished it when alive—
   I look for browsing deer, and slow
   For the tight down-curves as I drive
     Through deep oak shadows
   Over the back way to Ojai.
The October day burns quiet bright and dry
     In the brown meadows.

The thing he's playing's a rocky-riffled clear
     Mountain stream of a piece by Bach:

The bright quick-moving length of it's here
Along with sun and oak and rock
    O brief survival
Glittering in the light and air
And in the dark unbreakable silence there
    The new arrival.

He puts down his book—it is
the works of one of the number of
the old poets he still loves very much, has
loved for a long time—and noticing
the loveliness of the weak light
of the winter afternoon sloping in
and lying so bleakly and hesitantly
and quietly on the rounded upper
surfaces of the bare branches
and knobby twigs of the trees
he can see from the window,
he thinks, *And that, just as
it is just now—that is plenty.*

OLD MAN AFRAID

Whiskey of youth once mine,
White fire straight from the coil
    Of a hidden still ...
Cool, dark I keep the wine
Of age, that yet may spoil,
    Or handled, spill.

THE WATCH DOG

The terrier barks. I look up from reading and find
the afternoon is over. Voices—some people going by, their
movements just detectable through the high hedge. They are
out for a walk on this first spring-like evening of the year.
The terrier stays tensed—ears forward, she keeps watching
on hind legs at the window. She barks again—two sharp
hard barks, for good measure. The light is mild
on the new green already flecking the old, stubborn dark of
the oaks crowding together up the steep slope opposite,
mild on our apple tree divided by window squares, its thin
crossing twigs still bent from last year, still bare. The street
is quiet again along its length, moments are all we have.

GERON THE HERON

A fragment

There, leaning alone,
A thin crooked dark shape inside the blaze
Of the low sun and the blaze-back of the sea:
Now the breeze freshens, lifting his scant crest. He
Is finishing this one more of certain days
He has made his own.

II

Some Mountain Poems

———————

PROLOGUE

VARIATION ON A THEME BY FROST

Now in the soft spring air
familiar hills appear
bodiless as a fragrance,
successive shades of blue
that I could step straight through
once I had crossed that meadow
on mere green and cloud-shadow.

That's the old drunkenness.
It would with slight harm pass
if I should go in for it.
The pasture's partly marsh,
the hills run back to harsh
steep slopes and stony rubble—
I've learned that for my trouble;

therefore on poison oak
and toyon and sage that choke
the dry ridges and gulches,
and the one stream flowing out
(with shadowy pools, and trout)
through gorge and flat till sunken
in summer, I stay drunken.

A PASSING THOUGHT IN THE CASCADES
(UP ON THE McCLOUD)

From this retreating a glimpse
of a possibility of
a scatter of small unshowy
pieces as certain blossomers
in the left-over bits of habitat
along these streamsides and
tree-dark, cold rock-slopes, where
the ones in the recessive tints
take root, some down to pinhead
size in full bloom (with—bend
closer—sometimes a flick of
brightness, unpredictable scribble
or dot of crimson or swerve of contour
in the hidden celebrants).

AN EARLY SPRING DAY ON
THE UPPER SANTA YNEZ, EXPLORING, DOING A LITTLE
FISHING, BRINGING IN HIS DAYPACK, ALONG WITH
TROUT-FLIES AND LUNCH, THE PAPERBACK
GREEK ANTHOLOGY MADE
BY PETER JAY

Here were no noises of high-up water
dropping over rock ledges, nor had herders,
in the first big storms last fall, left behind
propped against trees their roughed-in
woodcarvings of the girls of groves, nor were there
young women in cut stone standing under the falls,
smooth beneath their thin dresses of the
creasing water; nor was there any tablet left here,
by a late-summer traveller, in thanks
for the shade and grass and running water.

He had leaned his fly-rod in the fork
of a weedstalk gray from a year
of the weather, and sat reading
Leonidas, and eating a sandwich. Below him
sprawled the remains of an enormous oak,
long fallen, the underparts softening
into dirt. The chill green fire of
the week-old grass worked into them, and on
downslope to the little river running clear
in sunlight. A pair of young oaks nearby
checked a cold wind. He was alone
the whole day in that backcountry. Once
he put the book down to rest his eyes on
the two oaks. They would move only slightly,
briefly, in the gusts. Fresh in their strength,
crisp, pitiless, splendid from stem outward
to their clear leaf-limits, hard trunks
stone smooth, stone colored, they were OK
as the small deities of this steep place.

The gods
of the Greeks
long gone, the
nature of things
from which they
arose is as
it was and
will always be.

MANZANA COW AND DRAGONFLIES

—there was a red lizard, brick
red—and a red cow in the creek,
showing through the willows, sloshing
awkwardly upstream bawling
frantically for her calf,
which she had lost somehow.

Diving from overhead
came skipping across the pool
where I had caught the rainbow
two dragonflies—Chinese red.
Then an electric blue
dragonfly shot by too.

Then finest of all came one
(Christ! this was years ago)
the color of the air.
I could best see her where
she floated on the stone
in shadow-duplicate,

distinct where she was not;
seeming, herself, almost
her own faint-featured ghost
over her charcoal show
of self on things below;
and free of anguish there.

1982, 1992

FALL IN SPRING
(BLUE CANYON)

During that time he was nearing
the far side of his own autumn,
with its grants of a certain number
of clear, still days, with a fugitive
richness of colors against the dusks
coming early across chilly ground.
And in that place, on that day, wondering
if there were trout back up in there,
he had caught a small one in the pool
above a crossing, and letting him go
stood for a moment, looking at the pebbles
in their different colors, in the shallows there,
thinking—not sadly, but as the outcome of a rough
calculation—This may be the last time
I'll be up here, and do this. And so it was,
on that shady feeder stream, in that steep place.

That the day is
unrepeatable
you don't think
of, at the time,
so much is moment-
by-moment fitting
together with
never a joint
showing and it
all on the go

He recalls how the road down to it had turned
to a little mountain stream, along a stretch
where the water had shifted its bed in a storm;
that he saw some Mountain Bluebirds in migration.

1983, 1991

A RECENT SPUR-OF-THE-MOMENT HIKE INTO THE BACK-COUNTRY ON THE WATERSHED JUST TO THE SOUTH

In this fifth year of drought
the Poison Oak has turned
the scarlet of October in
mid-June—an early quitter.
Before noon feeling worn out—
hot and out of breath, glasses
sweaty, up here with scant water and
no food, he was resting on a shady
boulder out in mid-stream.
The little stream had led him on.
He had not thought he would
go so far up in. Dry
through much of its course,
here the Matilija still
ran—slow, low, clear. (And
not potable.) Through the heat-tremors,
high on the stony slope, in full sun,
a scattering of that early scarlet showed,
in with a stand of the satiny white
flower-like dried bracts
of the California Ever-
lasting. It made a fine mock
wildflower stand astir
in the quivery glare

and gusts of baking air—dry air
streaked with faintest tangs
(was he imagining this?) off
the chaparral, off Yarrow,
off the bitter and the minty
herbs, the occasional rank
sunflower, the six different sages,
the streamside Bays, the Yerba
Santa, that tastes bitter at first,
later on, cool; all the while, from
upstream and down there came
the different water sounds
over various distances, changing
with the swerves of the light wind,
the occasional gusts. This was one
of the times when the more carefully
you listen to the water, the less
you can tell whether it's partly voices
of hikers approaching upstream
or down, blent over the middle
distances, varying in pitch,
in loudness—or is nothing but noises
of the water going fast
through the shallows, or slipping
over low sandstone ledges, or pooled
behind jammed boulders and splitting
into narrow falls—sounds
filtering through the shadowy Alders
and Bays, mixed in with their rustlings,
carried by the air currents
over water currents, or glancing
off the damp stone of a cliff, in
the near day-long shadow and coolness
of the narrows not too far up from here.

III
Over at the Academy

—————

MARTIAL OF BILBILIS

Nothing in Rome escaped his glance, he understood
    This touchy sort of verse,
    And mixed the poor ones with the good:
    Your even book, he said, is worse.

Old and fed up this son of Bilbilis went home,
    A harsh hill town with a cold
    River below, that shipped to Rome
    A lot of iron, a little gold.

SO-AND-SO REASSESSES YEATS

The mystery's not that like the poet you are made of dust & spittle,
It is that after all these years you'd look so hard & see so little.

READING

Doing my best, first with the intricate
    Bold sudden 'heart-deep' wit
    Of Herbert's poems, then
Out of a harsh professional obligation
    Turning to Maul du Pin
And Willis Hiller, is a revelation:
    For in these latter I find
Myself kept busy slowing down my mind—
Slow, slow, still slower … staying with the creep
Of the meaning there, the meaning of the creep.

FRAGMENT OF THE HISTORY OF THE WEST

… spat out the wine and wafer
One sour the other stale
(All institutions fail)
And wolfed down Marx and Freud
And felt a little safer
Tenting beside the Void.

SONG

O how much is missin
From poems by Thisson
Old life-denier
Groaner and sigher

In Eliot-tones
He sucks his despair
From the light and air
All skin and bones

So shrunk up and dry
He won't even smell
Once he climbs down to try
Rotting in hell.

Lord, if *I* go down there
Moanin and pissin
Stick *me* between a snivelling, snarling pair
Like Farken and Thisson.

PROFESSOR BATH'S TALK ON SHAKESPEARE'S SONNETS

Forgot his notes? Over-confident? While we waited
He employed charm, and when that dissipated
He stalled, digressed, tried more charm, made
One little point, digressed, once more delayed—
We writhing under the infrequent drip
Of meaning from a lifetime's scholarship.

ONE WHO IS CULTIVATED (AND CULTIVATES)

One finds that one
must say *one* rather often
when one wishes it
to be seen that one
is one of that class
of persons whom one
expects to say *one*
and not *you*. (Don't you?)

ANTHEM FOR THE NEW INSTITUTE

There is no such thing as literature.
—DEPT. CHAIR

Literature? We can shove it
No more fake that we love it,
We've got ourselves above it
And make a *good* thing of it.

IV
Far from Yoshitoshi

―――――――

A FEW ASPECTS OF THE MOON

Dusk—city and harbor lighting up below—how
quickly the Mission grounds become all
but deserted. She wanted us up here tonight
to see the full moon rise, having suddenly
recalled such a visit many Octobers ago. And these
others, left over from the day here?—the two
young Latinas idling, idling in silence
by the lavanderia? that young male lurking
(what for?) by the big arch? the middle-aged
bald businessman up on the colonnade, pacing
slowly back and forth, in shirtsleeves,
head down, puffing hard on his stub of a cigar?

'There it is,' she says. Immediately the young man
slips out of the tree-dark behind us for
a look. It is switched-on stadium lights
down by the beach, behind some trees

and this wait's tedious. We go for a walk.
The moon edges up from trees on a hill
and as we pause someone behind us says
'It's beautiful, isn't it,' and
stops beside us to add, 'We used to watch it
from the back porch.' An old man, he crosses his grass
to his car, we round the corner, head down the street
—she looking over her shoulder, for the back porch.

～

Have to find me a clump of grass
—Rabbitfootgrass? Rough Sedge? the
Giant Rye? or Fountain Grass or maybe
the tall, shivery, slim Wild Oats?—
to get down on the ground behind
and see the gigantic full moon through
as Shibata Zeshira has demonstrated, in
          ink, lacquer, and silver.

~

At last the big moon cleared the grove on the seacliff
only to catch in and then have to drag along
that throw of thin drab fibrous cloud.

~

How fine if Tsukioka Yoshi-
toshi could be standing here this dawn
at the window to see the white moon hanging
a little while from the white limb
high in the sycamore and the big flicker black
in silhouette against it, clinging to
a thin, jointed, sharply-bent-down twig
and jabbing the whole length of his bill into one
of our hundreds of prime, dead-ripe persimmons.

~

Going to Pine Mountain again!
after many years, and just because yesterday
a friend spoke of his own recent visit.
The moon will rise and entangle
itself in the huge old pines up there; and
when that happens—I'll be exactly where?

~

Smashed on the pavement up ahead
one mauled wing lifting in the wind
lies a hawk.—No; fooled by a torn cement bag
I'd already seen on the way up; and I see
your crescent cruising the blue
straight overhead—worn out,
gauze-thin, yourself bluish, you lean,
    take in this piddling incident.

~

One for the laments our time begets:
where I grew up the October moon
used to rise huge from behind
the Arms boys' paintless barn with its gambrel
roof and rooster vane, on the round hill
across the draw two farms away—
fit for a thirties postcard photograph.
Both Arms boys are dead. The barn got torn down
and its weather-silvered boards hauled off for use
in bars, barbecue joints and such—as for
the round hill—the 'dozers flattened it
for fill. What the moon rises on over there
tonight is not worth glancing toward.

~

    Out to mail a letter
    and there it is—
    the midmorning moon which
    Stravinsky in his last year
    of life, after surgery,
    said he was pale as
    (a glass of champagne
    left standing overnight

was the air the day
Stravinsky died,
the sparkle gone).

~

At 3:00 A.M. out of bed
with a belly-ache, see
no moon, only how dead
white are the red
bricks of the entry, how black
a roof-post shadow can be.

~

Darkness comes on. My 65th
birthday nears in the dark
of the year, dark of the moon
too: dark I have never feared,
but liked even when small; *e.g.*
getting warm under heavy
covers in the icy room,
sure of the coming on
of sleep, as I lay alone
in the familiar silent dark
upstairs. —Truth is, with you
though, moon, I can get into
difficulties: have sometimes a
nagging unease at finding
myself in your presence, have felt
more than once terror
at your full white face, can
be resentful at the
thought of your thin light
diluting the dark; dark
that Homer called the holy dark.

~

This cold full moon of
December will be shining
on the grave of CRAZY HORSE—
which nobody can visit, neither
Oglala Sioux nor White nor anyone
else knows where it is. Knowledge
of the location went with
those who buried him. (Like the grave
of that wrathful homeless old
blind man, the once King Oedipus,
whom the gods, having ruined, summoned
at the end into the sacred grove to die:
his grave itself both sacred and secret. And
in that grove's place now a bus garage in
an industrial slum of Athens....)
And, in our age, with CRAZY HORSE
the country he and his people
had for walking on got—let's say—
spirited away, so for them it's there
no longer, not for living in, not for being
dead in. Even so—tonight with the radio
announcing it's clear weather all across
the northern plains, let us say
that on the grave of CRAZY HORSE
this cold full moon of
December will be shining.

~

I lie awake in the small hours
and think how in the heatless
mind-light of a dream I never see
a shadow. Very pale shadows
of the old pine tree are moving
hesitantly, back and forth,

in the folds of the thin curtains, and
it is a half moon in the clear night.

~

Well, moon, enough of these
that your Yoshitoshi, who left us
a hundred moon-prints, started
me up on. You don't mesh with our
calendar or clock, or day
or month or year, you claim
your own month—*mooneth*—with its
bunch of ill-fitting moon
numbers, 29 (days), 12 (hours),
44 (minutes), and tonight you are
complete, O smooth one, and in
that matchless silence you
command, how you keep
perfect now at your maximum
brightness that delicate, clean rim,
as of what metal, hammered thin?

SOME-TIME-LATER WORDS

There was once, moon,
for some weeks, something like
an understanding between us,
and a traffic in lively,
if slight, considerations.
Then came this bare aftermath.
You were never more, never less
than yourself—than the moon
I am seeing now up there:
and this distance between us
eventless and vacant—a part
of that whole experience, now.

The general is seated
cross-legged beside the lamp
in the closed-off inner room,
on his knee rests the hand
gripping his suicide knife,
the just unsheathed blade
upright. Under his gaze,
on the floor, lies the poem
he has finished. It speaks of his
part in a disastrous defeat.
The tiger's head on the wall,
a great strip of shaggy pelt
looped around its neck and
hanging to the floor, glares off
above and past the seated man.
—Where, however, is the moon? Look,
the moon is in his poem.
      It is a summer moon.

~

The two scholars with their oarsman
have anchored under the Red Cliffs.
A little moon lights up the water
from a great distance, the water
is rippling, the cliffs lean
among themselves. The scholars wait.
Eight hundred years before them
Su Tung-p'o, coming here with friends,
wrote of the cliffs, the
little moon so distant, the lit water.
The scholars wait—for the way to be in

the presence of the moon, and water, and cliffs,
in that full understanding
possessed by Su Tung-p'o.

~

Stillness of evening: Murasaki
is sitting chin in hand
at the writing desk, set up
for her on a balcony of
the temple retreat; above her
a lantern glows, suspended
from an unseen roof-timber
over the railing; and blocked
in part by the lantern, shines
the full moon: a line-up
of three lights—Murasaki
being the greatest of these—while
everywhere both visible and hidden burns
the fourth light Yoshitoshi.

~

The courtier Fujiwara no Yasumasa stands
playing the flute, oblivious of the bandit
Hakamadare Yasusuke, crouched behind him
amongst the tall and delicately formed grasses,
unable to draw his sword, immobilized
by the beauty of the music: the moon has come
three-fourths out of a fog-soft cloud to watch.

~

The ebbing moonlit sea has drawn
from two ancient pine trees
the spirits Jo and Uba, old couple

of a long happy faithful marriage.
They stand upon the beach (she holding
her rush broom, he his bamboo rake) fixed
in fear and astonishment at their situation:
over them juts a tough and crooked branch with
the orderly, stopped explosion of its needles.

~

The child Kintoro, in build a
sumo wrestler in miniature,
(grown up he'll be the famous
samurai, Kintoki) leans forward,
hands on knees, eyes fixed on
a hare and a monkey just now
coming to grips at wrestling.
Kintoro is umpire. The moon
has edged itself out from behind
Kintoki Mountain to watch.
It is also illuminating, where
they lie undamaged on the ground
between Kintoro and the wrestlers,
two magnificent ripe persimmons—
there for the taking, so
intent upon the contest are the hare
and monkey, and Kintoro, moon, and we ourselves.

~

Flooded with moonlight the bald
round head and round bare belly
of this deity of good fortune
Hotei where he sits half turning
to glance upward and show us
how a finger pointing at the moon
is not the moon.

V

Two Women in the Middle Distance

On her way without starting. Gone without going.
—BECKETT, *ILL SEEN ILL SAID*

THE WHITE BOAT

To close out the year

Light fading and the marsh
Wide now with the tide out,
Darkening, sky pale, bright
Patches of water near,
Bright streaks of it far off
Over the flats. Bird-cries

Cross the stillness: black shapes
On the water-shine,
Willet, Whimbrel, Godwit,
Feeding in a hurry,
Much back-and-forth movement,
Quarrel-cries. Curved bills, wings

Clear on the after-glow,
Curlews glide in. Chitter
Of a Kingfisher: low
Whir over the water
Shoreward, to a dark tree.
Heron, dusk-blue in dusk

Where the sandy path bends
By the marsh-edge, listens
Dead still in mid-stride.

Air ripples the distance,
Small boats drift, fishermen
Hunched on the water-blaze.

Sky over the spit's gone
Smoky red now; low lights
Along the north bay, more
On hills across the marsh
Jump, air-jostled. A last
Puff of warm land air dies.

~

From the boat basin now
Through the late dusk the white
Rowboat comes sliding out
On the still water, white
Reflection under it
Slides along upside down.

Oarsman's figure just
Visible through the dusk
Moving off rapidly
In the silence, without
Noise of splash or creaking,
A good hand at the oars.

Night Heron flies over,
Squawks once, the marsh is dark
Inlaid with thin pale strips,
Oarsman rounding the point
Now heads up bay and boards
A sailboat at anchor.

Breeze now, the bay glimmers,
And that oarsman's in fact
A girl, her silhouette

Miniature in distance;
Wearing a dress, her long
Hair and long skirt blowing—

She sets out to work on deck
Without delay, bending
This way and that, cranking,
Lifting, rearranging—
Every movement practiced
And quick and unhurried.

Then the girl goes below,
Is all; her disappearance
As brisk as her other
Doings. The boat rocks, stays
Dark on the bay's paleness.
Then light at a porthole.

Night nears now, fishermen
Heading in, clear voices
Come small over the flats,
Birds settling in, restless
Bustlings, creaky cries, some
Still feeding in tide pools.

The fishermen arriving
Cut their motor and coast
On the quiet water
Of the small-boat basin,
Through the dark a man's voice
Sounds close in the stillness.

~

This is how it is here
And will and will not be
Again, these small doings

Each an end, a beginning,
A middle, overlapping
Momently, here only,

This year, and then next year
Again, especial, late
In the day then, in late
December, this is how
It will be, and not be.
How it is here.

Morro Bay
December 19, 1979; 1992

MOLLY BAUGH

Of the first sights we saw
When first we settled here
One would be Molly Baugh
With dachshund on its lead
And husband with a cane,
A red-faced silent man
With carefully combed hair
And trousers sharply creased
And his gaze aimed with care
On the ground just ahead
As if that were the scene
They came out to walk in
And not the pleasant park
With poplars, and old pines
The mountains show between.

Big, Mediterranean,
White stucco and red tile,
Was the house they lived in
With children grown and gone,

And all dim, trim, and calm
That we might glance in on
Up there (we are below,
One of a crooked row
Of various small houses
Strung out along the creek)
As we went driving by
A time or two a week
And often as not saw
Out walking, with her husband
And dachshund, Molly Baugh.

And this, you understand,
Passed in the middle distance
Of our own lives, to the end—
My wife had met her once
Years back, at some fundraiser:
For twenty years and more
I only knew her look,
Her thoughtful way of walking,
Tones of the evening shore
In the wool and silk she wore,
Sea grays, and duns of beach,
Or the like quiet colors,
And her keen, pleasant eye,
And alert, slight tilt of head,

As they went slowly by:
And our talk of her
Brief, casual, infrequent,
And the years passed, one day
It was just she and the dachshund
Out walking, side by side
Taking their usual way,
Both showing now some gray,
Later we saw just her

Alone—still with her air
Of pleasant alertness, then
We heard she had moved away,
And then that she had died—
But no details—last year;

And now I want to praise her,
For where at times I find
Her passing through my mind
The air is sweet and clear.

VI
Odd Pair

'IS THE UNIVERSE TRIVIAL?'

(Title of forthcoming lecture by physicist up here from Cal Tech)

And is the answer 'Yes'?
I have a hunch it is.
I know I'd leave the hall
Uncomfortably full
Of mathematical
High-powered subtleties
I couldn't even guess
The strangeness of, much less
The forces that they show
Held in their symbol-net;
So I'm not going to go.
I have a hunch it is,
Though; having lived in it
For sixty and more years
And heard the news one hears
From the astronomers,
Of bent space going on
And on and on and on
Before you've well begun
To drift much past the sun;
Where, for people at their lives,
Roads and rivers and trees,
Bookstores, gardens, cafes
And theaters, and baseball,
Music, and pictures, all
You get's dark vacancies
And silence going by
With your occasional

Physico-chemical
Huge whirler hurtling through
Their remoter distances
(Airless, and what is more
Too cold or hot for you)—
Urania declares
That if your ship arrives
You'll be freeze-dried, or burned
Precipitantly away—
There's inconceivable
Violence ashore.

—I have a hunch it is,
So far as we're concerned,
Until it comes to us:
We hold it in our heads,
We featherless bipeds.
—Where it alone begins
Is where the meaning thins:
A horror, truth to tell.
Here's paradise, there's hell:
Oh yes, it's trivial—
Apart from the not-so-small
And inescapable
Fact that it has us all
      By the short hairs.

BALLAD OF THE SUBFUSC DAY

Gray inside, and the overcast
      Outside is staying put
When I get down to it at last
      Doors and windows shut.

But words don't crowd in now, the way
    They did last week for me—
Gave them some shoves and there they lay
    Fitted like tesserae.

Silence. I probe with a broomstraw
    Inside a lampshade pleat
An odd shadow I just saw:
    An earwig lands on his feet.

Oily and slim, he trots along
    My desktop, hunting a crack;
I place him where earwigs belong,
    Between two bricks out back.

More silence. I get up and gaze
    At the woodpile and pine tree
Thinking of certain sunny days
    And wishing I might see

The big Fox Sparrow, say—the one
    Last year who came and went,
His sides and back rainy-earth brown
    And a magnificent

Central chest spot, irregular
    And bold—as for his song,
He was a rich, clear whistler.
    Nothing in him not strong.

What did I see out there instead
    But a rat—a young one, shy,
Intelligent—almost, as my wife said,
    Pretty, in silvery gray.

He matched a silvery stick of pine
    I'd left there, at the tip
Of which he paused, working his fine-
    ly whiskered upper lip:

The first rat here we ever saw.
    And we two stood entranced
Watching him daintily withdraw.
    And the dull day advanced.

And inside, in the same gray air
    Alone once more, I sat
And made place for that seemly pair
    The earwig and the rat.

Water Among the Stones

Along the Matilija
(1987)

*To the heart that has felt it and that is the
true judge, every loss is irretrievable
and every joy indestructible.*
— SANTAYANA

An inordinate attachment
    to the Matilija
Brought on these poems
    with the grief
That love of a place
    will come to
In time—even
    so unbeautiful
A place as this one,
    mainly,
Is—or used to be,
    till destroyed.
For what is one
    to do?
—Belittle the whole
    experience,
And let it rot
    in you. Or
Yield to homicidal
    fury—and
Kill whom? how many?
    or take
That old man's way
    up in Maine
Some years ago—in
    the flames
With his house, condemned
    alike
By the state, for the new
    overpass.
Or, as worker in a craft
    and art
Nobody asked you
    to take up,
Do what such a person
    can do,

Hammer out a set
of poems:
This occupies a few
weeks....

December 27, 1986

I

TO MY MATILIJA

Where the canyon walls
Close in, and the air cools,
And the little green trout flick and hover
In the clear green pools
Between the falls
Where that sturdy solitary, the slate-gray dipper, year round, sings
Till the steep stone rings
Is where I'll go, still unforgiving
Of others' and my own poor past
(How keep my mind clear and not curse
Doings that make life worse?)
And be, Matilija, your lover
When I am dead, and at long last
Won't have to make a living.

~

As for the agony
Clenching in me:
My own and others' imperfection,
Killing delight ...
On those clear pools my own reflection
Is broken light.

And in that steep stone cleft
What will be left
Of me is not the middling lover
Here, of a wife
With whom he gladly would live over
A second life —

Nor that one who'd begun
A better son,
Friend, father in his own thinking,
Than he became —
So maimed in the doing (heart here sinking)
And yet the same.

Say all these disappear
Into the sheer
Fire of that anger — what's remaining?
Stranger, the sight,
Say, of the tall slim pale wild oats leaning,
In the late light,

Beautiful, on a stony rise
Before your eyes,
While you stand making out a crossing
Down where the stream
Slips roaring through boulders, and the spray's tossing,
And the alders gleam:

At such a moment, here
I'll stand, tho' not appear
But be coincident with your seeing
The shining scene
And in that moment have my being,
Unhuman, and serene.

II

FESTIVITY

The early morning air at streamside—
  criss-crossed, hung
With an intricate lace, then long
  streamers, of the birdsong
As I tie on a fresh Royal Wulff,
  size 14.

III

ON A HILLSIDE

There's a movement, and a snake suddenly underfoot
  sliding in the heat, through the dry tangle
Of brown grass and thistles, dead stalks
  of wildflowers. A California Kingsnake it is,
In plain view; he's entering the rock-pile
  beside me, out on his rounds.
The fresh enamel gleam of the close-fitted
  scales unblurred by the dust
He goes upon, his bands of ivory and black,
  crooked-edged, ride motionless
In his gliding. Now, fine-tapered tail-tip quivering
  into thin air, he inches
Himself through a tight bend. Now
  a three-inch section of him shows
At an opening, the bands like box-cars
  travelling past steadily.

Note: The quotations at the top of the poems are taken from Isaac Walton's
The Compleat Angler, except for the couplet from John Weever above XVI.

IV

CATCH AND RELEASE

Now the wild trout comes in, tired out—in from the roar
    and splintering light at the falls past the bend
Just upstream—in through the glass-smooth stretch here
    that travels dark green, clear, noiseless, over a great slab
Of sandstone—in toward the black shadow and the dank, sweating
    stone fragments tumbled to the water's edge
Under the cliff.
                    He looks transparent as he nears
    my hand, the green ridge of his back
Being exactly the green of the water. Fine and icy,
    hard to the touch, he waits quietly, gills working,
After a last strong slippery lunge, the mist-bow colors
    intimated nicely in the polished steel of his flank.
And my Royal Wulff makes a striking rosette
    in military scarlet, green of peacock, white, cinnamon,
Against the dark shine of his jowl.
                            Released now,
    he drifts sideways a bit, hesitant, hovering under
The opened fingers, next to the fast current. Then bolts,
    himself a green smudge above the distinct
Shadow shot downstream, skimming the white bottom sand
    in the sunlight then suddenly accelerating
Toward the scant shade of a young alder standing straight
    on the far bank, thin-branched, its leaves just opening,
A lyrical green light in them; and, back here now,
    on the hands, clean chill scent of trout.

V
STUDY OF WILD OATS #1

Wild oats agile in the wind
at day's end, along the dusty track
going down-canyon—*Avena
barbata* said the flora, 'common
weed of waste places
and open slopes'—now
frantic in their innocent
agitation, twitch and thrash, now
looking but the more graceful
as they swing violently,
the strong sun of this late evening
burning white through the dried-out
husks that dangle, spaced
evenly in the loose
open panicles, little
shining spearheads, all of them
pointing one way and the whole
shining stand bending lower
under a stiffer wind—they
vibrate, bright rustlers, shy
hissers of early summer
under the brown, still mountain,
its flank filling with shadow—
later on, after nightfall, and
the wind down, their exquisite
shapes standing motionless
unbroken in the clear night.

VI

THE HARBINGER

You soon drop down to the place,
taking the turn-off, an hour
up-canyon, from the main trail.
Willows and an old, broken alder stand
along the far side of the pool,
above the crossing. Trout lie
out near the middle, now holding beside
the main current, now drifting backward
a foot or so, and, slow-finned, easing
forward again, looking faint
above their shadows; the pool,
with the air quiet, all sleek,
till a dragonfly scrapes it,
or a fish takes a fly wrinkling it.
On the near bank huge boulders
obstruct your way upstream.
There, just this morning, lay
the Alpo can, on its side, new,
empty, clean, on the clean sand
under a shady overhang
of sandstone. What a brisk blare
the orange and blue of the label;
how tight and sure, the fit of the label.

VII

STUDY OF A BABY RATTLESNAKE

The little rattler sleeps on, snug
On the sunlit sandstone boulder, tho' oak shadow
Laps over him now. He has tucked in his head
Near the center of his close coils and folds.

It is getting on toward mid-morning.
His luck still holding, there in the open,
Against a cruising hawk or kingsnake,
He collects the stillness of his boulder, and its warmth,

Into a fine heavy medallion,
In his dark bronze markings.

VIII

AT THE CONCERT, AFTER A DAY UP THERE

The succession of bright scenes passes through
involuntarily, over this fine old music:
you, Matilija, in the sun, spilling among boulders,
flashing in the shallows, pooled
beside damp shady stone, quick sway of leaves.

IX

HOMAGE TO W.C.W.: THE PRICKLY PHLOX

The tiny alpine flowers, tundra
blossomers in the Arctic, the wildflowers
of these coast mountains, say
this prickly phlox, this April
in the hard canyon wind
down the Matilija, amid
the drab hugeness and harshness
all around, half frozen, by gravity
gripped and splayed; bitten,
wrinkled and dried by the heat,
whipped by winds, burnt down
to a black stub by wildfire—
look, made small, made
definite, here it roots,
under the brush, in the rocks
with its clean pink petals
arching back, flared from their centers, all
straightforward ardor, distinct
in its requirements and opening out
completely with a delicate fragrance:
intricate and exquisite grave system
of living, in this just-sufficient zone
of indifference where, for now,
the big and little forces,
just balancing, cancel out,
amid which protection
unprotected (the physical universe
being Greek, as under that hard
to make out, fearful 'justice
of Zeus' you find in Homer

or Sophocles)—to feed,
to flower, again and again
to bear and be, in toughness
and delicacy, this strictly
conditional existence, small,
swift, incidental beauty, persisting.

X

VISIT

Patch of wet sand there
    by the water's edge
Packed with butterflies
    doing what—drinking?
Till one tottered upward
    to circle me, then others,
One or two at a time,
    and for a moment
I had going around me
    in the playful silence
A big wreath of butterflies,
    that broke away then
And went staggering high
    above the Matilija

XI

DRAFT FROM THE MATILIJA

Down off the burnt-off slope
    for a drink, the big snake
Stops me on my way
    home at mid-day
To responsibilities (miles from here
    in what is, for the U.S.,

A well-built little city)—how
        quietly he lies,
In slow, slack curves, broken
        by shadow, among three rocks,
Lowering his chin daintily
        to the Matilija.

                    ~

Having paused to judge of me
        by tonguing the air,
He resumes drinking now,
        letting down and lifting
His U-shaped, thin, flat jaw.
        On and on he drinks, taking
A very little at a time,
        unhurriedly
Slaking the whole length
        of his thirst.

                    ~

Earth's a great harsh gaunt garden
        here, made of spiny chaparral,
And cliffs, bare crests, dry stony slopes,
        the fan that opens, desolate,
Scattered with boulders, below
        this canyon; and, running through,
Narrow, bright and chill among its stones,
        the Matilija.—Born
Somewhere in all this, on his own
        from birth, in the fit
And hard gloss of his scales,
        eye of translucent, dry horn,
Or some clear stone, for his seeing, strange
        but, still, seeing:

He lifts his head at last, done
    with drinking, and without haste
Or hesitation winds out over the water—
    not toward the far bank
But downstream, steering purposefully
    between the rocks, the current
Very fast down there, he lifting his head higher,
    moving rapidly now with an air
Of matter-of-fact eagerness into the loud water
    smashing itself solid white
Among the boulders jammed together
    below, where he vanishes.

~

What is it, to be? Slowly to find yourself
    already alive to some place, alone with
Purposes already forming; what is snake
    intelligence but intelligence
First and last, snake experience
    but wholly experience?
No king of darkness, no god, but something
    as good, I think…. To live,
To live and at midday there, to be
    a snake completely, very thirsty,
And drink your fill, at length, of
    the clear Matilija.

XII

STUDY OF WILD OATS #2: THE FISHERMAN

It is something unhuman in us,
    doubtless (serene,
Though, for what it's worth)
    which now has that figure

Pausing a moment, as if interrupted,
    on a stony rise, to see beside him
A stand of the slender
    wild oats bending
A little stiffly, shivering,
    each long, smooth, hollow
Pale stem filled to the top with late sunlight,
    the husks even brighter, swinging
Under their spikelets, ablaze, in shape like
    narrow fine-pointed lance-heads,
Or, sprung open, bird-bills held wide to call—
    and the creek below them
Splitting to pass between boulders,
    roaring and misting,
The mist carrying away rapidly
    on the up-canyon breezes,
Over the boulders the cold shadows of alders
    beautifully sidling.

XIII

JOHN'S LIZARD

The little lizard waits—slender
    fingers outspread
And long thin whip of a tail
    straight as a ruled line.
Resting quietly on John's palm,
    having been caught
With a looped fiber from a stem
    of grass, he tilts his head now
To hold both John and me in his calm
    direct gaze: entirely
In the moment. Things Florentine goldsmiths
    hammered, enchased, smoothed,
He resembles in elegance; likewise

the Samurai weapons—stirring and
Practical. By day he hunts and suns, by night
    sleeps undisturbed,
His blanket, his roof, his local government
    the starry universe.

XIV

A LEOPARD LILY

The other flowers are long
    finished, and mix
With the dead weeds and grasses
    on the slopes, in the gullies,
Among the rocks. So for you,
    leopard lily—
Tired as we are, late
    in the long day—
We leave the trail, cross
    through the charred brush
To see you: against
    the black hillside
Sending your tall stem
    straight up, your five
Great bright flowers tilted
    at various angles
Way out from the stem
    like bells swinging,
Not knowing—or maybe knowing—
    the festivities are over.

XV
IN LATE MARCH UP THERE

Under the hillside ceanothus
    in pale bloom, blooms
A nightshade, bright fresh blue
    in shadow. Here below,
Sits a tiny stone-colored frog,
    looking very knowing in his stone niche …
Bitter scent of skunk on the wind, ahead
    old tortoise on poolside rock
Head and neck outstretched,
    sunning his throat.
And the fishing's in low, clear water
    the sun pouring straight down,
And scarce cover, just the shelving
    shale and the boulders,
The set of difficulties
    slightly different
At every run and pool. Working
    upstream, a happiness near complete,
Among such quick-to-declare-themselves
    factualities.

XVI
THE END OF SOMETHING

I have come here late in the day.
    Now the light is failing, and
What I've just seen's the dead
    gleam of aluminum,
The shape of something, across
    a half mile of chaparral,
Up near the lovely pool
    where the snake was drinking.
When the end of something comes, often
    the signal is ironically
Slight. Goodbye Matilija.
    By the time I reach it—
It's a house trailer, laundry
    flying on a line
Strung on the low bluff
    above the pool—
I have passed two others,
    assorted bulldozers,
Dump trucks, trench-diggers....
    Nothing is ours,
Matilija, I well know.
    How often though
Through how many years—but
    time to go: to
Go and pack out with me
    my useless grief,
Of which neither this place,
    which I know I've loved
Too much, nor any other,
    will bear a trace.

XVII
YUCCA WHIPPLEI

This big capsule
I plucked green
reaching high
along the stalk
late this spring,
and week by week
let it brown,
and wither, and crack.
Pick it up
and shake it now—
Cha cha it
whispers here
in my study
Cha cha
Cha. Faithful,
dry, and shy
sound of the promise
of *Yucca whipplei,*
calm presence
sending high,
out of its fierce
tipped-with-spines
rosette of blades,
that stout stem
tapering green
above boulders,
in dry gulches,
in strong sun
on stony slopes,
breaking out
its white blossoms,
a great cone of them,
curled and tumbled,

where, in the quivering
heat the light
comes in and is creamy,
cool and still; where
the mind can go
when it wants to.

~

... and a low wind in the alder grove —
or is it the little waterfall? —
mutters from ancient Isaiah thus:
Thou hast multiplied the nation
and not increased the joy.

~

from *Goodbye Matilija*

On the North Fork
(1992)

*All stories, if continued far enough, end in death, and he is no
true-story teller who would keep that from you.*
—HEMINGWAY

DREAM VISION

Well, it's an old affair—
Stronger than ever, though,
This twenty-seventh year
That I've been coming here.
The memory stays clear
How other places, too,
Brought transient happiness;
I was just passing through
And therefore could avoid
Seeing them destroyed.
But much the same is so
Matilija, with you
As from the first I knew:
I have been passing through—
The difference being, here
Your ruin, though delayed
A bit will be, I guess,
The one I'll stay and bear.

~

At the ranch headquarters, which
you have to walk through
to get up here, an old
yellow Lab with flabby,
drawn-down dugs and, this past
year or so, a bad shoulder,
stands waiting to greet me, in
her usual quiet good humor.
I am an old admirer.
Last year she'd still join us,
lame as she was then,
to fetch the sticks she'd have

one or another of us fling
again and again into
the icy currents.
     She can just bear
the pain it costs her now
to take a step. As I push on,
she stands there a bit, before
making her way back to the porch.
Her eyes half close with the pleasure
from our meeting, her tail wagging
just a little, reminiscently.
Still the enthusiast; while
in her whole manner you see
her unreluctant recognition of
the scope left to her now, including
the clear if receding view
of how, with her, things used to be.

     ~

Over and over the gods
Fail what they came to guard;
Yours too, poor little stream,
With your lower crossings all
Dry stones, bulldozer-scarred;
Slammed through by mountain bikes
I wonder what god likes,
That's now having his day
(Sees 'em come slashing down
At top speed on their way
To get trucked back to town),
All your bright-bodied trout,
In your shrunk pools, jerked out
By jerks with spinning rods ...
Well well, let me be fair,
The herons took their share.

~

The upper gorge: rest stop,
Midday; and half asleep
I hear your waterfall,
Maybe six inches tall,
Through alder and foothill ash
Gurgle hiss glug and splash
Between your banks and steep
Clean sandstone, that goes up,
Up to the yucca, small
With distance, along the top.

A coolness on my face
Breathes from the whole place—
Your remnant song, that seems
Reflective, now, subdued,
Sounding entirely good.

~

With such things on my chest,
And with my Thermarest
Between me and the stones
And sticks, to spare old bones
That have no flesh to spare—
Outstretched, with eyes covered
Beside this upper reach,
With your much dwindled stream
Still making itself heard
I went down into sleep
Through the leaf-shady air.
In my sleep came a dream,
And in the dream (I swear)
A vision, then a speech,
Abrupt as a sonic boom,

That broke into the hush
I faced in a long room
In which I used to teach—
Broke, then went on in a rush,
In which the vision hovered.
Here it is, word for word:

Our little earth's a goner—
As anyone can see
With or without a book,
You only need to look—
The whole revolting disaster
Being inflicted on her
North south east and west
Now uncontrollably
Coming straight at us faster
Than anybody guessed.
Once and for all, right here,
Come drop with me, a tear
For her, as dwelling-place
For us, the one earth-race
That hasn't belonged here
From the outset: the ones
Whose hearts have been elsewhere,
In this or that Elphame
I won't take time to name;
Neither would I seek
To parcel out the blame:
By nature, so to speak,
We are space aliens.
The space, between our ears.
How lately we have known
That we are on our own.

And after we are gone?
(Be sure that we'll be gone.)
If anyone should care,

So goes one prophecy
Fitting in its grandeur,
And true, for all of me—
A various multitude
Of the bacteria
Will rule the biosphere,
Their center everywhere,
Humble inheritors
Guarding the true and good;
And all we've understood
Of all that has most mattered,
And, understood, have spoken
In music, paint, words, stone,
In number, and the rest
Till it all stood complete
As nearly as could be—
And perishable, though
After each overthrow
Learned all over again
And more still—all this broken
In ultimate defeat,
The litter of it scattered
On earth *that spinning sleeps*
On her soft axle, while
She paces even, and bears
Thee soft with the smooth air
Along (that's as she crossed
Our gaze in *Paradise Lost*)....

For us, though, let's not grieve—
Nor turn in treachery
On our own kind, at heart
Finding life hard to leave,
Finding it sweet to be
Even if in prospect
Only, for the most part,
As certain sages claim,

And likely to be wrecked.
And deeply as fear goes,
Having in view a good
That, clearly understood,
Comes always at great cost
And always incomplete
And sooner or later lost;
Even so, to repeat,
Our being remains sweet
Under the deepest fears,
In human hardihood.

The vision paused, then said,

Last night I heard a song
Coming through leafy air—
Though fading before long
It sings on in my head:

The earth that once made us
Being the same earth that made
The dragonfly, the deer,
Lizard and mastodon,
Worm, leaf, stone, bright green blade,
Hill, river, and so on—
When we, in what we do
Ravage it all—this, too,
Is a natural result
For us, the boldest one
Of all her experiments;
In which to fail, long since
We've learned is not a fault.
Experiments mostly fail.
Ours had a good long run.

"Many the wonders," so
Sophocles long ago
Remarked, "and of them none
To match us."
                    Let that be
(With ambiguity
Worked in by history)
Of all that we can see
Of what, now, we have done,
The thing to reflect on.

Just so the voice-vision spoke,
And cold and stiff I woke.
Whether the dream was so
I'm not the one to know.

~

Pretty tired coming back down
today, too. Birds are difficult
to identify against this light.
Sudden black shapes bank and vanish,
light flashing, uncolored, off a wing,
a glossy back. Meanwhile just ahead
beside the trail the little sycamore
with its as yet entire and at the moment
motionless set of yellow and bronze leaves
has lit up like a lamp, backed by
the cold shadow of the great ridge
where the sun just now touched down.

~

The whole day I've been alone.
And now I see a woman
a fair distance away,

standing just off the trail,
and looking up intently
into the dark treetops,
quite unaware of me
under my big daypack
approaching through the dusk.

Since she still hasn't moved
I click my walking staff
against a trailside rock
letting her know I'm here
before I come too near
and perhaps startle her.
She gives me the briefest glance
and goes back to her gazing
and soon I am drawing near her.
She is a tall, plump woman,
well into middle age,
dressed in T-shirt and jeans,
looking as if she'd just
stepped outside the house:
no hat, no jacket, no
binoculars, no daypack;
up here alone, it seems,
maintaining this rapt stillness
in the stillness, as the birds stir
high up in the foliage,
darkness a half hour off,
the canyon chill increasing.
"There's a lot of birds up here,"
she says, an eagerness showing
a little, and a slight shyness,
under the factual manner.
I nod and mention seeing
some signs of bear up above.
She rounds our meeting off,

"We saw bears on Pine Mountain,"
releasing us to resume
the solitudes we broke,
she mine, that is, I hers.
I go and she stays on.
I meet nobody else
The rest of the way down.
The appearances all say
she has come up here alone
and on the spur of the moment.
It is dark when I reach my car.

RECOLLECTION

I saw a ballpoint pen,
of clear plastic, like new,
its vein of blue ink full,
lying athwart the trail
just where it starts to dip
down to the twelfth crossing
and the pool and the bigleaf maple.
I paused considering
what should be done with it,
not wanting it myself,
not wanting to leave the thing
there in plain view, either.
With the worn toe of my boot
I worked it underneath
the slightly raised underside
of a small sandstone boulder
till it was out of sight.
There it will be, just where
the trail begins to dip....
The boulder is on the right.

Not half an hour later
the pencil I'm so fond of
and carry everywhere
but into bed with me,
fell and began to float
away, Matilija,
bobbing and swivelling on
your currents—playfully, though,
and slowly, slowly; so
enabling me at length,
having roused myself, to retrieve it.

AFTER-WORDS

Each of us varyingly
Has come here from the ocean,
And once here each waits
On a set of varied fates
Now and then not kindly. Still,
Despite my streamside vision,
I've left off sermonizing.
The frayed old pack I carry
Back down this long-loved trail
Contains no remedy.

My spirits have stayed high.
If asked for a reason why
I'd use this mystery
In indirect reply:
The blinded Samurai
Taira no Tomoume
In Yoshitoshi's print
Declines to stand apart,
Fights in the thick of it
Bearing, as talisman,

A poem-slip, that says
Even in darkness, one
Can see the moon with the heart.
But there's no moon in this print,
No indirect sign of it,
In shadow, or weapon-glint,
For us with eyes, to see.
(It is this print alone
which is without a moon.)
Say Yoshitoshi meant
To say a no-moon is
An aspect of the moon
Which he cannot omit,
That once, there was no moon,
And that there'll be no moon
Again, in time; that these
Twinned non-existences
Accompany the moon,
It never goes alone;
Which a blind Samurai
Found with his darkness-eyes,
Leaving him battle-fit
On ground two no-moons lit.

Note: The print is number 33 in Yoshitoshi's *One Hundred Aspects of the Moon.*

from *Stubble Burning*

(1988)

THESE TOO, FOR FRAN—

Poems are not what you head for
When we go into a bookstore.
Handed these, maybe you'll recall
How, without fail, when they were small
The boys brought home their dinosaurs
(The long flanks brightened up with flowers),
Houses with slanting chimneys, trees
Of course, a dog complete with fleas …
We taped them to the walls and doors
So you will understand with these,
The bringing of them makes them yours.

AT CHARLOTTE

Eating alone, what shall I have along
        For company
    At my small table, while the young
    Mostly it is who'll neighbor me
In twos, threes, fours, clear-eyed and smooth of face,
        Inside this place?

—Old Bridges, yes; the secret of a few,
        Not doctrinaire,
    Who see the firm shapes, lovely, true,
    Stir in that style 'so worn and bare,'
Stone-carved and weathered, rose- and ivy-trace
        Still twine in place;

This Hume, which from its unfrequented, dim
        And cool recess,
    His minor works, I pick by whim;
    Prose at its ease in formal dress,
Genial, stately as if in stellar space
        Wheeling in place:

My dark blue, gold-stamped duodecimos
        Beside my plate,
    I'll start at random, verse or prose,
    Read on, or stop and meditate,
Or gaze and eavesdrop on the human race
        But keep my place.

…Though what I hear when I look up at last
        Is this catch-phrase
    And that from a decade well past,
    Phrases the old rage still replays,
Habitual grievance, now, that words encase
        And keep in place,

While from the table on the other side,
                Psychology
        Fastened on friends, and self-applied,
        Grapples poor human dignity
Into its mechanisms, to debase
                Or take its place …

Serves an eavesdropper right. And anyhow
                Clinking of glass
        And sudden laughter drown them now …
        Outside the window tourists pass
Our old drunks and young toughs with averted face
                And know their place.

And I, all the while hoping to outguess,
                Outwit, outwait,
        The subtler forms of foolishness
        That have been crowding me of late
Inside and out—I study to outface
                This commonplace:

The old wisdom and the old beauty both being gone,
                Their imperfections
        Forgiven, now the harm is done,
        At least by me (in my reflections
A trouble still)—what now, for wit, strength, grace,
                Will take their place?

Make us our buildings (say) that the light fall
For your material
Intelligent delight
Across them handsomely all day, let night
Show dark on stars some shape of ornament
That opens on the deeps of your intent.

Now that we've quit that cant about sheer need
(That less was less indeed
Being plain now everywhere)
Speak of needs rather: which ones? whose? and spare,
Spare us mere NOVELTY *that stale confection.*
No, draw your art up through severe reflection,

And lay it out for us once more complete.
Sidney, on his defeat
At court, living apart
In Wales one summer fashioned anew the art
Of English poetry. Look what there is
To be engaged: hungers, abilities—

Well, well. Charlotte has chosen to locate
   With a sure wit,
  Just here on upper lower State
  Between the chic and the misfit
Making this calm and airy and clear space
   Stand, in their place …

And late as it always is to build by it,
   In the debris
  Here, there, intelligence is lit …
  Let it be for a tough subtlety
Of beauty, and a roughed-in wisdom for the race
   To hold in place.

The boss meanwhile moves easily here, there,
   This late fall night,
  The soup and bread and wine her care—
  That some small gain for our delight
And dignity can be, is the clear case
   Inside this place.

November 1982; September 1985

GERON MUSES

Such ancient commonplaces as I shunned when young,
They rustle around me now, untended old olive trees,
With their roots driven so deep and wide, their branches so strong,
In winter storms they only gleam and sway at ease.

GERON AMONG THE LIT REVIEWS

Though by our century's failing light
Our poets can't find much to write,
They're safe enough, with our new breed
Of critics that can't learn to read.

GERON'S GUIDANCE

Seek truth—slow truth, exacting truth—with the
saintly Darwin, son, avoid
Orators and literary fellows such as Marx and Freud.

THE TWO FIELDS, WHERE I USED TO LIVE

*Nothing lasts, and ... in that very fact lies some of
its glory; the sadness ... is really not so terrible.*
—ISAK DINESEN

Where each oat tassel turns
in its own air
On its own white fiber
well out from the stem—

And the barley beards out, rasping
      the fingertips,
Both oats and barley bending
      bright metal they made
Of brightness, dryness, heat
      in authoritative silence—
The fields two shining rectangles,
      below them, black there
In the tangle of rough grasses
      at the fields' end,
The shade of the big glisteners,
      cottonwoods that found
The little stream underground
      before it rises
Where the three fences meet, where
      the gully opens,
Where in the quiet the redwings
      sway the cattails:
Small grain fields of our high country
      with the cold mountains lifting
Above you the crooked line
      of their crests!
The whole scene nears and clears
      now, across fifty years—
Though now, where the great trees grew,
      now, where the stream came up
Whirling a little bright sand,
      the traffic vrooms—
Though the houses of strangers stand
      where the grain bent,
With its own innocence and
      wisdom implicit—
The whole scene nears and clears
      now, across fifty years.

GERON STOPS LISTENING

At a lecture by a young woman

And no thanks for this power of vision
Granted as my eyes fail,
To see with pitiless concision
Whole lives unfurl, or furl—
Which grief is greater?
Seeing that smooth fresh face suddenly later
Sag, seam, and pale?
Or in this hag nearby glimpsing the girl?

DAY THOUGHTS, NIGHT THOUGHTS

Politics is like the air: necessary to life, insufficient to live on.

I

That was a long time back
When Solon, spending his days
On the unruly ways
Of your ordinary Greek
And the rank sons-of-bitches
Both poverty and riches
Can make and make attack,
Rose to speak.

2

What Solon had to say,
As he already knew,
The many and the few
Alike would hate to hear.
They heard him out at length

Such were the grace and strength
The words moved in that day.
        Sound and clear

                3

He held 'em—for a time.
'Hard to please all' in just
The things that matter most—
That, if at all, are fixed
In a hateful compromise
By creatures that even when wise
Come from a dab of slime
        Chance has mixed.

                4

Ruin a delightful city
For money or for spite.
Do it in broad daylight.
Then you can see the law—
On rich gangs, on poor gangs,
Violence boomerangs—
That half in hate half pity
        Solon saw.

                5

All sides are wrong. He'll rule,
Though, that you'll take a side
Or be disqualified,
Citizen … and perceive
In the weak collective mind's
Twitchings, and your designs,
Both drawing from one spool,
        One tight weave.

6

In crisscrossed tedium
And danger the whole day
He'll bargain time away
For his and both sides' sake
And watch with the setting sun
The little that he'd won
Lost, it may be, to some
    Known mistake.

7

And Solon wants a long
Life (and a death to grieve
A city that he'd leave
Less open to outrage),
Arguing with his friend
Who, saying life should end
At sixty, going strong,
    Dreads old age.

8

And after hot daylight
The spacious, lamplit night—
Among its goings on
The glowing Cyprian
(With luck) helps from above
Delicious physical love
Up to the cooling, white
    Touch of dawn.

9

And there's time in the night
For the god that makes the bright
Splash of the wine and then
That gleam and splash again
That frees both heart and head
To let his warmth and light,
In all that's done and said,
    Slowly spread.

10

And music and the rest
The muses shape is best,
Too, while it's happening—
He made his nephew sing
Some Sappho twice, and why?
It seemed a thing he might
That very winter night
    Learn and die.

11

And all that the muses do,
At once lovely and true,
Starts, not in public light
But somewhere in a night
As private as—the slight
Sound of her quick step through
The door (being for you
    All delight).

12

I have his own words here
On all this—brief and clear:
Let's think of them, my dear,
Sometimes when we two mix
In tedious politics
With its transparent tricks,
Much being under threat
    Since we met—

13

The doings of the lady
From Cyprus I love now
and of Dionysus, and
of the muses, for these three
give people happiness
(so he wrote having written
also the laws for Athens
    at her best).

14

And though whatever we do
May scatter in defeat
At last—still it is true,
For these three time slows down,
While they are going on,
Until, in them alone,
Happiness is complete.
    Solon knew

15

That man is 'all accident,'
Though, all things intersecting
In us…. As the night passed,
However well it went
In each particular,
Politics was protecting
And menacing all we were
        To the last.

AFTERWORD

A friend dislikes the Day
Part of my poem. It
Is 'crabbed,' he says. I say
The anger's deliberate;
Yet aimed at nothing clear
But what to be against:
All politics that claims
To be salvational.
You know the various names
It goes by left and right….

I have my politics,
Living here in the sticks—
Not looking for a fight
I won't inquire of yours,
Of mine will just observe
It never offers cures
(Since cures in politics
Wreck what they're meant to fix),
Is slow to pick its spots
For palliative changes
(Having kept well in mind

There is another kind,
Most thoughtfully arranges
to keep back the Pol Pots),
Tries to be practical,
And not to lose its nerve
When its benefits have a way
Of turning into curses....
(So much for those crabbed Day verses—
At least they led to the Night
With what—but did you guess?—
Would bring us our happiness.)

GERON AT 3:00 A.M.

August, a full moon.
Avoid that window. The lawn
Is cold white marble.

GERON'S SONG

Spring again and now we'll see
If a bent, stiff tree
That the gritty north wind scours
Can put out some flowers.

NIGHT PIECE

also he hath set the world in their heart

I

Back from a trip up north,
From the big bridges over the bays
From the fast or slow, squalid or clean, old or unfinished, sad freeways

With their quite elegant curves
From the seedy cities squeezed in hard
(Hard on the nerves!)
Around the windy shores
To extrude their immaculate glassy high rectangulars,
With cash or credit card …
And so forth;

2

And at the same time back
From the fine old streets under oak shade
Calm airy rooms where you can hear the old music beautifully played
Shops intelligently run
For cheese, fruit, wine, bread—all in trim
In the morning sun;
For books, the bright Black Oak,
And, in the City, that lovely old lady's, with its choice stock
Hid in a cool and dim
Cul-de-sac;

3

Back (and I'm motion-dizzy)
From too much desired and undesired …
van Gogh in Arles thought it a pity that Parisians never acquired
A palate for such crude
Things as a rough-hewn wooden chair
Or earthenware,
'But there, one must not lose
Heart because Utopia's not coming….' Rather choose
To buy paint (then maybe food)
And get busy….

4

Oh you that are the saint
Who shows us best of all,
From your day down to this,
Man free of cowardice,
Living as you had to,
While you could live at all,
That lone life, terrible
In all but the main part,
To paint as you could paint,
'meditate and paint,'
Making red and green display
Man's heart at its ugliest
In a poor night cafe;
Paint for the brain's rest
Or blazing substantial bliss
(And write those thought-tough, true,
Warm, and full-spirited
Letters to your good brother)
To you as to no other
I've turned, to clear my head,
And bring home, to what's mine
Of a more spare design,
My miscellaneous heart,
Now that I'm back from where,
Brainy relentless place,
Offers of everything
Multiply their embrace,
Show how to hold the string
Quartet and cyclotron
Together, and apart—
And, infinitely supple
In everything that's done
All the old ways to couple
Intelligence and pleasure—

And take no quiet measure
Of human life.—I know,
I know this trite complaint
Is half of it the way
The mind takes when it's tired
Or frightened. Still it's so,
All this we have desired
Builds higher the mind's load,
I mean even when good
And calmly understood.

A long day on the road
Has ended in this night
Settling in around
The house and the one sound,
The friction of a pen
On paper by lamplight,
Saying I'm home again.

Now that I've suddenly struck
The last part of the way
With something still to say—
Now that I'm growing old
(And still find with a shock
The spirit never wise
For long, although with luck
It has so far when blasted
Come slowly back, and lasted)
Before I am stopped cold,
I will make here and there
Along the way ahead
(And then let be, together
With whatever else of mine
I leave behind to weather,
Including a daily curse
Posted on likely walls

And trees at intervals
For travelers who make things worse)
—I'd like to make, I say,
Here and there on the way
A little rough shrine,
Something for contemplation,
Like your own kitchen chair,
That's surely now a shrine
And asks for no oblation
From us but contemplation.

Help me when I raise mine
Without an architect,
Made out of words alone
(And for no creed or sect,
And for no personal need)
Along the open way
Spirit comes on today—
To be detected in
The evident and near
And plain and secular,
Drastically puritan.
(Bringing back pure, I mean,
Into our glutted scene
A meaning all but lost
When the Mayflower crossed,
Or St. Francis stripped bare,
Or Christ hung and was broken,
Or Aeschylus had spoken,
Or time-out-of-mind sages
Further and further east;
Always there, though, not least
Glimpsed in the worst of ages:
A mundane pentecost
The mortal spirit makes
Even as it breaks.)

Here put into a book
And each word like a stone
Found where I chance to stop
And thus irregular,
Hefted and so piled up
They all, though out of line,
                Interlock.

GERON'S WINTER WALK

What, stirred still again as I stepped outdoors,
    Mind at idle this winter day,
By how the low sun so lightly lay
    On the leaves of my creekside sycamores,
Thin copper and bronze all bent and bright.
    —And you, brushing the tips of the dark boughs
of my old pine listing over the house,
    O mild-in-mid-December light.

In Plain Air

(1982)

*And let me in these Shades compose
Something in Verse as true as Prose.*
—POPE

Years pass and there continues in me a preoccupation with what it is to be in the physical universe, with its always individual near-at-hand doings and beings, human and otherwise; the whole show shading off into immensity and vagueness, and (however splendid or frightful or dull or, ultimately, unimaginably strange) with its bare unrelenting factuality hurtling along impassively as it does, in a kind of final dignity. Some sense of this preceded by a long time the writing of the poems, I suppose, and has something to do with their unreconstructed realism and particularity.

The poems are nonetheless meditations, and, as I said about some of them in another place, where descriptive they are descriptive meditations, and not meditative descriptions.

Something else. Among the new poems are poems I wouldn't let out by themselves but that—like an "openwork" line in a stanza—make their contribution to the ensemble: what counts for me in any collection is less the individual poem than the individual life, finding its way somehow, anyhow, directly and otherwise, into the whole work....

A.S.

Winter Dusks

AUTUMN: ISLAND

after Jorge Guillén

Autumn, an island
with a severe
profile, watches the combers with their crests
that waver, race forward
to their glistening destruction.

A love for line, and
the grapevine is stripped
of its overlapping green

and a small basket
filled with clusters
out of—good luck: sealed in them
a balancing of dreams
about things possible.

From secret high spirits
a clean style; wisdom the more definite
as it becomes the more inconspicuous, a plain
branch above the hurrying colors.

_________ AT EIGHTY-SIX

This last photograph, for the book jacket,
and you the next thing to the corpse

you will be in a month or so,
the abundant white hair stiff and dull,

the shadows black and sharp in a face now
papery skin over bird-bone; here's

a condescending introduction by a principal
silly ass of the current literary scene.

Never mind, never mind! it chill
and nearly dark now, and you the vesper sparrow

still twittering! no matter that the twittering's weak
and repetitive, in the black locust tree

that holds its thorny old branches, iron hard, above
the frozen ground you criss-crossed when young; winter fields,

bare and rolling, run to the dark East, where shines
through trees a long familiar house light;

but here, it's just you and the dusk, and a gaunt God
with his speculations, joining you now—the three

of you plenty of company for one another.

THE FALL PLOWING BACK HOME

Young, and I burned the world away
Ahead of me, anywhere I went,
With my personal blaze.

Now the world is filling back in.
How I like the plain details,
Complete with shadows, in the low sunlight.

When did I empty?—it's as quiet in here
As a cobweb furred with dust.
Let the harness on its peg

Harden, let the green build up
On the battered brass knobs of the hames.
This old manure scent is dry, and very fine.

Long blades of the afternoon
Slope in through the drop-siding,
Slit the dimness. The light wind

Of late afternoon carries clearly
The fly-buzz of a whole fleet
Of tractors, over the flat brown fields.

THE MAN OF FEELING

Let it go on, he says,
The sweet, steady humming
Of time, and leans again
In the light of the lamp, outside
The gray and dripping day,
Its light entering the window and setting
Its pewter-colored shine
on the back of his hand, his books
In reach, the three or four people
He loves best, at their own doings
In the near middle distance
Of his life this wintry day
As he enters his fiftieth year,
Let it go on,
That sweet hum, let there be
No end to it, ever.

~

Curious how ready he is to die
At moments when he looks around
Quite happy with things—driving

Through town this afternoon,
Heading home, looking forward
To dinner and the evening with *her*,
The town so pleasant in the clear, late light
Reflected from the white undersides of clouds
Pushing out over the rooftops
From the mountains, the air
Chill, fresh off the ocean—

AT LOS OLIVOS AND ALAMEDA PADRE SERRA

Below St. Mary's retreat
In its greenery, on its hill,
Are some unowned olive trees
Backed by a stone wall
In a crook of the busy street.
You can visit them when you please.

Though trucks gear down and brake,
Growling and hissing, and cars
Whoosh by the place all day,
The light's clear there, the gray
Grove whitens, when it stirs,
As if for its own sake,

The ground is packed and bare
And stained bright purple and black
From the unpicked bitter fruit
That spurt from underfoot.
Walking, I do not lack
For quiet in that air.

~

Winter dusk, and I peer
From the stone bridge nearby
Through alder and sycamore
At the stream racing high
And red with mountain mud
And listen till I hear
Under the water-roar
The streambed boulders thud
And see them gone dead white
and silent at this spot,
And the last pool sunk from sight,
And the clear, weightless current
Of the air quivering hot
Over the solid torrent.

~

A place being manifold
With more than the eye can hold,
Was I once Spanish or Greek
To like these gray trees so—
Or a solitary kid
From the dusty plains,
Much to wonder about
Inside himself and out,
Sent to school in town,
Shown a few things to know,
While, in a country drowse,
All but completely lost—
Who came at last to seek
Clearness in all he did,
And had for all his pains
The thing in itself clear
And the meaning disappear
—A strange curse to bring down
On much that he loved most;

Latterly come to stray
Under these twisted boughs
Of the old wisdom, where
Mixing leaves with air
Off the sea below
This is what they say—
Σοφία first was skill,
What a craftsman knew,
Physician, sculptor, smith,
And it is so still,
Being just a way
Not a thing to keep
Or a state of mind
That we stiffen with
And go slowly blind—
But an act of mind
In the course of being,
Going with our seeing;
To sit still and know
Is itself to do,
In our moving through
With the rest of things;
Standing here, we go,
Passing we stand still
(So the gray grove sings
Whitening on its hill)
Till at last we see
Or rather, learn to guess
In our doubleness,
That awake we sleep,
Sleeping we're awake,
And all these mixtures mean
That no thing can be
For its own sweet sake;
Clearness has its source
In the Vague and Vast—

Shapeless, these two last,
While clearness's green leaf
Shapely bright and brief
Consummates their powers;
That the seen and unseen
Send into each other
One another's force,
Separated die
Quicker than cut flowers—
As for what you write
(Rustles one old tree)
Why, Athene knows
Every poem goes
No matter at what height
Over rails of prose,
Length on length on length
Shoved by smoky strength
Straight and smooth and bright,
And the ugliness
Where the iron is mined
Of necessity
Has a dignity
She could not but bless
—If she, brought to birth
by Hephaestus' axe,
Shouting her war cry,
And without a mother,
Were the blessing kind.

~

Such is what I heard
When the branches stirred
In their dialect;
Now I look around

And this bare dry ground
Prompts me to reflect
No man walks beside
Athene the clear-eyed,
She was born complete
Of the bright-lit myth
Where she keeps her distance
From the shadowed earth;
From the twisted trees
Standing here, for instance,
Catching the sea breeze—
Slow to grow and bear,
Whether here or elsewhere
Cultivated stocks
Grafted to the wild
(Mixture in the shoot)
Able to hold out
For the dusty farmer
Through the longest drought,
Grappled in the rocks;
The black, bitter fruit
Yielding a clear oil
That once symboled human
Plenty and good will,
Bitter turning mild
In the hands of skill
For the kind of peace
Households need—all this
Sponsored by a woman
Who was born in armor
And who bore no child.

MID-OCTOBER

And such
things as he achieved are
to him now as its ringed
wood to an old tree, firm
and of the essence
and utterly remote
from the present quick
movements of the leaves, whereas
from the most recent
of a varied assortment
of misjudgments in the life
the pain is as keen
as it is familiar, joining
the life's quite particular
griefs that, subsiding of course
in time, run fresh nevertheless
as when, years back,
they arose, while it is now, now
with the first cold wind
of the fall blowing
down the empty road
that he's walking, one more
aging man, lights
from the house windows
piercing now here now there
the wind-roughed trees,
the first leaves
to be torn loose in the season
skidding wildly past him,
he gaining the hilltop,
looking across the canyon
at the mountain, trickling
headlights along its road,
the trees roaring now and

dark below, their wrenching
tops catching the red
of a last flare of the sunset.
No car passes. Nobody else
out here. The wind hurries
its new, clean, cold volumes of air
through the big vacancy between him
and the mountain: old elation,
come of this icy freshness
in things in their clearness,
shapes—in the sharp air
of this one deepening dusk—black
now and unreturning,
though a man travels
no more than a tree.

NIGHT PIECE

Last night I lay awake
beside my sleeping wife
at four a.m., and listened:
wind sifted through the pine tree
and made a branch tip finger
the roof above our bed
as if reflectively.
Then I went in my mind
the way the wind was taking—
down through the winding canyon,
shouldering past the trees,
and onto Hendry's beach,
across the channel waters,
gaining the channel islands,
and then the open sea
and moving by itself
over the dark swells
and nothing more to seek.

~

My dear slept on beside me
I knew; I had for proof
her light breath on my cheek.
The branch kept fingering
the same place on the roof.

A LIGHT RAIN IN THE LATE EVENING

A green bush in the shower
That bleared the window pane
Stood shining when it stopped
In its new skin of rain:
While leaves and eaves dripdropped
I stepped out on the scene
To breathe the late cold air,
When the sun broke through again
Forming a leaf of light
On every leaf of green
Making a bush of light
Still green with all its power
In the approach of night
And I could find nowhere
To put the credit for this
And similar unsought pleasures
Various in their measures
In things that barely mattered
That I never thought to keep
And certainly can't miss
When I dissolve in sleep
Leaving them where they're scattered

A Puff of Smoke

A PUFF OF SMOKE

When my old friend writes to me
Of the 'stark fact that the mind
Appears to be infinite
And to have nothing to do
With the scientific "law"
Of dispersion'—I don't know,
I'll have to write in reply,
Maybe it is infinite
As the world of numbers is,
His purlieu. Immortal, though?
Why, it's an activity,

And it stops. Smashing the skull
Ends it—the anesthetist
Interrupts it, telling you
Mildly, 'Let me see how wide
You can open your mouth, now,'
And the next thing is a flood
Of bright gray light, followed not
By immersion in darkness,
But a moment's consciousness
That the light's gone; and then
Not even darkness. Nothing.

What is this nothing? Nothing.
Where is this nothing?… Think how
When a reader finishes
His reading, as an event
Of his attention, it is
A memory—a different

Event. His book's an object,
Gathers dust among objects
In no terrible darkness
Or emptiness, but only
In things around, continuing.

There are no gaps in the world.
If spirit's intermittent,
A flickerer that at last
Goes out, the body goes on,
Disintegrating only
To other bodies. The fine
Chemicals…! (While the body
And its habitat were what
Spirit had burned for its warmth
And light. In the beginning,
Spontaneous combustion.)

~

—Conscious again; shaking, cold,
Interstellar cold sunk in
To the middle of the bones.
No doubt from the shock. A new
Numbness down there, and fresh pain,
And a meek feebleness, and
Morphine, all teach the spirit
How it sits reliantly,
Precariously, astride
Its old mule, the body, now
Tottering along strange roads.

I am still musing upon
The horrors that shape themselves
In the gray country of drained

Vitality, foul places
And presences that we two
Innocents visited, with
A sighting one night (eyes closed)
Of death's door, going past it
In the hospital basement:
Bare concrete, tall, wide, unmarked,
Set flush in the concrete wall.

~

The stunned spirit monitors
The shocked and wounded body
And itself; and puzzles how
The mind includes the body
The body includes the mind
Equally.
          —I remember
Using the body the way
One drove a car when a kid:
To see what it could take, from
A curiosity quite
Disinterested, from anger

At a world so impassive
And clearly uninterested
In the spiritual (no
We would not have used that word),
Authority of energies
Our own yet not our own; and
From exuberance.... When young
We are I think but distantly
Attached to our bodies, being
Ill-informed still on any
Necessity we live by.

Years pass and we sink into
The body. Now warily there
I find I take a kindly
Interest in the more or less
Faithful old mount (that is
When fairly healthy), wrily
Admiring its survival
Of pain sickness and danger,
With recollections of work,
Food, sleep, love, talk; of places
Where for moments all was well.

And one day we are body,
And nothing more. Though spirit
Is instructed by the body
Not the other way around,
It's in the spirit only
That instruction can take place
—Of what grand elaborate sorts—
While a definition of
The body might be: What knows,
Really knows its lessons, so
Is a fully accredited

Member of the cosmos. While
The spirit, born ignorant
Of its own rules, and the world's,
At the end has, at best, earned
Only a provisional,
Temporary membership,
Still more ignorant than not
(Which must befit it, must be
Of its nature)—and at worst
Will be all but blackballed (yet
Never quite, even at worst?)....

~

Home again! I write my friend,
And at such a time as this—
To be driven home and see
On the way people's fruit trees
Bright with blossoms in back yards;
And on the hills above town
New green from the recent rains
After a dry winter; that
Was a piece of good timing
I tell you; and once at home
Green fresh outside the windows.

~

Still, what the wan spirit knows,
After its late adventures,
Is a world surrounding it
As nicely put together,
And frail, as the seed crown of
A dandelion; and I walk,
Gaining strength, the grassy hills
Through the wildflowers, little
Fire shapes in the green, fading
Here and there with the approach
Of summer, and its routines.

FIRST DEPOSITION

A trout stream in the high Rockies,
my wife's laughter, a little brass whale
from Taiwan, the sight from my study window
of the two blue hills above the trees,
all kinds of cats, the high desert
of northern Nevada, all particulars
concerning the life and writings of Pope,
the time of sundown and just after,
the grammar of any language, a flawless
sea urchin shell found on Hendry's beach
and kept around and looked at
almost daily for ten years now,
all the birds, the look of Greek on the page,
cottonwood trees in summer, glistening
above the ditches in the dry country
of the west, the words of English songs
of the period 1580 to 1620,
the smell of lumber, of the iron
in a hoe as you file it, of a horse;
bolts of fine woolen goods;
the Indian head nickel; rain,
snow, sunshine, wind, darkness,
the game of poker, discovering used bookstores
in large cities, the clear recollection
of the house and farmyard of early childhood;
driving through streets to meet someone
at the airport, at an hour, late or early,
when you are not usually out; bare trees;
the rhythms of iambic trimeter;
granite boulders; coffee; the coming
of the early darkness of December.

Work

PURE PERCEPTION

And I woke up this morning
    To nothing on my mind.
Friends, it was putting to your ear a watch
    You had forgot to wind.

It was walking through the half-dark
    Of a sales barn after the sale;
Litter and echo; light from a far door
    Falling still and pale—

Was the barren clarity
    Of a February sun
And you look up at a stony peak and see
    That the stone is stone.

O all day long the air
    Will move clear, cold, and thin
Over things that have come up too near to me—
    It will razor off my skin,
    And no event within.

THE WEATHER MAN

Cold and from the wrong direction
a cutting wind out of a raw
blue sky, the feelings have shrunk back
and frozen, a swamp iron-hard in the cold,
all the lively emotions of yesterday
not even a memory, but like hearsay.

My brain's been taken out. All day
I go about my duties as usual
with a headful of icy air.

THE GNOMES

Months pass and still
they come squeezing out—
little deformed pre-poems
between crammed duties
and whatnot, the attention
wrenched this way and that.

Keeping their distance
they look at me
with their lopsided faces, one eye
higher than the other,
in those eyes the light,
a pale, clear green,
of an unworldly
wisdom; they stand there quietly
for as long as I look at them.

WORK

And I wake up,
yeh, it is dawn,
the young helper, waiting
pale and serious
outside the window.

INSIDE INSIDE

The Japanese farmer
in Rexroth's translation
hoes weeds all day
and then hoes them again
all night in his dreams

joining a memory of hoeing all day
forty years back, and all night
dreaming of hoeing
till I was so tired in my dream
I found a pile of gunny sacks
in the noon shade of the tree
between the well pump and the garage
and sank down on them and slept,
a dreamless sleeper in a dreaming sleeper.

LATE SONG: AMBUSH

I see my bones lie white
And shining in the Light,
I need the darkness here
Inside me to repair
Old purposes much frayed,
Or shelved, being so ill-made,
Parts of my life now broken
For clear thoughts left unspoken,
Things I uttered, too,
Made some of it run untrue,
Of all that's mine alone
Little fit to be shown—
With more work crowding in,
A fresh page to begin,

And a recent bad mistake
To fix, lest the Light break
And my case still not made,
My meanings all waylaid,
And all I am lying clear
With no interior,
And my bones sprawled out white
And shining in the Light

SECOND DEPOSITION

Sometimes I look inside
and see a mountain slope
in Colorado. There
my grief comes trickling down
from the packed snow of my hate
freshly, spring after spring,
through darkness under fir trees.

You've seen such places, maybe.
There breed the little wild trout,
the brooky and the cutthroat
in their icy brilliant colors,
there, under branches sagging
or broken from the snows,
the thin song of mosquitoes
criss-crosses the chill air,
there, tiny colored stars
on the dark of the wet moss,
a few mountain flowers tremble,
fine roots washed in snow water,
the colors clear and cold
—almost too small to notice
should you stray under there,
certainly too small to pick.

And These

AND THESE

Out of an occasional delight
in those icy vacancies
that stretch away
from the 'comforting stench
of comrades'
        mostly
of a simple, bi-partite
structure like the fungus
living with an alga
to make a lichen, some
2,000 species of which
inhabit the Arctic, fastened
to rocks, pieces of bone,
cast-off antlers, so cold
and barren and dark
their situation, some of them
may grow only during one
day in a year—in the long
darkness each bright patch
holding fast to its object.

FIVE O'CLOCK

Just before hitting the turn
and entering the down ramp
hunched up and tensed again
and the little new moon in the west
by herself in the early darkness
cocked backward so jauntily
on the steep downward slope
into the wintry ocean

DEC. 19, 1975

A malformed and much sophisticated world
it is, and I in my fiftieth winter of it
with a few ordinary things known, matters of doing,
matters of desire, and there's the full moon
in the workshop window again,
with its old silent abruptness, light
held cleanly inside its firm rim,
lifting so clear and cold
over the wintering poplars—scrawny
columns of brush upfountaining
through how many years? over
the worn and frozen lawn, grove
and grass burning white together

THE STUDY WINDOW

All tired out in the morning,
yeah, and the moon there, old
in the midmorning sky, white
and worn away on one side
so thin, the sky shows through,
in the stillness above the crisp
snow peaks of the winter mountains.

MARCH 16, 1976

Home for the convalescence, stepping
Out on the patio, the sun
Shining at full strength on me,
And there, aslant in the shadow,
Is our young maple, that had been

A forked stick all winter,
With its new leaves, each pale,
Just uncrimping from the confinement
Of its bud, individually distinct
At the tips of the thin twigs—
Dark, overlapping, they will make
Heavy clumps in the summer and be
The main fact of the tree, but don't yet
Belong to it, still glistening
In the film of their newness, out in the air
Like a scatter of little green birds,
The pointed lobes of the leaves
With the shape and tilt of wings.

THE WINDOW: IN TIME OF DROUGHT

The camellia leaves against it
will be sleeked with the cold
wet, despite their jouncing
under the big drops
and then the air going
gray-green with the rain
clattering suddenly,
water bunched, quivering,
dragged by the heavy wind
in long diagonal welts
across the old window,
as if the glass were melting—
as it is, in fact, the panes
being thicker at the bottom,
ever so slightly,
after all these years, from the slow
downward pour of the glass

A YOUNG SLUG ON THE COUNTER

Brought in unawares—suddenly
Airborne as he was clambering
Over the *Times* in his cruise
Across the rainy sidewalk
In the early November dark.

And now on the move again,
Singlemindedly, belongingly,
In the warm lit kitchen,
His rain-freshened, mucusy skin
Glistening, clean as the porcelain tiles;

And meanwhile, to imagine, still
Travelling through his tissues
Toward the immaculate dark
At his center, the phosphorus-cold glow
Of his wonder: shy, by itself, slow.

SOLILOQUY

Home as are his brothers on a visit
and now saying as we sit at dinner
'After dark I walked out from camp
under the pine trees and wondered
where the light was coming from,
there was no moon. I looked up
and it was stars, I've never seen
so many big stars so close together,
and right over me was Orion,
with his legs down in the branches.
The sky had more light area than dark;
And in the trees, stars were shining
in the smallest openings.'

THE ROSS'S GULL

Whenever the Arctic winter nears
and the white sun just clears
the earth's rim and the tundra colors go
under the new snow
and the terns and plovers make their flight
away from a solid night
and ptarmigan, fox, owl, hare
turning white, disappear
on the white space under the black sky
and the gulls, too, fly
by coast and open waters down
to where there's green and brown,
the Slaty-backed, the Glaucous, the pale
gray Iceland gull—
then the little Ross's gull makes a strange
migration from his summer range
in north Siberia—heading northeast;
most lovely and known least
of gulls; his plumage a delicate rose....
Northeast then north he goes
beyond Point Hope, and Icy Cape, and past
Point Barrow till at last
he disappears, with his graceful, wavering flight
into the polar night
and his cry *a-wo a-wo a-wo*
kiaw! drifting back slow.
There he will fly and sleep and eat
for some nine months in the complete
darkness—God's own darkness, surely—
over the Arctic sea,
feeding among the open water cracks

Note: "graceful, wavering flight," and most of the information, are borrowed from
Arthur Cleveland Bent's *Life Histories of North American Birds, Gulls, and Terns.*

in the shifting polar packs
(so the authorities suppose,
nobody knows)
in his fresh rose feathers no one can see
up there, not even he.

IN THE CANYON

More distinct
than ever we

can be,
their ways

remotely
crisscrossing ours,

gods
each

with his one
virtue

(or maybe two
or three)

by itself
simple,

disclosed
with such unintended

sureness and
so glancingly

passing across
the eye-piece

of our
complicated and

clumsily aimed
attention

~

Of birds the big flicker
his cry from a treetop clanging
in the first light: how to begin.
And the deer, for the body's lightness, surprised
at mid-day, russet and a hint of antlers
over the green bushes then gone,
as if he had not been in motion but hanging there
when the whole forest shifted a little
and concealed him—
the bear for knowledge
in detail—there is no other—of his terrain, and
for his unhurried gait
that takes him so rapidly
where he wants to go, his company
his solitariness—and for his capacious
robe of sleep for the long cold and darkness,
and in the new grass by the footpath out back
the green and yellow striped
garter snake that shows every time
how innocence startles,
the snail for his hush,
the grasshopper, of insects, for alertness
and his lucky look

SPRING

We two at our reading this evening
making a busy stillness in the room
when the singing of a mockingbird
came fresh and loud
straight into my ear
from the long empty, black
cave-mouth of—the cold dark lung
of the fireplace, beside my chair.

END OF SEPTEMBER

However it may be with me
Lying wakeful in the old bed
This night is cool, fresh, quiet,
Moon-blanched, a few late season crickets
Trill under the oaks across the road,
Some of the moonlight, coming through
The pine tree by the window,
Burns like lumps of phosphorus, on the bedclothes.

READER LISTENING

Rain now with dark coming on
after the chill clear day, and it makes
coming against the roof a roof of sound.
Many mild little comments,
with the occasional loud drop,
the faint ones, the pitch
differences, the many drops striking
at almost the same time, the
individual sounds still audible
in the general run of sound as the rain
comes down heavier, loudening

on the roof, the sense of this change
belonging with the sense that comes
when an animal one has been watching—
say a bear, soaking himself in a creek—
suddenly & calmly changes position—
when on the window ledge
a series of drops begins falling,
starting up an excited little
local tempo, and then, oddly, slows down
and at last stops while the heavy rain
continues

~

… and leaving, then,
for that first companion
of your mere existence (before
you established relations even
with yourself, or your human mother)
the immense brood-beast
the natural universe, where
for instance Homer's 'dark earth
and starry sky and strong-running ocean'
are a corpuscle eddying—
                              not
to be home any more,
with a consciousness like the house
built joist and stud and rafter
in time, in human lengths, not
to pause even at the nestling
of chemical to chemical,
but entering those subtle barrens
where billionths of seconds go,
under the whole show
(leptosome to the last!),
into the sheer and clear
orderliness of chance

where the numbers do their dance
of no location—haunt,
if what I've read is so,
of Heisenberg, and Planck,
and the quiet magister, Gauss

THIRD DEPOSITION

The lamp throws a pleasant warmth
on the back of the hand, its soft white light
floods shoulder fingers pencil note pad
and desk surface, notes on old soiled scraps of paper,
the Hölderlin, the glasses case, the black bowl
by Blue Corn, the Hokusai Fishermen Draw in Their Nets
While a Poet Meditates in a Distant Hut,
the Porsche ad, The City Porsche, cut out
of an old *Time* years ago, a blue-silver 914
driven by a blonde up a hill in San Francisco,
the 0.5 liter earthenware coffee mug,
the drafts of a poem, "migraine's fancy
stitching" a phrase at the corner of the eye,
piles of old letters—the latest from Helle—
a lucite box of dry flies, clippings of reviews
of books wanted, a lump of turquoise and
a piece of white granite veined with green
from the Snowy Range in Wyoming,
white glue, a pen light disassembled
its batteries exposed, a bit of paper folded so
that a quote from Pope sits up, and crawling across
all this comes the black cat, Christmas, so much
admired by the family, cautiously lowering
and lengthening her body, one glossy paw
testing for a spot to sleep in, settling instead
for the window shelf, hind quarters on a *New York Review*,
front quarters, and cheek, on an old rabbit pelt,
a paw curled over her eyes.

Toad Sweat

τεττιγα δ'εδραξω πτερου

FRAGMENT

... Self
the sly continuator; peevish; writhing
knot of flat-eyed appetites,

no one of which ever notices
the others it's tangled with; old

shapelessness, incessantly bringing on
disorderly assemblies of shapes;

busy attractor of swarms
of gnat-miseries with its sweat; deep

well of pity for its own plights
and tireless accumulator of grievances; inflamed

and swollen with the merit
so gained, with gleeful resentment

concealing its own indestructible
talent for moderate happiness; constantly

aching to be changed into now this
now that icon of calm felicity

FATHER AND CHILD

These are the case-hardened fingers
With which I bring to your pink
And drooling mouth your food
From farther away than you think,
      But sleep,
Sleep in the natural dark.

With this electronic sound
I shall teach you what to do,
My son, as I now sing
Lullaby for love of you.
      Now sleep,
Sleep in the natural dark.

Fetched from the polymerized
Thermoplastic womb,
Now blue-eyed and golden-haired
And shapely and firm of limb!
      Sleep, sleep,
Sleep in the natural dark!

Under this coat spun of cooled
Chemicals is the shoulder of chrome
That will edge you after a while
Out of your gleaming home.
      (Now sleep,
Sleep in the natural dark.)

Whereupon you will ascend
Chock full of your own desires
On your own titanium wings
Driven by chemical fires,
      But sleep, now,
Sleep in the natural dark.

The night wind and a bough tip
Brushing the pane make a mild,
Serious, purposeless music,
O my strange human child.
    Sleep, now,
Sleep in the natural dark.

MEETING OLD MR. JIM PORCUPINE

At the reading—somewhat country-boy,
it's just you people and me, here;
open, simple, sincere—mind you,
clever enough never to be
anything like them. There are certain ideas
none of us would be caught dead with, which makes
our being here together—well, pleasing.

The trouble is, I remember
how very savvy, how cagily nice
and quick on his feet the fellow was
when he stopped by to visit earlier,
though I sat there supposing it was just conversation
after a while I began to feel in my skin
the fine little needles of—what's this, malice?

Friends, imagine seeing out in the woods
your ordinary old lumbering porcupine
and he commences capering around you
with, by God, the smooth quickness
of a monkey, and while you stand there gaping
he's busily firing his quills into you!
I know, porcupines don't do that.

But your canny, enterprising sentimentalist does.

THE CAREER

By means long since too commonplace to mention
(Taught, therefore, in the classrooms of the land,
With diagrams) he captured their attention.
How anxiously they came to see him stand
With a loop of his intestines in each hand!
        He was no Indian giver.
He fed them with his two lungs and his liver.
His call was 'Come and see a man unmanned.'
He diced his heart and kidneys. He became
        All mouthed name,
And then they took the blame.

WINTER CHILD

        Never mind now, I am delighted,
        my happiness is complete—
        the individual human now recedes
        with his motley moderations
        on moderate little earth
        these days of October,
        November, December, when
        the mother darkness and cold
        come back and the father light
        wheels low, aslant, unconcernedly
        withdrawn into remoteness,
        in the extravagance
        he blazes with, and we
        come back into the mineral
        sleep (a little way) from which
        rousing so keenly
        in the cold
        we see and hear nothing
        but the Heart's red fires in the dark, in

the end Silences
where reign the archaic King
and his Queen, that was
before him, in the Beginning.

IN THE HABITAT OF THE MAGPIE

Oh, we will get out of here
Where everything's impure, not clear,
Where, as they say, it's all shades of gray,
Won't we, old self (though time I fear
Is getting on…)—like the magpie
We saw springing up today
Lightly from his putrid meal
On the pavement, his feathers
Such a fresh black and white.

THE ACCIDENT

"A poem does not come into existence by accident."
—PROFESSORS W. AND B. ON THE WAY TO DISCOVERING
THE INTENTIONAL FALLACY

Dear Mother Muse,
We *thought*
we were being careful.
But it appears to be
a very healthy little poem.

NEAR THE STAIRS

This busy lame-brain,
This picker-up of ideas
Discarded by their owners,
This maimed intelligence
Hobbling to catch up,
Eager to compete, arriving
At the arena after
It has emptied, this
Challenger and flincher
With the wrecked, zestful mentality,
This poor devil, pity
And keep clear of him,
He'd trip you with his crutch
Should he find himself beside you
At the head of the stairs.

FRAGMENT

... and still, deep down, in your personal
La Brea Tar Pits, sunken
some of them these twenty years,
like so many mastodons, sloths,
sabre-toothed tigers,
this hulking collection
of old hatreds, perfectly preserved.

Running at Hendry's

For head with foot hath private amitie
And both with moons and tides.

—HERBERT

NOTE

I've always loved the old sonnet sequences more than any of the sonnets in them, magnificent or lovely as these may be. The sequences take up as no single poem can the unpredictable mix of experiences and themes with the prevailing passion, all going on during a longish stretch of time. Then there are the scraps of narrative that come out incidentally, the shifts (alas) in the passion itself, the sense that each poem is being done at a sitting with the time passing, that an idea that doesn't come through satisfactorily here may turn up later (only now with a fresh secondary theme jostling it which later becomes itself a main theme), the untidy couplings of metaphysics and peevishness, jealousy or other unworthy emotions, this or that unrelated preoccupation obtruding along the way, the speaker himself changing willy-nilly, the bits of news, glooms, dull stretches, elations—and the old types, the anniversary sonnet, the insomniac sonnet, the sonnet about the sonnet.

When I found myself taking up running at the height of the craze, a byproduct was that phrases kept coming to mind, pieces of poems, having to do not only with running but also with the not especially beautiful or otherwise remarkable beach where I ran. I had come to love the place for its shapes, tones, smells and the rest, not least the people that showed up there. All this, with its daily, hourly changeableness, I was each day looking forward obsessively to visiting. So here was a passion, and it occurred to me that I could cross the new craze with an old craze and do a sonnet sequence, drawing on whatever came in handy in the older craze, for treatment of what I was doing down at Hendry's nearly every day, over the weeks, the months, the unspectacular seasons.

A.S.

AFTER WORK: FOREWORD

Home, then out of the canyon and inch past
Shopping center, school; inch over freeway;
Veer with the creek that notches the pale clay
Headlands and I am at the place at last.
The shoreline hereabouts runs east and west.
Clear days there's islands to be seen, any day
Sky, sand, waves, light, birds, dogs, people. I'd say
Late in the day in winter is when it's best.
Down the long, slant beach, and the wave-tips catch
The sun's low fire, the wet sand's all red light,
The shorebirds eat red light—and all goes gray
The moment you turn back the other way,
Cliffs, sea, and sky a great cave, in dead light;
And the fresh darkness settling, in the stretch.

1

DOWN HERE AFTER BEING KEPT
AWAY THREE WEEKS BY SICKNESS

How much I missed this place. While I've been gone
The season has turned, the winter birds are here,
The sand is firm, clean, smooth, and the air clear
With a wave flashing cold in the low sun
Under the slow wingbeats of a pelican
That three pilfering gulls keep swinging near,
Whimbrels and godwits and plovers and killdeer
Work the sleek shallows, I begin to run:
Easy, now. But I swear the beach gives back
My footthuds like the tightly stretched buckskin
It looks like here, the blazing water track
Of the sun's running beside me—coming in
The old ocean commotion and the dark mass
Of a jogging girl's hair jouncing as we pass.

2

COMMOTION

Under a low fogbank, the blackish tone
Of its belly darkening the waves and sand
And cliffs that block all view of the high land
Where the town sits in sunlight, I'm alone,
The beach is bare, the hard brown sand slopes down
Steeply to the low tide. From where I stand
No jogger rounds the point to scare the band
Of godwits from their meal. I'll start my run
Together with the dark sea running in
From a horizon turning steely bright
(Sun finishing its run where the fog's thin)
While jaegers and gulls keep up a running fight
Whirling sharp black against that piece of sky
The beach and cliffs run toward and likewise I.

3

LIBERTÉ, FRATERNITÉ

More fog.—Have you seen a gross, heavy-legged deer?
Or in a flight of terns some with the bill
Twisted and blunt, some with stub wings, some small
As wrens? Imagine an ectomorphic bear.
No, shaped by the shapes of water and earth and air
They move in ruthless grace and crucial skill
Unfree and strong and evenly beautiful,
Unprovided with souls, completely clear and here.
I pass a poor old woman, six foot three,
Mannish, who has a heron's jerky stride,
Just as a well-built fellow passes me.
Next, hairy breasts swinging from side to side,
An obese youth rounds the point; and better weather
Brings many another of us out here together.

4

BEACH LITTER

Slipped through the fingers of my writing-hand
Already in these dozen days or so—
The grove of winter trees, intaglio
Complete with twigs, carved in the hard smooth sand
(While the waves keep rushing in to land
In the old uproar) by the trickling backflow,
And running in fog, and the young pair who go
Down beach apart, I see the fellow stand
With his back to her while she with her eyes
Downward walks this way, that way—coming in
I pass and hear her humming cheerfully,
And the cold light one dusk far out at sea
And the time I finished fast as if to win,
Some girl's clear laugh away down the beach the prize:

5

—Or the man and the old woman seated at either end
Of a long bench that leans and sags rustily:
Though sudden raw weather has cleared the beach, and she
Is dressed none too warmly, she keeps with a thin hand
Her jacket collar closed and reads on as she'd planned,
It looks like, in an old paperback, all the while he
Dressed up as for a party—a party refugee?—
Stares, with his elbows on his knees, at the cold sand:
Or the leopard seal lying long dead and swollen tight
Getting his spots changed for him, all right, by the sea
And the sea air: or that strong old man in serious thought,
Bareheaded, in a workman's clothes—a machinist, maybe;
The last runner in, I met him stalking doggedly out
Between dark sea and cliffs in the fast-failing light.

6

THE PELICAN-WATCHER (1)

Dusk under fog; and under fog a mist
Grays out the view three hundred yards off shore;
Ocean, though wind's no harder than before,
Smashes and roars where it had slapped and hissed
All week long; beach may be at its ugliest
Heaped up with kelp torn from the ocean floor,
Huge clots and strings of it, yellowy brown, and more
Comes heaving and sprawling in on every crest.
Few birds. It's townsfolk out for the spectacle
And hundreds of surfers: black torsos holding still
As tree stumps in the troughs, awaiting the right one.
No pelicans. I miss them, on my run.
Then, five of them! infixing their reflection
In the wave's wall they fly along to perfection.

7

THE PELICAN-WATCHER (2)

There must have been five hundred here last week
Not grazing the waves like these but swirling high
Their silhouettes jagged against a sky
Bright silver in the west over a sleek
And blazing evening sea; slow, homely, meek
Amongst the agile lovely terns and sly
Gull gangs they flapped deliberately by.
Ungainly dives get them the fish they seek.
They look like so much scrap-iron hurled in the air,
But they belong. Archaic and venerable
Their ugliness no less than their steady skill
(And now alas who's jogging toward me there?
A handsome colleague whose talk is a display
Of intellectual cowardice and decay…).

8

RUNNING WITH MY SONS

Two of them home by chance the same weekend!
I fight a fear that's like Ben Jonson's fear,
Of being too glad of having them down here
Running abreast with me on the hard smooth sand.
And all the better it is for being unplanned:
I have no heed for shorebirds, or the clear
Sunlight inside the wavelets rippling near,
Or other runners, or the familiar blend
Of surf- and gull-noise.—One of them sprints away
Spattering through the shallows like a pup,
I say to the other "Don't let me hold you up,"
And off he spurts. I watch them happily.
How they shine! across the difference of years,
And will shine in my day fears and night fears.

9

RUNNING WITH MY SONS

Fifty-one runs with nineteen and twenty-three
Thinking "by hap of happy hap," the phrase
Cast by the crude old Tudor well displays
The kinship of happiness and luck … I see
From the corner of my eye how springily
The boys are striding, how their breathing stays
Easy and light. Not so with them always,
Both once rode crutches after surgery.
We round the second point and they run on
Into the haze, down beach I've never run,
While I turn back, and think of how that stretch
They're running is like the years I'll never reach;
And think helplessly, how will it be for them?
It'll be the same and sharply not the same.

10

MORE HAP

Bad omen in the morning and once more
Late in the day, encountering face to face
Two sons of bitches, each at a time and place
I'd never seen either one of them before.
And the day, picketed by this polluting pair,
Went wrong; running in the dusk I now retrace
The slight brain-lurches that put me off my pace …
The slippages of heed that are my despair!
So I run along full of my latest blunder—
And everything's still, but a distant simmering
From the sea, the light rakes low, the tide is neap,
In the strange peace I nearly halt in wonder
At water in thin clear layers wavering
On the flat sand—a kind of shining sleep.

11

DELIGHTS OF WINTER EVENINGS DOWN HERE

Saturday night. The ranger's shut the gate.
In the deep dusk I make his figure out
Eyeing me as I wheel the Z about
Five yards from his white gate-bars and hesitate
At the open Exit. Never before so late,
I park on up the road. He has the clout
To turn me back, I half expect his shout
As I slip through the nearly dark parking lot:
Cold wind. Dark sea with sharp little peaks all over.
This long bright strip I'm running on is lighter
Than the sky! Back where the beach is dark some water
Or foam—no, the white patch on a wing is flashing.
Five terns—still seeing fish!—plunge, wheel, hover.
Black stubs of surfers lift on a swell—*that's* passion.

12. GOD-LIGHT

Low dark cloud-cover and ocean make a pair
Of jaws held just apart; in the opening,
Where I now run, no room for anything
But the cliffs, now bleakly pale where they are bare.
At the horizon, a low, cold light just where
The sun has set; I watch it briefly cling
At the sea's rim—clear God-light, the real thing—
While I run on through suddenly darkening air.
Under the cliffs are sanderlings and plovers
Busy with their last feeding for the day;
And a few people—a lone girl there, two lovers,
An old lady with her dog; and part way
Down the cliff ahead a house hangs, with a flight
Of stairs down to the beach, and window light.

13. HOUSE

Though days may pass and you'll see no one there
The place is lived in always. There was the sight
You could have seen in clear, still evening light,
Of a girl trimming a bearded young man's hair
Out on the littered deck, and you might hear
The little dog's wow-*wow!* when running late
And alone below; for months a drying skate
Swung under the deck, wetsuits and suchlike gear
Hang from the railings. Looks like a fine life.
Sometimes one of them waves as they come and go
Casually in view of us passersby below,
While they hang half in the air on the steep clay;
That the house is going, waves chewing away,
Is habit-knowledge with them, as between man and wife.

A big storm struck shortly after this was written, some of the cliff gave way, and one of the family was interviewed in the paper: "I know what it's like to live with the sound of concrete popping, but when you love to live here …."

14

RUNNING LATE

Last class goes overtime, there's some delay
Getting an ace bandage on an aching knee
At the right tension, and then hurriedly
Into slow, slow traffic: the last light of day
Fades off the clouds above my getaway,
Though there at last and running I can see
The sickle moon reflected, glittery,
Like a surf-perch, in a wave; under the play
Of water sliding in and sliding back,
This sand is a seal's flank, the inch-high hiss
Of that foam edging somehow throws a black
Shadow in this faint light; my emphasis
Was haste-blurred on those lines of Herbert's. How
I'd like to have the class back (briefly!) now.

15

RUNNING LATE, HAVING HELD THE CLASS ON
HERBERT OVERTIME TO LOOK AT THREE LINES

Deep dusk, the quarter moon strong enough now
To show in the wave's flank with a fish-like glitter,
I run on the dark beach thinking, This is better
Than the delicate orange clouds two days ago
In pale green sky, too pretty. (Are there no
Other runners here, for once?) Thinking, That wetter
Sand there shines like some membrane, this twitter
Of sleepy sanderlings says it must be so
That I'm the last one out, that subdued roar
Of water's a not-word I have heard before,
And suddenly there comes the one thing more
I ought to have told the class, that not elsewhere
In English is that thought thought—and see how clear
And passionate and quiet it is there.

16

RUNNING AGAINST A COLD WIND

A bleakness about the place, with the wind keen,
Dark ocean under it running like a full
Rough icy river. A bright diagonal
Of orange cloud slopes over the whole scene,
The sky below it's turning that strange pale green
Coleridge in his dejection couldn't feel
The beauty of. I think of the tall girl
Who glanced my way as I came driving in,
And again later as I began my run
And passed her with her friends, and how her presence
Filled for a time the whole place like a fragrance.
Hard going now! lungs hurting, and she long gone
And everyone else but me, the whole scene stark,
Even the cliff house windows staying dark.

17

AND THE FAT ONE GRIPPING
A BOTTLE OF WINE

Blazing November. The wrongness of this weather's what
Makes my being here for anything all wrong, the sea
Having gone slack and pale and bland and summery,
The air since the first light this morning dry and hot
And motionless. Broad day's brought everybody out.
There goes a runner threading through a family
Straggling along in street-clothes. Surfers unseeingly
Step around three elderly ladies. All tramp my holy spot.
I run on sand where multitudes lay and strolled and sat.
It's scuffed and stale. And heading through the overused scene,
Around the last point I see alone out on the flat,
Where the sand's newly wet, one fat girl and one lean
Briefly link arms and dance, whirling this way and that
Over their clear, prancing reflections in the sheen.

18

RUNNING WITH A POEM FROM
THE LATEST *TLS* IN MY HEAD

A hot breath off the land at my turnback spot.
A streak of skunk-scent a little further down.
Sea quiet in the late dusk. No moon
As yet. The hard sand uneven underfoot,
Much trampled on. An airliner's headlight
Makes a big white star in the orange coming on
In thin clouds fanning out from the set sun—
Orange, and a real green, staying clear and bright!
But what I think of's the Britisher with the dripping nose
Who thinks we'll think he's tough because he says
Evil is tough and sure of itself and Good
Is gentle, irresolute. You know how it goes?
St. Thomas More, for instance, living in a daze?
Samuel Johnson, so lacking in hardihood?

19

MOON MEASURING

Moon'll be rising. There's a few people here
In the chill of the sundown, some of them regulars—
Old tilt-hat's there on his bench, photographers
Stand waiting for the colors to appear
As the sun drops. Pelicans swing in near
The flat beach where the sea now mildly stirs.
They fly in line, casting a row of blurs
Of pelicans on the slick swells they barely clear....
The boys are home, all three of them this time.
But they ran earlier. Turning back I pause
To watch the dead white half moon on its climb,
Which one of them said, a lunar month ago,
"Looks like a helmet" as he rejoined his slow
Parent along this stretch. And so it does.

20

SONNET IN PRINTER'S GREEK

Than sky or water. freenn tthom her hands,
How can they see? Bylypsoorr else a lover.…
Mallards float in the color. Llcck stobs hover.
Msidli advationfir ent shining bands.
A liitle bleak. yllongg undulant ands.
Smell off slifftop, excloomong. Woll uncover
Not much rmmm. And veers abruptly out over
Face tense. Breathing iv arq demands.
Or flash of foam. Blicypp, old sonneteer …
Abwarss in hero telic imperfection
Whyever not, Considerink the clear
Though sanderlings ssyvrrr which one's direction
Swer.kho in concert almost disappear.
Abdi nec dog runs on the red reflection.

21

DEATH SONG

Not the dead seal swollen tight as a football
That I saw, clear in the midday winter light,
But my students at their final exams last night
Was my death vision. And no, not Nancy's skull
Under her smooth skin. I saw death edge them all
As they toiled there, it rested at the white
Surface of the papers I had, curved with the tight
Curve of the c in 'precise,' kept the interval
Between each letter (and gives this cold salt air
Its underlightness, the moon its bright rim because
Death is what does not happen, around what does),
I held in my lungs its imperishable elsewhere,
I saw creation being supported by
Death's tortoise—not on his shell, in his air-clear eye.

22

VISITATION

No running is the doctor's order. Glumly enough
To walk along and watch the other runners run,
And the sky fires up smoky crimson, and the sun
Slips into a sea suddenly darkening and rough
Out from the shore. Tide's out. Where the sand levels off
And where I like to go, the water's coming on
In terraces, shining layers, the nearest one
So thin it is a skin of light to trudge and scuff
And watch the slowly deepening color on, until
There is my holy of holies: a sandy-floored recess
Under the cliffs, half hidden behind a rock outcrop.
Always when I am running this is where I stop
And turn back. What now? Careful! A brief pause, I guess,
With the merest sidelong glance will do or nothing will.

It was a Greek mistake to connect the sacred with the permanent, the sacred being phenomenal like everything else, and the transient conjunction of chance and those necessities whose most apt expression is mathematical. Three weeks after this poem was done, the holy place was destroyed by the combination of a high winter tide and huge waves that changed the shapes of the cliff-bases and heaped storm-wreckage—much of it freshly splintered trees—high up against them.

23

COLLEAGUE WITH A NOTEBOOK

Beach wide and flat. I run, dully, on a sheet
Of neutral-colored light, slipping along
In the wet is a blurry quarter moon, a tongue
Of water pushes in quietly over the wet,
Quick-sliding, low-hissing, its tip of foamy white
Entering up the sand. Then I'm among
The seal brown, seal high rocks—old seals and young
Seaward they slant, alertly—exposed of late
By the winter tides ... slowly, on the way back,

Darkness coming, the horizon turns a bright,
Deep orange-red, the exact color of the throat
Of a cutthroat trout! Pass a man writing a note
(His camera's set up) and look back—beach black
Where he stands, crossed with great slashes of light.

24

LOITERER

But the water—a half-inch deep there, sidling in,
Rumpling to sharp little ridges, with elegant
Black shadows, in the level light ... ripplings sent
At an angle through other ripplings cross-hatch, then
The surface quiets, and, smooth once again,
Shivers all over ... two tiny waves, blent
Head-on emerge, each going the way it went ...
New water foams in, slides back clear and thin:
The lovely loiterings, with darkness coming on,
Stay with me as I finish up my run,
Having had to hurry all I did today.
And nothing done well, getting it all done.
"That most exciting perversion," said Hemingway,
Of such forced haste; the feelings fray and splay.

25

THE BIG WAVE

To Michael Ridland

Others are leaving as I pull in tonight
Dressed for the chill, and under a dull sky
Gray surf from winter storms is lifting high
Far out from shore, then bouncing in loud and white,
But a kid in trunks straightens to his full height

By his old VW, powerful and—hell, I see
He is one-legged. Now he vigorously
Swings by on his crutches in the failing light.
When I look next he has got off alone
—Christ, to do what? Way down the beach, he's thrown
The crutches down and is hopping, his one thigh
In the boiling white, toward a wave three times as high
As he. Hesitates, though. The wave comes on
And he hops back. In the sad, bad light I start my run.

26

RUNNING IN AMERICA

Saint Kenneth Cooper, with your stethoscope
Stopwatch and clipboard, how they run for you!
Eager and obedient in every thew
Having had courses now on How to Cope
With Death, on how to eat, to screw, to ope-
n doors, breathe, spit, work zippers ... they can do
The running but you make it all come true
In charts, with points, paying off Faith and Hope:
Dad in his old sweat suit, running head down
Doggedly in the dusk, the stern beauty with the frown,
The young couple goose-stepping *shoulder*-high,
Eyes straight ahead, to warm up—none of them smiles.
I've heard at parties the questions ... "How many miles ...?"
And the really serious runner's shy reply.

At the New School for Social Research you can take not only "Coping with Death" but "The Philosophy and Psychology of Death." "We were early in death studies," says the New School's proud president, John R. Everett.

27

LIGHT LIKE THE BEAUTIFUL TROUT FLY NAME:
PALE EVENING DUN

Cold spatter of rain, then wind. Last night the tide
Covering the beach and sliding up the rocks
Along the cliffs, driving the sanderling flocks
And me elsewhere, now a beach five yards wide
All kelp-heaps and scattered stones, and a rock-slide
At the point, wet shale in jagged blocks
Angled for twists, foot-slitherings, bone-shocks;
And pooled and trickling water on every side.
I rock-hop past the next point. Here the air
Is quiet, the ocean crump-crumping its tons
Well out from shore, the nearby water still …
Stretch of smooth sand! with a boulder here and there,
Standing alone—black rock, gray water, duns
Of wet sand, cloud-roofed, in the even light; so beautiful.

28
RUNNING IN THE RAIN, HIGH TIDE

Rain slanting past and no place here to run.
In the cold deepening dusk there comes the roar
Of water much too near; as the car door
Caught by a gust swings wide, I see the brown
Waves smack the cliffs. Well, head for the next beach down.
Bulldozers have gouged it up and gullies pour
With the runoff, crumbling, forcing me to detour
Through garbage to the blacktop (it's near town).
I run in a dazzle of streetlights and car lights
My glasses streaming, and splattering along
Alone, think of the swaggering word invictus;
And sprint back through the drench against a strong
Headwind, wearing as the car comes into sight
A combination grin and runner's rictus.

29

CHRISTMAS DOWN AT THE MISSION

Tonight sun and moon and earth line up and drag
The sea far back, the still tidepools, like light
Solidified, mirror that great headlight,
The low sun, beaming on … but here's the snag:
Been reading in the latest lit'ry rag
From Britain, and in this one doing right
(As with the Pauper Witch) is their delight
In tight-lipped "leaders." Made my spirits flag.
I know it's for your own good when they say
"Sit down, my friend, this chilling Christmas day,
Though the bench is hard, the table bare of trimmings,
Hold out your bowl and heed our bracing hymnings!"
Meat gray and stringy, gravy gray and thin,
Served up by the clammy enemies of literary sin.

30

FREEZING

I pick my way through a parking lot nearly full
As a miscellaneous, chilly crowd straggles in.
The sea is pale, a barely fluttering skin
Of light, and everywhere, an uncomfortable
Clearness and separateness to things, they have all
Hardened in this sharp air, and I begin
My run bleakly, not much helped out when
A new girl jogger flashes me a smile
For my weak smile; much less when I look off
From the stones underfoot to where there glows
The sun, low now and like a blurred red rose
In its cold cloud. The cold moon clears the bluff,
Full, and almost too bright to look into.
I head home running moonlit through and through.

31

RUNNING IN THE EARLY JANUARY COLD

The near water heaves bright gray, then deepening
Outward to a dark horizon line as keen
And aloof as the evenly moving, clean
Crest of a wave, or the edge of a gull's wing:
That pale sunset out there hasn't anything
To do with me, with its cloud whorl, its icy green;
There's nothing in the few people I've seen
To catch the eye, and take away the sting
Of the raw cold look of things; and thinking I run
Upright and briskly, I see my shadow: a tall
Pinhead aslant on stilts, going at a crawl
Along the sand; and in that room today
The neutral silence, I feeling in all I say
The desolateness of what's barely begun.

32

THE HOUSE THAT CLIFF-HANGS

Sometimes my run down here's like putting on
Music and after a while not listening.
I tell myself I spot every least thing
As the same, or changed, around me as I run,
And now I see, as the last third of the sun
At the horizon lays a glistening
Road to the house and reddens the west wing,
That the cliff has fallen away. The deck is gone.
There's a piece of railing stopping in mid-air
Above the expanse of raw vertical clay,
Loose dirt, iceplant, and planking sprawled down here,
Storm-loosened—not today or yesterday.
Coming back by in the late dusk I see
The bearded young man contemplating me

Or else the wreckage there,
    Through the salt atmosphere,
Straight down, from his high, narrow balcony.

33

WILLETS UNDER AN OVERCAST

This new and winter term is a stopped wheel
To push against, it budges and rolls back
Into its rut in a hard-frozen track
Through the inside country where I think and feel:
Outside the willets land for their evening meal,
Their lifted wings exposing elegant black
And white zigzags, beside the tidal slack:
Gray clouds, gray ocean, and the light still and pale.
Whatever was missing from what I did today
Is the second overcast to run under here,
I puzzle and puzzle under it all the way
To my turn-back place—willets again, a pair
Alight on a black rock offshore, crying *kerlear!*
Teetering prettily, above the sloshing gray.

34

THE NYMPHOLEPT

The crimson sun slipping down through the haze
Smoothly as I arrived is now half gone,
Its color riding the backwash; and I run
And sketch a plan to draw out of her daze
Of shyness Pam who writes so well, and faze
The Marxist glibnesses maybe of Juan,
When the girl walks by, barefoot, putting down
Footprints still clear under the water glaze.
Later, it's two girls writing in notebooks

As I come in, in the deep dusk they lean
To see their words. Then still another looks
My way as I get in my car, to say
"Yer a good runner!" I, startled: "Nah."—"I've seen
You often …" drifts through the gloom as she goes her way.

35

THE BARE WINTER BEACH

No kites, no frisbees. No baking half the day
Beside her friend, a radio in between.
No babies. Not a six-pack to be seen,
Even gulls are scarce (no garbage). Far away
Is the big brown belly July puts on display.
—Two lovers, and one walker, dark and lean,
And two runners, are strung out on the clean
Smooth beach ahead, with the light a misty gray
Coming from nowhere and everywhere alike.
A good place for a passion to be worked out
Or up. Near here last night my young friend Mike
Whose wife left him and took their child, did not
See me run by, his eyes so fixed on a pair
Of beauties running by with streaming hair
(Eyes that have been in training on Vermeer).

36

RUNNING WITH ANOTHER *TLS* POEM
IN MY HEAD

The bulge of the sea above the benches shows
High tide, and I'll be driven off the sand
Onto the rocks. I should have calmly planned
My run, by the tide-chart, but old drip-nose
Reading his Homer troubled my repose,

Reading his *Times* indeed almost unmanned
Me with his questions. He can't understand
Why gods and heroes cause so many woes.
Odysseus, with his lies and murders—not a bit nice!
Couldn't he practice a gentler kind of vice?
These Afghans, skinning the Russian infidel
Alive! Blood-smeared old Faiths, awake and well,
Inflicting on us still their gruesome folly ...
Why can't we all be good, and kind, and jolly?

37

RUNNING IN THE RAIN AGAIN;
A SWEDE WITH STOUT LEGS

I run and think of running here the night
After the first big rainstorm of the year,
And the tide low, just a few people here,
Wave-watchers, mostly, shapes making upright
Thick ink-strokes on the louring watery light
Between gray waves and low clouds, and the air
Sharp and the beach vast, gaunt (with here and there
Rank kelp-heaps), bending flatly out of sight.
I'd finished fast and started cooling out,
There's a big Swede nearby doing same,
Stretching and bending and then gazing about—
And edging my way, I see, as if by aim;
He says, "It's beautiful, in its own way,"
Walking past. "Yeh, it's beautiful," I say.

38

RUNNING

Driving down with KABC Sports-talk on,
Author of *The Complete Runner* is the guest,
"How should you breathe?" he's asked, "What is the best
Surface for running?" "Is the backbone jarred when you run?"…
Now that the days are longer, now that the sun
Is up where it blinds me when I'm running west
And the plovers are leaving, all too soon the rest
Of the signs of winter down here will be gone.
Still, Dad in his old sweat suit and salt-caked shoes
Sends me a wave this time, abrupt and shy,
Without turning his head, and others smile
As *they* pass, and now my mind cuts out, while
In that sudden sort of silence that ensues
When an engine stops, the cliffs blur by.…

39

BIG WAVES IN WIND AND CLEAR COLD SUNLIGHT,
AND THE INTELLIGENT NEW SECRETARY
FROM THE MAIN OFFICE

Clear from the entrance I could see the spray
Glistening above the cartops like the snow
That banners off the drifts in a big blow,
And once I'm running I watch the falling away
Of waves heaved house-high, and the steady play
Of the cold light on wave-slopes bursting snow
Over the snowy rush and crush below—
Too much for surfers: wave-watchers here today.
And up the beach, a girl sitting quietly
On a big rock, with those waves roaring in.
And it is Marilyn, I recognize
As I come near; sun lights her gold hairpin,
And I start wondering if her blue eyes
Are seeing more than the rest of us down here see.

40

OLD ROCKS OUT IN THE LATE LIGHT

Chill air and the sea sunk, like a lake
In drought-time, back from the gray sand,
A bright place the size of a man's hand
On the waves, where the light comes through a break
In low clouds. And the striped rocks. They take
The eye between flat sea and land,
Humped, leaning, pale band by dark band,
Green-bearded, dripping, with pools that quake
In the raw breeze. Here's one pokes out
At our cliffs a heavy upper jaw
That with the lower grips in its maw
The sand I cross. Surely the brief light
Is holy, and holy the darkness light
Makes when it goes, but not that snout.

41

A QUIET FOURTH

Homesick, building a fly rod on the patio
All the fresh sunny breezy morning; a calm blue
Sky and green leaves close me in. Low tide's at two,
And I'll run then. —The dusty parade and rodeo
Took place in town, all right, forty-five years ago,
A thousand miles away; fireworks afterwards, too,
And then the ride home on the dirt road, winding through
The cool fields in darkness, hearing the water flow
Over the weirs; and then our dogs, at the driveway turn.
—And winter's the time for Hendry's Beach; therefore I'll write
This one, to do for my few summer runs down here:
Beach flat, trampled, sea flat, slack and warm and clear;
People little black figures against the big silver light;
Close up, it's beer can, frisbee, radio, sunburn.

July 4, 1978

42

A QUIET FOURTH

Fran and I much alone this bright mild day
With the boys scattered, friends too, mostly, so
It's Sousa and Ives out on the patio
(And how subtly the Ives lets the attention stray);
Then work on a fly rod, later get away
For a run at Hendry's, when the tide is low.
My last run down there was six weeks ago—
Summer crowds, and a new fee I won't pay.
But on the Fourth you want a crowd, I learn,
So down I go: beach flat, sea calm, clear, warm.
In and beside it, in every tint, size, form,
People, with frisbee, radio, sunburn.
—Drive back, see centered formally on a top stair
A beer, beneath a flag limp in the cooling air.

July 4, 1978

43

THE OTHER RUNNER

Recalling, during a drought, a rainy day last year

Wind spread the rain across the glass, I hearing it
While reading Milton all day long, and looking up
From time to time, to wonder when it would stop,
And then forgetting rain, in the warm room where I sat.
Then arriving at the beach: yellow-brown breakers lit
From under a slowly lifting ledge of cloud—the tops
Catching the level blaze, and darkness soon to drop,
And for my run the sand wave-beaten hard and flat.
I ran alone, leaving some saunterers behind,
Beside a set of fresh footprints so far apart
I couldn't match them long, and slowed my pace, resigned;
Thinking of Milton, no, of every excellence,
How it exhilarates and humiliates the heart;
High waves nearing both sets of our footprints.

44

DOG-DAYS I: RAIN-RUNNING RECALLED

Hard wind, rain; I the only one out here.
Wind on my back, rattle of rain on hat,
Hissing of rain on sand, and beyond that
The noise of the big waves; and small and clear
A whimbrel's call in the din as I draw near
A roaring down the cliff and over the flat
Hard beach—an hour-old river I halt at,
My glasses streaming. The world is a bright smear.
Into a gale now, and the ocean sound
Drowned out by the new howling of the air
Around my head, then even louder pounds
The *hough! hough!* of my lungs inside this blur
Of boisterous air, cliffs, water—startled mind
Along for the ride, body with its old kind.

August 11, 1978

45

DOG-DAYS II: INCIDENTALLY RECALLING
A DYING SEAL

—Not that its old kind give a damn for it.
For us who live here, the impersonal
Bright quiet gaze of that dying animal
Put rightly the relation of the fit
And unfit both, to that of which we're knit.
And once the indifference is mutual
Shall consciousness here in the individual
Turn with the whole? the light of light be lit?
I know I saw that seal dying his death
Half sunk into the sand, on the sunny shore
In the tide-wash: with each wave coming in,
The sand sucking him deeper than before,
The water swirling over his head again,
Subsiding, he catching another breath.

46

ANNIVERSARY

Life's uneventful, and while we were gone
The season turned; the winter birds are here
And the crowds gone, and the salt atmosphere
Is sharper, with a low hazed-over sun
Laying its wide and glittery roadway on
Gray ocean that looks lonely. Like last year.
—Over the cliffs two hang-gliders appear,
Slope in and land nearby; I start my run.
Sand smooth, smooth! for a runner or a flyer
In this gray light and chill air's misty blend
And the sanderlings, lively, lovely, never tire,
And the sun suddenly lights a deep red fire
Up on the sand, using a beer can end,
And all of it makes up my heart's desire.

47

THE PARTLY-WRITTEN PAGE

Life's uneventful. What I remember most
At the odd moment or lying awake
At three A.M. is not the storms that shake
Oranges from the groves on up the coast
And wash them out to sea (this year some crossed
The bows of fishermen watching gray whales break),
Litter the shore with splintered trees and make
The news: X houses ruined, X lives lost.
What has stayed with me is such a thing as this:
I come in through the late dusk from my run,
A girl at the picnic table glances over
A half a page of writing she's just done,
Then stares out where the dark waves slap and hiss
Under the darker rainy low cloud-cover.

48

COMPANY

There's Giles again, the lanky fellow who,
Working toward a Ph.D. in Greek,
Likes girls (and always runs with one, a sleek
Beauty at that, mirabile dictu).
—But there's one running because she was told to
By *Runner's World*. And some journalist has the cheek
To call on us to go, seek out the weak
And sick and scorned: we happy running few …
Loneliness is not possible for this
Long distance runner; I spend my mother wit
Dodging the latest book you dare not miss,
This goddamned merchandiser plucks my sleeve,
Holistic priests approach—I bob and weave,
I detour past the bull- and the horseshit.

49

THE *REBECCA MAE*

After the loud storm she lay off shore low
In the water, grating on rocks. Then a huge wave
Beached her and she looked good enough to save,
Engine and all. Half sunk in sand now, though.
All of us eye her as we come and go,
Runners and saunterers. But she never gave
When kids tried prying her from her half grave.
Soon her name's under. Just her gunnels show.
Still the big seas aren't done with her. One day
We find her resurrected, all the way
Past the next point, then later scattered out
Against the cliff, till her last splinter's under
The sand we pad on; now a well-buried boat
To muse on running through the water-thunder.

50

NIGHT-PIECE

Lying in the long dark, insomniac,
I see it clearly: sea and beach and air
And a red winter sun, down low, for fire,
For the fourth element made out by the Greek
On Sicily's coast two dozen centuries back—
Fire that'll turn me into atmosphere
After I'm dead, and ashes tossed out where
Maybe they'll wash ashore. I hear gulls creak,
And put my being in with the elements
We share with the whole show, rather than
With the odd creature in it that is man
Or with my self, still odder … till the tense
Weavings of wakefulness begin to fray
Loosen and come apart and float away—

Phrasing in lines 11 and 12 taken from Santayana's Dialogues in Limbo.

50 CONTINUED

Not bad, for night thoughts, but as Hemingway
Noticed, night thoughts on recollection,
Deep as you went for them, don't pass inspection
Laid out and drying in the light of day.
Something on which there is not much to say,
Sheer Nothingness, once more escapes detection,
Though disciplined minds can reach by indirection
What the imagination hides away …
Yes, *darkness, sundown, water*—take your pick
Of pictures: wings, a little boat, dark blue
Of gentians, you can't make any of it stick.
So human, moving, lovely, and untrue.
By the fresh light of morning being bound
To thought that makes the phrase, if not resounding, sound.

51

SANDERLINGS HERE

A low fog bank to run inside today,
Wave-noises muffled, near cliffs blurred and pale.
Fog-puffs come down, each spreading a black tail,
A black bill aimed at the sand. And a slight gray
Movement ahead suddenly swerves this way
And a whole flock gleams cleanly purposeful
Against the drifting vapor. Now they all
Vanish up there, sheering themselves away.
And near the finish, a flat stretch, bits of shells
And pebbles lift a little and begin
To travel along the water ahead of me—
Sanderlings, running in the fog or else
Low-gliding, I here running heavily
As faintly they shape unshape and shape again.

52

"WHO PROP, THOU ASK'ST, IN THESE
BAD DAYS, MY MIND?"

Yeh, summer beach, young riders thudding past
Punching out clear hoofprints beside the white
Spill of the waves, against the low sun's light
The black shapes of the horsemen dwindling fast,
And here, attached to each of the sand-crumbs cast
Beside the hoofprints, a little stalactite
Of shadow, while I mope along and fight
The gloom my reading's put me in last …
Cheer up. What if you must throw in your lot
With Gittingses and Thompsons now, and not
Go back to those they've told on for the ages,
Those monsters Hardy and Frost. You'll get, God knows,

A generous friend in Lawrance Thompson's pages,
Largeness of soul in Robert Gittings' prose.

Gittings records with approval the verdict of Mr. Clodd that in Hardy "There was no largeness of soul."

53

RUNNING WITH THE POLLUTION

I run and coordinating agencies
A panel of experts new measures called for
The decision-making process funding more
Multi-disciplinary activities
Are in my fatty tissues and all these
Are in my liver supervision war
On crime fact-finding panel a hard core
The underlying causes facilities:
Well, that's our social climate and the air
Carries their fumes and particles everywhere
We breathe. But here's one runner that keeps clear
Of *etic structures* and such—I hear the first
Fibers of these, if you come in or near,
Will cause the alveoli in your lungs to burst.

54

SLINKING OFF

Open the morning paper, what do you see?
Tom L. and Abby W. in full stride,
The splendid young pair running side by side
Their dog loping between them happily
The finishing touch: I wish them well all three
And damn the lurking journalist who eyed
And caught them coming toward him in their pride
And put them there, a soon-yellowing cliché.

Picture one now, with his thin legs, gray hair
And turkey neck and flapping khaki pants
And nylon shell from the discount drug store
Slipping along down here and wondering
If some other poet ... deepening in advance
His shame at doing *so* fashionable a thing.

55

PELICAN HALCYON

Low tide of winter, beach shines to the eye
Wide as the sea itself for my late run
And the sea light-streaked and smoothed out to a sun
Red in horizon fog, and already high
A piece of the moon's rim, in the neuter sky.
Quiet. Sun flattens to an oval on
The fogbank; to a glowing bar; then gone.
And in the pallor, one pelican flaps by,
Black on the afterglow; and another, black
Out on the pale sea, silently splashing down
Makes yet another pelican silhouette
With the thrown water; I seeing this all alone,
It happens, with the one sound as I head back
The slip-slap of my feet along the wet.

56

SPELL BREAKING

That is soon over, others come in view:
Old man in street clothes down for a beach walk,
Three women heading back absorbed in talk,
A guy surf-fishing, the odd runner or two.
And no more pelicans: gulls now skreak and mew,
I scare a willet that flies to a safe rock
Kerlear-ing his hurt feelings, a godwit flock

Reflects in the shine they poke their long bills through.
And here's my old friend Herb, facing the sea,
Musing, quite motionless, holding, curiously,
A folded newspaper level with his waist:
Day-offering to sea and sundown, he the priest.
I can't not greet him though the spell will break,
He jogs on in with me for old and new times' sake.

57

COMING DOWN TO RUN IN DARK AND FOG

In the near dark two runners stagger in
Out of the coiling fog along the shore.
Another lurches in, and then two more.
But nobody else here after I begin.
Once I am startled, when the fog-swirls thin,
By a movement I glimpse behind me on the shore.
That's the moon's hard reflection. Airliner's roar
Joins wave-roar for one huge roar coming in
Straight after me; and then a hooded form
Comes by with darkness where the face should show;
It's a runner, though. Small light, with sea below
Is the cliff-house, fog-faint, the one a storm
Last year brought down in part, to crash and splinter,
What's left now pushing into one more winter.

58

HERON OUT THERE

The first cold day of winter, darkness near,
A stiff wind coming in and a high tide
Roaring inshore and everyone else inside
Or heading there, what am I doing here
Plugging through mushy sand, with a wind tear

In either eye, up a beach three feet wide …
Chased by a rush of water up the side
Of the shale at the first point, I slog from there
To the furthest—and the heron I know by day
Is a slab of the dark rock, breaking away
To pass me in the dusk. Down beach again
I spot his still shape—leaf with a long stem.
When I come near he flaps unhurriedly,
Belongingly, into the icy spray,
    Then back the other way
    From me, this time to stay
The long night undisturbed, by the loud sea.

59

THE HONESTY BOYS

I run along beside the little wobbly blur
Of the moon on the sleek wet sand (whereas in the sky
It's holding motionless, hatchet-sharp) and have an eye
On the just-after-sundown ocean's crinkling stir
In the beautiful steel-blue light that suddenly appears,
And find myself thinking again about the way
Certain poets are always putting on a display
Of *honesty*—they bring up yours, and of course theirs,
To your face; sometimes slyly, showing how others are
Dishonest—as one of them just lately tried to tell
All of us Hardy was. That didn't turn out well.
However, credit for trying…. On with the essay-war
With each name mentioned being a piece of disputed terrain,
Or outpost in the latest *honesty* campaign.

60

THE DESOLATION LIGHT

I came down here one dusk and the beach was gone.
The winter tides were easing it out to sea,
Shelving it down and down, when suddenly
A storm came through and scoured it to the stone—
A jumble of stone; and the sky having done
Its damage loosened up, pale vacancy
Between a lot of ragged cloud debris
Scattering fast, foam yellow and waves brown,
The sea, too, loosened and sprawling, sunk so low
That stubs of rock under for months now showed.
Air darkened as if a curtain had been drawn,
And shining as if for meditating on
Was a tidepool that the gray light had filled
To brimming where a simple stillness held.

61

NEWS

RAVAGED BY NATURE, says the local News,
BEACHES ARE DYING —naturally I read on,
How one day these thin margins will be gone
For good, new sand held back by the dams we use
On our best streams while the sea slowly chews
The old away, back to the cliffs and down
To the stones. And nowhere then to run or sun.
Any dark place can say what else you'll lose:
The canyon air that floats the alder leaf,
The light on the creek, and the creek too, will go;
And the ground under, where it had to flow.
Your sons, and the dear woman who is half your life,
And the two eyes you see both with and through
Will go; and your skeleton; and your spirit, too.

62

HERON SHAPES AT DUSK

I know the heron that's made this beach his own
Between the headlands, slants like a poised spear
Invisible in the driftwood where I peer—
And there he goes now, flapping off alone.
Later his shape breaks out of some gray stone
That the low tides leave bare this time of year,
Then further down, in deeper dusk, lifts clear
Where only a black tangle of kelp had shown.
Then over by the cliffs, in the near dark there,
I see a heron shape become a girl
Hunched with her trouble there on the driftwood.
The shore a place of human bad and good,
Not herons now, so stony stark her stare
At the late red fading from a cloud-swirl.

63

NOON SWIMMERS, PLOVERS,
A YOUNG HERON, A GREBE

People are black on silver this mid-day
Far up the beach, the waves withdrawing show
Light rustling in the grit, the plovers throw
Shadows appearing solider than they,
And the young heron that lives here flaps away
And alights up ahead in the backflow
That glares more silver as it slips below
The nubs of the bright foam, the sunny spray,
While the grebe I come on has been lying dead,
At the water's edge, on his back. His wings are spread
As if in flight. He looks heraldic, too—
Like the scrawny phoenix D.H. Lawrence drew.
But this bird's missing an eye; draggled and sad
Lies here for a little the only self he had.

64

HERON TOTEM

Up the long beach, a flock of sanderlings
Will swoop past a ridge of ocean roaring near
(Their white chests flashing), tilt and disappear,
Or pelicans line up, dark, heavy things,
And form one body with a dozen wings
Approaching me head-on, or godwits flare
Warm cinnamon wing-linings on the gray air
When they veer off in the big flocks winter brings.
I love them all, and most this homely one:
Color of driftwood, among the bustlers, the wary
Swervers, he leans inquiringly, and waits.
Slow, frail, ungainly, set for the long run,
Silent with hope, by nature solitary,
He picks his spot, stands still, and concentrates.

65

POLITICS: READING THE PAPERS

On the first page, review of Brecht by Spender.
Asks the tough question last: how come he
Clammed up about Stalin?—Because, you see,
Brecht could "play games with evil," with no tender
Conscience, for the sake of future good. (I render
The prose down to its shred of meat.) Page three,
It's Solzhenitsyn—getting by memory
His prose and verse, in the gulag. Old non-bender.
And in the *News*, Bukovsky (Vladimir,
I mean): "I don't like certain ideas because
They bring terrible results." *His* prose is clear.
"The most dangerous thing is when you start
To limit your conscience" *for the noble cause....*
Cold dusk, and time to run ... where's the tide-chart?

66

SUNDAY RUN: STARTING OUT

At the water's edge a baby smacks the beach,
Seriously, then casts me a grave look.
A woman wades along reading a book,
Surf tugging at her legs. And the gulls screech,
And a girl makes a staggering run and reach
For a frisbee through a haze of charcoal smoke
Sharp-scented in the cool air, from a nook
Under the cliffs. We brown and burn and bleach.
And the sober sun, half through the afternoon,
Throws iris-leaf shapes, and squarish glares of light
Along the rollers, sends a quick-sliding thread
Of light along a crest, and overhead
Makes on a softball on its climbing flight
In the blue, a tiny daytime quarter moon.

67

IN PUBLIC: *LIBERTÉ, FRATERNITÉ*

A photographer sets his tripod up and waits
Among various types down here for the sunset;
The unlovely public—whatever it is creates
Us bungles us.... And no colors as yet;
The scuffed-up sand shines gray where it is wet.
The place seems idly jostled, by the gazes
And glances of all these folk, their grunts and phrases.
On the bright gray they bulk in silhouette.

~

And home now, out of the salt atmosphere,
With these things written as I pleased I feel
The doubts crowd in (like a real crowd, watching me

Running along down there), each all too real
And undisguisable deformity
Passing in plain view, in the open here.

68

WHAT THE SEA MUTTERED

With a variation on a theme of Goya

You haven't kept the reader busy enough.
I know, I know—it comes of my long affair
With the clear and ordinary; all my care
May fail to hold the intensity in the stuff.
Too many off-rhymes, rhythms strained and rough,
You crash the delicate old barrier
Between octave and sestet. I declare
My shame before the masters. *You sheer off*
From the whole truth: not even writing of
That day you found you'd fallen out of love
With running down here, much less of harder themes.
—The reason sleeps, and monsters shape the dreams
Which are the things we're doing in broad day,
The monstrous half-done.... Nolo contendere.

69

WHAT THE WIND HISSED

A chill gray day and a wind began to blow:
Where will you get with that plain water style?
Running's a joke that long since has gone stale,
Seascapes were old a century ago.
I like plain words, I always have been slow.
And the names you drop. Milton of course is vile,
And Hemingway! pathetic macho male ...

And that brute, Robert Frost. I like them, though.
Why Santayana? Surely you want Saussure.
And Rilke's missing. Really I much prefer
Hardy. *He's fading fast.* Herbert? *OK …*
And Homer? *Fine.* My dirty words? *Passé.*
Here, try a Barthes. Somehow it lacks allure,
Such is my hesychastic mood today.

70

TOPOPHILIA

Cold dead light, and the beach, from the long rain,
Like a mud-flat under this low cloud-cope; though where
Sun lights the cloud's far edge a pane of clear
Yellow sky joins it to the steady line
Of the horizon; and tiny and black, and fine
In detail, an oil rig sits precisely there
On the skyline, like some miniature
Electronic component, the thin struts showing plain.
And the space out there clear and empty and fine,
Ready for God to fill—like an Inness, a Lane,
Or even a Hopper: and I think of their
Frank and mystical love of light, and plain
Shapes in the great vacancies of air,
And taking comfort in the bare and spare.

Hopper, to whom the 'mystical' doesn't exactly apply, said, 'What I wanted to do was to paint the sunlight on the side of a house.' Inness spoke of 'the hidden story of the real.' With Lane I had especially in mind the wonderful Owl's Head, Maine.—*Santayana writes of the 'something in the human spirit (which is not merely human), something unreclaimed and akin to the elements,' that is perhaps at work in these things.*

RUNNING AT SUNDOWN AND DARK

Well, it's a pretty sunset—sherbet green,
Orange, even some raspberry, streak the sky
From sea horizon to cliffs. Pelicans ply
The offshore reaches and fishing boats careen
On big waves, giving substance to the scene
With their everyday skillful efforts. Meanwhile I,
Pondering a talk that may well go awry,
Run on the tide-zone's particolored sheen:
Mind pawing obsessively at certain unclear
Distinctions.... Pass two more runners; lovers, one pair;
A lone girl walking slowly back. It's night
When I come in, distinctions still not right,
Past black stumps in the water just off shore—
Surfers, in the dark there, waiting for one more.

from *Tree Meditation and Others*

(1970)

NOTE

The poems are descriptive meditations rather than meditative descriptions—I mean that they are first and last about subjects, not objects, despite what may be appearance to the contrary. They arose usually when I had some time to myself, which perhaps gives them their pre- or post-social character, and they are put as plainly as I could manage.

The voices in "The Green Cape" come from an article about New York City in *Look* magazine (April 1, 1969), by Gerald Astor.

A.S.

—suppose the words came in
the way a flight of blackbirds
I once watched entered a tree
in the winter twilight;
finding places for themselves
quickly along the bare branches
they settled into their singing
for the time.

TO FRAN

Out in the rain all afternoon
hands and neck chilled—
some trouble, anger

and late supper, the rain
smacking and clicking
outside the room

plenty of chablis
our sparse reflections
on the black window glass

where space comes pouring in
all the way in
from between the stars, in past the blacked-out moon—

desolately it enters the room
and streams around your shoulders
without harm—how curious—

and enters my grizzled beard
stopping when it arrives
at the skin warmth—

~

it must be we belong in it—at once remotely
and intimately; the way a sheepherder's fire at night belongs
in the distance on a desert upland

THE WHITE DOG TRUTH

I make out the white bulk in the dark—
the dog approaches at a quick pace
and goes by showing no interest in me,
and such is the quiet of the street
I hear the clicking of his toenails
on the blacktop, quick, business-like,
even half a block away, the sound
growing fainter very gradually
and already, while I keep an eye
on the wire-thin half rim of light
the moon shows in a sky jagged
with trees along the bottom—
already this encounter, the white bulk passing
in the dark, the diminishing click
of the toenails along the stretch
of silence back there, cannot be forced
not to have been, the lords of creation
themselves will have to submit to
its having been, if they should find it
some day blocking the way of a desire.

THE THREE SISTERS

River, dangerous—green water
going over a ledge, it smashes
into a mixture with the air
a flashing white, the lava

it cuts through having a purple cast
where it unites chemically with the air—up country
lie the great lava beds of the Three Sisters,
new, like melted metal poured out
over the mountains, the sharp raw masses
enter the air like hot metal splashed up
and hardening before it could subside.
A sharp thin cold air
moves in hard breezes over the place.
In the distance the Three Sisters—austere
ones, the three bare cones, snow-streaked.
Guard me, guard me, O Sisters of the desolation
of bare beginnings.
                    All of it under streaky clouds
that slowly become uniform, then drop rain,
a cold rain. It instantly forms runnels
that head down across the slag, moving fast.

THE GREEN CAPE, WITH VOICES

green, Pacific Northwest; voices, New York City

    —evergreens gravely
    flourish below the fog

        —on the beach the gulls stand
        in disreputable-looking groups
        and appear to be waiting
        stupidly for something

        but fly alone, intelligently

        —where we were this morning
        greens springing out
        above other greens,
        greens against greens

spear points, rays,
ribs, arcs of green

    (ocean makes a hush-hush
    hush hush sound
    with varying rumbles
    under it: the sound
    looms inland

—green clasps the eye wherever ...

    yesterday at nightfall when
    you and I bedded down
    in the lee behind the dunes
    by the fire's flicker
    we listened to the ocean
    sounding overhead—
    it was as if we lay
    beneath huge trees
    in a wind storm)

*Mrs. B.—"I went back down to Georgia for a couple of days. I don't
like it down South, too many trees."*

    —shapes of fern splashed up
    in green by the rains

    the ribs aslant along a narrow
    arching stem with plenty
    of springiness in it
    when caught in air movements

    even when still they seem active
    above the ground where you stop,
    your figure clear, remote,

set back in a dusky luminosity
of greens separated like sections of stained glass
by the heavy black strokes
of the major branches and trunks—think

of the long soft steady rains
the glass ablur

     on this entirely gray and white scene
     this morning seaward from the cape
     (the whole cape, be it understood,
     in its eternal aspect, as we in ours)
     ocean terracing itself comes in
     hurriedly pushing along its walls
     of bouncing white water—seven of them
     I count approaching at one time, descending
     to slide, at last, easily up on the gray
     shine of the beach, and this solemn
     and orderly commotion continues
     helplessly. We have contrived
     to be idle—and alert, for a time,
     but to the firm sand and to the air
     moving as if with brisk intentness
     and to the light busy at being light
     on the water
              —for ourselves are
     (with you dozing away in scarlet)
     off somewhere on vacation

—listen: in back of the rain forest
on a cold flat shining loop
of the river are some old logs
abandoned I suppose long ago
by a lumber company, and on the logs floating
near the bank, long grass was growing

—from this dune we can see
the cape as a completeness

to the left the cape headland
darkening as the fog thins toward the crest
the crest spikey and heavy-looking, black
evergreens in the fog pallor,
ocean big and burly along the brown beach
to northward, backed by dunes, then flats
with salt grass and bushes and big Sitka spruce,
then the steep green hills, and the rain forest

~

—looking inland, late afternoon;
sunlight sloping in under the fogbank at last; through
the bare gray Sitka trunks, over the salmonberry bushes,
you see a logged-off hill with the old stumps
shining—bright gray in the direct light,
against the ground greenery; how much the hill
overlooking the ocean appears at this distance
like an old-fashioned graveyard, giving off an air
of mild, decorous expectation, with its marble headstones
in various shapes and sizes placed unevenly around in it

—at a rotting trunk we pause—I see
you noticing with well open
steady eyes what is to be seen:
in the one place alone
grow various mosses, three kinds of vine,
a mushroom, several smallish plants
with prettily cut leaves, and numerous
pine seedlings, inch-high sprigs;

a flourishing of distinctions
in the same air, the same
half light

*Mrs. B. one more time: "Harlem be the onliest place in the world you
could have a headache, be broke and hungry and still laugh."*

—yesterday (another yesterday), drive upcoast a few miles;
edge down tall cliff to sandy and stony isolated beach;

huge rocks, black in the offshore glitter, form islets, close-set;
holes like doorways or gates eaten through them to sea-light;

sea lions loafing out there at water's edge, seafowl gray-white on crests;
the place is not of the land (which is shut off from it by the cliff);

the sea is shut away from it by the great rocks standing offshore;
the place is unfrequented by people; a violent cold wind is blowing:

behind a black rock that rises
straight up out of the beach
we encounter a collection
of huge stumps and logs,
each one weighing tons,
lodged everywhichway
(showing the strength
of the waves: how light-seeming
the logs would have spun
and tumbled in end over end)
their bark taken off cleanly
by storm, glare, wave-blow
they have acquired a sheen
of curious fineness—transmuted,
a silvery white, they
are phenomena of light,
LIGHT (that were never

formed to be in the light
living under moist bark
on a green slope somewhere)
now in their casual magnitude
and stillness they seem of the gods,
seem like the white bulls of a god
driven into this place between cliffs
and sea, and possessing it
now in the repose of their might

*Mr. J.: "People are out all of the time. Life. You walk at midnight,
people are in the streets. In other cities, streets are deserted in the
evening. You walk by yourself, emptiness, emptiness."*

we climb where a huge tree went down
heaving half its roots into the air
(out of the dirt still gripped in its roots
a group of ferns and vines is growing)

and throwing to one side a smaller tree
that leans upon another tree, in turn
holding bent sharply beneath its weight
an even smaller tree—it is a system
of disasters criss-crossed, still happening
slowly (a violence of placid monsters) in silence

~

—a huge old tree beside the path
on the way out—in falling it, too, turned upright

much of its root system, in a matted
disc shape perhaps eighteen feet high:

visible at the center of it is the ringed
heart wood of its life—a huge crude medallion:

when I dig some out and squeeze it
it becomes a rich red mud in my hand

Somebody else: "I like the smell of the pavement here."

~

leaving under the fog,
past the rain forest,
the wet green hills,
a few small houses
solitary, at intervals
in small clearings
in the greenery—fog
with us still, moving
among the treetops,
the Sitka spruce, the hemlocks,
the red cedars, the firs,
in dark assemblages—
rounding a curve we see
a faded Mobil red horse
full size, fastened
on a sagging shed
in the yard of a small house
set well back from the road—
fastened at the proper angle
for ascent, aimed upward,
forehooves striking at the air
on the weathered drop-siding

WELCOMER

Just in time for the fog arriving.
It pours around the streetlight, drifts
Through headlights swinging stiffly
On the curve at the foot of the hill.

On the high ridge
Behind the trees the lights of the houses
Look weak inside the heedless
Placidity of the fog.

A helicopter making a last
Pass behind the ridge, broadcasting
Seed on the blackened mountains,
Makes a rapping in the air.

Fog enters the tops of a grove
That nearly burned with the rest
A week ago—whole groves would ignite
Even before the flames reached them,

From the advancing heat. Into the huge
Eucalyptuses that stand over the house
White moisture motes slowly swerve,
Navigating the blackness, among the still leaves.

CLEARING

No longer muffled in brush
contours are clear

subtle blades of grass
come up in the blackish ground

behind the twisty black branches
stand chimneys and pieces of walls
broken glass around the foundations
a sterile glitter

vacant
of human tones and scents and looks

like the rest of the mountainside. Mere weather
has cleaned them out

higher, sycamore
and oak and bigleaf maple
and occasional pools
and trees blasted
along one flank by the heat

a squirrel crosses
a branch over the road,
his fur fills
with light,
spilling it off.

VARIATION FROM A THEME BY MARSDEN HARTLEY

Hartley, summer was plainly for you,
    remarker of joined clearnesses, plover noticer,
    savorer of 'infant clams' and campestris, among the opulence,
    'the look of bright everlastingness'

But it is not for me, in summer
    it seems there's nothing to do
    but continue what's become obvious, greens
    overlapping soberly, whitening sky,
    stationary August.

An upper rocky field, and the way
    begins to open, a few bright
    stubble stalks leaning among the clods, nearby,
    and red light flickering in the distance, on the blue flats
    where they're burning off the cattails in the sloughs,

And 'shall the cold flowing waters
    that come from another place

be forsaken?'—I'm on my way
up to a wind-swept place
of darkness, snow, and some lights, and further on
a granite cave, icy water on its walls
black flecked with white and pink, the good
lair dark I dream to; start down fresh from.

DESERT

This bad country in the late afternoon wears us down,
The rocks with their dead purples,
The scabby cactuses, trees with tiny oily leaves

And thorns so big they're visible from the road,
Shrubs that look made out of old wire. Finally it all says:
That hard life of yours couldn't live out here, the bad country

Would free you of it; then the spirit, turning
Ruthless as it was in the days of the anchorites,
Could have a respite and stand empty on some hillside.

THE FUGITIVE

Quick slapping, shaking of fronds,
something heavy jolting around
in there—merely pigeons: they began to coo.
And a squirrel, perhaps young
and inexperienced, came out
on a frond and crossed over
fastidiously to the adjacent oak
leaving the place to these others
that no doubt satisfied themselves
with only approximations to comfort
and promptly fell asleep.

ONE MORNING

The white
Of her flowers against the white sunlit wall
Is excellent indeed to contemplate

And
Similarly
Her silence

Inside
The prosy silence
Of the house.

MOON, RAIN

Homeward, and how sudden
The round white moon
Above the winter poplars
(Bunches of broomstraws)
And the gray
Of the sky in that quarter
A silence for the moon statement
And she is indoors at this hour
And the moon not visible anyway
From down in the canyon
This was yesterday—
Today where she is, at the window
Rainy light on the faucet chrome
And on the sheath of wet
On the tree, the bare
Apricot the rain sparely decorates
A knop of silver
Here and there, before
The window where she is

Coming back to the house through the dark
I see a flashlight come on
at the dark window of Tim's room—
as I enter he trains it on me
and greets me.

He has climbed out of his bed
to look at some tomato worms again
which he put in a can today with fresh tomato leaves
fragrant with the scent
of tomatoes themselves—
he explains: he could hear the worms
chewing the leaves in the dark,
he imitates the sound for me,
a slight sucking sound.

The broad scars or scabs
on tomatoes are made, I suppose,
by these worms. We sit a moment
watching them in the flashlight beam.

Big fellows, a clear, light green,
built high and rectangular
like boxcars, and with a thorn
like a rose thorn set in their hind ends;
on their flanks are stripes,
diagonal, crooked, black with white edging;
between each stripe is an imitation eye—
we look at it, it looks back at us,
a clear black pupil
rimmed with a delicate white tissue
that makes the eye appear to glisten
with moisture. The expression, we decide,

is that level, considering regard
you meet in the eye of a toad
or a lizard.

HOME ROCK

This chunk of mica-flecked rock I took
Off the mountainside; one fleck
As I look catches my lamp's light
Eagerly, and from within itself
Dartles red and green lightnings back,
That blaze at the edge of my mind half the night.

SURF PERCH AND WANDERING TATLERS

Those migrants
rush back and forth importantly on the beach
and point with agitation and work their wings
with a curious proprietary air
and make excited sounds, aroused
by the uproar of the surf, and we are
at ease, usually, inside
'the wave that cannot
halt' and is for this
no less secure
in its character
(the glittery bend of its
on-hastening wall)—
at ease and alert
to the likes of pelicans and fish hawks
(naturally) and not often thinking about the lively water.

A BREATH

A quiet, cool, spring morning—
the sun up, and its light
crossing things without emphasis,
merely bringing out the pale colors.

Before breakfast, stepping outside
a moment, you can see a part of a
fair blue, distant mountain above
the mixture of neighborhood trees.

It is all so. You want to put it somewhere
inconspicuous in a heavy, dark frame.

LATE TO PRAY

All around the infrequent little towns
(a few gaunt old stores still in business,
elm-dark residential streets half-way
abandoned, a broken-hearted silence in them)
lies the shining wheat country, gold white
and open, all visible or else nothing;
hill gleams above hill to the smooth rim
of the horizon like the sight of excellence itself.

If you are still holding out here, every street
an elm tunnel opening at either end on the dazzle—
in the afternoon silence all the bright grain
standing motionless takes on a distant look;
and is again a goddess, with child,
and absorbed in that, in being nothing more.

BALANCES

How strong the young tree is, and heavy
    for standing so easily, and
    so readily shaking and bending
    in the light air

The small limb I saw at, drops and swings
    behind me unexpectedly and claws
    a rip in my shirt in passing ponderous and
    quick as a bear

SEASON

September night,
a long time over
notes on a hummingbird
that fed at the flowering
bush by the window—
thought unexpectedly
of some trees in winter
on a hill behind a bare field,
black limbs stiffly
forking in among
themselves, stern scene
under a colorless sky
of some fifteen years ago
—some forgotten old affection,
not modified, where now hummingbird
wheels again aglare....

CUBE BALANCED ON ONE CORNER

The mockingbird is quiet and stays out of sight.
Absence in the trees; in the heat and bad light
A turtledove begins despairing loudly, across the way.

Home again. The looks of things in each room
Belong with our feelings of two months ago. So this
Is a surprise visit to their wistful presences
When what we'd been wanting was merely to get back.

The yard's inhabited by strange grasses.

The hollow in the top of my great boulder—dry!
The oak has thrust a harsh little thicket
Of new twigs into one side, in the other
The oleander has thrust a blossoming tip.
In the bottom, yellowed blooms and dry oak leaves, horny-edged.

Dog days. Too late for any but small measures. I clip off
The intrusive growth, brush out leaves and dead blooms,
And brim the stone hollow with cold water. Now, near noon,
Absolutely still, it contains a sharp-cut reflection
Of the oak bough and oleander leaves and blooms
Arching irregularly over it, with the remote blue
Of the August sky filling in behind; a summer-crystal.

AS IT HAPPENS

It was in early middle age
That I saw for the first time
The legendary event—
Fresh water entering salt;
A creek came out from under
Darkness of pines and firs

Then down a stony beach
Pouring still crystalline
Among brown sand and stones
To the silent shock of entry
In a fogged, booming ocean,
Grays, grays and muffled whites,
Vague parallels hurrying in,
Creek shooting under, straight in.

THE DRAGON OF THINGS

I

Silver Creek isn't silver
but dark, for the water flows, clear and shallow,
on a bed of black lava,

that flowed in its time,
thick and slow, over a sandstone bed that in its time
was slowly drifting sand.

Firs, cedars, and maples
shadow the thin soil that formed in time
upon the lava

—shadow Silver Creek
(among the shadows the streaks and blobs of light
are silver indeed)....

2

Where the lava flow stopped
the stream wore a gorge in the sandstone in time,
over the gorge hangs

the lava lip or ledge
from which the little stream drops free to its pool
among the rocks:

3

Water entering air
is elementary, something important but not interesting
except as belonging

back among elementary things
and here having come forward, separated out
at the heart of the scene,

a violent exception
that sustains itself, making the uproar of the time that is
at the heart of the scene,

a "local dragon" sustaining
its presence in quiet start, loud close, and varying descent
all taking place at once,

hung timeless in time,
medium of the timeless—time taking its course,
gathering speed

in effortless accelerations
the dragon (tail gripping the ledge) arched out in the hissing pour,
scales streaming in heavy gouts,

U-shaped, pulling apart
in threads, spatterings, whitening all over as at top speed
it enters the uproar

where, inside the bouncing spray,
among overlapping explosions and thudding sounds, the head
moves quietly from side to side,

at his distance. The dragon
in the falls is a kind of summary, and like the rainbow
in the spray it is vivid

with an intrinsic distantness....
Beware the Dragon, I tell myself, as we are entering
the outskirts of the mist and din.

4

On the spray-slick rocks,
we watch the thing once more. How slowly it bends
at the top, then parts

as it leaves the basalt shelf
into heavy strands that speed up promptly and start to tear apart,
losing shape as they push harder

into the air, falling faster and faster
and in your last glimpse dropping like lightning, headlong,
disintegrating into the roar.

Fast as it happens, you can watch it
all the way down; you feel yourself involuntarily jerking back
at the last moment,

when the water goes on to smash itself
among rocks invisible but for a dark place now here, now there,
that suggests the snout swaying—

vivid with your attentive presence
at the danger, the near-far roaring of the dragon (or say heavy
machinery) back in the nature of things....

LATE FEBRUARY

The man down the creek owns a fruit tree
on which the white blossoms have just appeared
directly on the bare, red wood; how
they shine against the tree shadows
behind them—unaware that they are classic
Chinese plum blossoms ... their owner
is idle, white-haired, and in manner
unlike the people in the plum blossom
poems: he nods to me with a look that says
he knows something about what I think
(which is not the fact), when in the evening
he saunters past with his basset hound.

SCRIBBLING POEMS ON A VISIT HOME

Poor little bastards, is
no provision being made
for their future?

They just scatter like beans—
the pod splits and curls back
spring-like, and out they fly

during these dry August afternoons
while the tremendous, dazzling thunderheads
white as the original white

of creation, build up in the west
like the springtime fathers that drenched
fields they knew not at all,

and passed through never to return.

August 27, 1967

LORE

At the museum (O Mousa) I learn
from the stuffed specimen
that the brown pelican
(I've watched his homely flight
through binoculars from shore)
wears a crest of down
too small to be visible from shore;
and it has nothing to contribute
to the legend of pelican charity.

Then there are the living owls
in a cage outside; they glare out
with a pre-Hellenic stare
like the old Athena—glare
at nothing, apparently, soberly
astonished.
        The porcupine nearby is
humped up, motionless, reeking,
against the dirty glass—his dull
eye opens and peers up
through the stench incuriously.

Once a neighbor told me
that when fighting forest fires
as a youth he saw porcupines burning—
they'd run screaming into the brush
spreading the fire up a hillside,
and the men would curse them, and to whose credit
or discredit should this be accounted.

SHORT WALK ALONE

Cool air just arriving; half moon
High, keen-edged.
Air still and town still,
Lights on the mountain shine
As through punctures in the blackness,
Shapes like tiny explosions.

High, high in the eucalyptus—
Black bough tips in a black
Star-mild—a nighthawk cries out,
Twice, a gravelly scream,
That it's his darkness.
Coming back, catch a fragrance like cloves,
From some flowering bush or tree,
Near where the hawk claimed the dark.

Merely walking here seems
A kind of right spending
Of good, built up by the nature
Of things, by the race, by myself,
Brought within reach by the hang
Of the world as it has come
Quietly round, just here, just now.

A DAY IN THE BACK COUNTRY

I

Strong cold gusts rake the ridge;
I drive into the east light;
The roadside wild oats shake,
Glisten delicately
—Silver for a girl's wrist.

But here sea haze to right,
Mountain chasm to left,
Against their small clearness.

II

Miles, and nobody, then
Two helicopter crews,
Machines idling nearby,
And this whole back country
Seems theirs—they criss-cross it
As they please, their faces
Interested, easily
Looking out over it.

III

More miles, and I wonder
Am I lost? A deer stands
Quietly in the road,
A flowering up, it seems,
Of the dust of the road
At just this moment,
And the road itself wild.
The deer walks off, down the slope.

IV

Down steep, tight curves, jolting.
A strange rattle starts up
In the steering column.
Mudholes from the oozings
Of roadside springs. And there,
The shine of the river
Winding in the open
Valley. And no one down there.

V

Much of that day is gone.
Half careless as I was
Of it—since it was mine,
I chose that, rather than
Become cautious with it;
So, much of it's well gone—
Into my bones, maybe;
Certainly out of reach.

VI

Sycamores and alders,
Grass turning a bright brown;
In the vertical light
The loud water ablaze,
Skimmed by green-backed swallows—
Hawk, black in the distance,
Calling down at it all—
Now from these I recall:

How in the unknown
River with nothing
Promised came the jolt
And quiver of the
First trout (thereafter
How readable were
The pools and riffles!)—
How then I kept on
Fishing past lunch time
Knowing the fatigue
This would mean; then ate
Somewhat hurriedly
At last with my boots
On a log to dry—

How I went downstream
Barefoot, astonished
By the pain! each small
Rock made its own pain—
How slowly that pain
Drove back the idea
Of a pleasant walk
Barefoot to that pool
Downstream; how I caught
Two fine trout while each
Move I made meant pain;
How the log had spurs
On it, like pinpoints,
Entering my bare feet
When I came back; how
In midafternoon,
Tired, I took my last
Good trout, at a bend
In dark blue shadow,
Under a rock ledge;
How then I rested
In some tall grasses,
How they hissed loudly
With the gusty wind
While I on the ground
Lay in still air; how
I thought of sleep, slept;
And woke in changed light,
Glare and shadow strange
On the water—late
Afternoon now! How
Fishing back upstream,
Seeing the water
From the other way—
Alien—chilled me;
How in my fatigue

I went by riffles
I'd have fished, before;
How in that estranged
New-shining water
I caught two more trout,
And, leaving them cleaned
On a streamside rock,
Turning back found one
Moved—then saw the snake
That moved it, his jaw-
joints unfastened, whole
Head of fish inside
His mouth, his own head
Startlingly deformed,
Eyes looking close-set
Now that the small head
Had been stretched so wide;
How, motionless, he
Watched me, knowing well
That I might kill him,
How his eyes asked, "Well,
Will you?" and waited;
How, as I held still,
He moved, ever so
Slightly, stealthily,
Looking right at me.
How I went upstream
And from being tired
Lost three lures in quick
Succession, thinking:
I'm skin-tight, aching
With this day, bone-cracked
By it, like my friend
The snake with my trout
All but disabled
By the good fortune.
—Time to crawl home, then,

And sleep it off. How
A big, bushy-tailed
Ruddy coyote paused
On a stony spur
And watched me a moment
As I drove toward him
On the road out; how,
Truth to say, the sight
On my return, of wife
And sons distressed me
—I distressed myself
Among them, come back down
As I was, unfit
For human converse,
Drunk with the dry, bright
Liquor of the day.

SOUNDS

At my desk, the house still;
Somebody's dog barks again
And again, steadily
Through the late night silences;
I step outdoors; a full moon,
And the pour of its brilliance
Catches me full on when I emerge
From the black shadow of the house
Into the pallor among the boulders and bushes.

Huge, scentless, the moon
Has changed things. That dog
Does what he can about it,
Off in the dark of the grove
Barking on, in the dim torment
Of his poor eyesight and blurry brain.

Faithfully he barks for all the silent,
Irregular shapes on this wooded slope
Where the moon is shining
And the house stands;
I go back in and hunch over
The familiar hiss of my pencil tip
Racing across the lighted page.

THE HEAVILY WATERED WHISKEY
OF THIS DECEMBER SUNLIGHT

… if time is friend
or enemy? we stand still
by going and go
standing still:
along a hillside this
midwinter afternoon,
"An old thing to be doing"—what?
"Filing down a trail like this,"
I tell her, the pleasure of it
that we are partly roused ancestors, or
as if we were an old trellis
with a young vine in it
where now the air is moving
birds visit the grapes
the season lives
a sunny and windy freshness
so ancient—this
or nothing for us.

The Heat Lightning

(1967)

I

FIRST TWENTY-FOUR HOURS

4:00 P.M.

The enormous silver maples by the house:
their leaves are sleek and dark green
on the upper side, and a clear silver gray
underneath, and just now a strong wind
bringing thunderclouds struck suddenly
from the west as we watched and these trees
changed over from dark green to silver,
bending massively all at once, their own
agitated ghosts in the darkening air.

7:00 P.M.

On the side to the west, with the light
of the low sun striking squarely
on the flat of the leaves,
the old cottonwood sparkles like a pond.

8:00 P.M.

Now Seeley's Lake, eight miles distant,
looks like a long slit, in the bluish gray
landscape, through which light is shining.

9:00 P.M.

The moon—not long before going in
I saw it appearing low over the knob
on which the Arms boys' place stands,
the color of an orange; a little later,
stepping outside for something, I was startled
to see it reflected in the thin bright strip

of water, a coppery flare, in Latham Lake
over in Beebe draw, a full ten miles away.

12:00 MIDNIGHT

(There is nothing here, says the midnight,
but the lineaments of the real, resort
and support of every implication.)

9:00 A.M.

The brown water flows along soberly
in the main ditch; out in the beet field
water from this ditch appears as silver inlays
between the dark green rows.

11:00 A.M.

Late morning and the children have been playing
in swimming trunks on the lawn for an hour or so,
resorting from time to time to a sprinkler
that has been turning out in front long enough
to have made a big disc of darker green, mottled
and glittering—countermeasures successfully taken
against the rapid approach of high noon—and
the sparrows have not once stopped chirping
in the trees in the yard—big trees dark with summer.

2:00 P.M.

Surrounded by the hot fields the Russian Olives
make a brightness, growing along the draw—
the gray-green boughs are as clumps of frost
to the heart's desire that sees itself entering
that foliage from the heat and the light
as deer step into a grove and break up in shadows.

II
SECOND EVENING

The sense of the real thirty years back in this clearness—
I could hold with my eyes, it seemed, the body
of the air; it was like standing at a fast stream
up in the mountains, seeing down through the water skin,

through the fine streakings of light, gripping in my vision
the whole crystalline heaviness of the water—clearness
right down to the toothed edges of the elm leaves,
almost black, stationary against the streaked colors

in the sky; cats emerged from under the granary, and taking
no notice of us, disappeared in high weeds; Seeley's Lake
started shining through the mild darkness; lights came on
near it, an uptilted glitter; heart's desire picked up.

About then I might stand up casually, half thinking
of those cats out in the weeds, and with hands in pockets
take a turn out on the lawn, and stop, and seem to myself
to be in the clear dark like a trout in its pool.

Later, air movement in the elm: night proper had begun.
One or two of us would rise, re-enter the house; and others
follow, I too, and meet in my turn, at the threshold,
the shock of the day's heat held still in the house.

III
TREE MEDITATION

πότνια ἀγλαόδωρ ὠρηφόρε …
*— ΕΙΕ ΔΗΜΗΤΡΑΝ**

In this country, of the few
native trees the commonest
is the cottonwood. Settlers
planted it for windbreaks, for
shade; it grows in giant rows
on irrigation ditches,
and stands over the houses
shading them in the summer
all day; it grows in the draws
and in great dark glittering
groves on the North and South Platte.

It takes the classic tree shape—
a round symmetrical crown,
a trunk short and straight and thick;
up close, you see that the leaves
grow in loose swinging bunches
out on the periphery—
the interior is gaunt
and the few major branches
form powerful, still arches
that contrast with the quick leaves
throwing off sharp bits of light.

Considered thus, the whole thing
suggests perception combined
with imperviousness. But
I turn to one specimen:

*From the closing lines of the *Hymn to Demeter*, referring to the lady
herself: 'Queen, giver of shining things, bearer of the seasons....'

viewed up close its old trunk
with its deep rough crevices
and hard ridges covered with
sharp protuberances is
a badlands: there's nothing here
to penetrate to, it says;
impassive, unmoving, dead.

Whereas the leaves, with their fine
patterns and movements that take
the eye are transitory
and expendable—thousands
of them in agitation
all over, to the one trunk
almost featureless and like
nothing that's alive, whereby
the tree lives—holds out and lasts,
standing over the big ditch
steady and astir also.

The brown water runs past it
in the summer; in late fall,
the ditch dry and the weather
dry, the leaves turn a brilliant
clear yellow—it is startling,
the rough shining globe, against
the clear sky. The leaves fall then
in the ditch and are still bright
and new-looking when the snow
covers them, below the wood
that stands patient in the air.

The tree has had its full growth
for some thirty years at least,
bears its multitudes of seeds
regularly—small white dots

in cotton that expands vaguely
and goes aloft on breezes
looking supremely idle,
to drift up against fenceposts
and weeds and along the sides
of farm buildings and upon
the crops, irrelevantly.

The tree having grown from one
white dot, you know that of course
on the microscopic scale
in the seed's interior
it worked as distinctively
as it does here, fully grown—
below those microscopic
particulars, well below
the molecular, there lay
at last vagueness, though; vagueness
is ultimate. Thence it came,

thither doubtless it will go;
but here it stands out clearly
against a sky, it traffics
with the world intricately
and persistently, fastened
by many ways into things;
moving to the world's movements
its cotton drifting thickly
through the air on certain days
in midsummer is a sight
ordinary and solemn.

I spend half an afternoon
underneath this glistener:
in a light breeze the leaves make
a fine pattering sound, like

gravel sliding down a slope;
if the breeze strengthens, the sound
becomes a voluminous
general hissing; stronger still,
and the hissing becomes a
roar of massive excitement—
as if a cyclone had struck.

All these sounds are the sounds
of her present, passing, while
her trunk and limbs, hard things, dream
permanently, beneath sound
the dream of air and rock
and water, things around in
inorganic splendor.—Now
from the leaves I can tell how
at its quietest the air moves
in eddies, isolated
short currents, streams with dead spots …

Each leaf in a given bunch
is behaving differently;
none are the same size or shape,
all are versions; one flapping
while another seems to whirl
though in fact it oscillates;
another swings hectically
back and forth while its neighbor
hangs still; one flops over and
back, now, slowly; another
vibrates, the whole cluster sways.

I single out one leaf: it
begins to tremble, then wags
violently. The breezes
start, quit, and start up again

all afternoon. The musings
of the tree, on one calm day.
Now agitation up high;
below, not a leaf moves. Now
a breeze pours through the whole tree
and it rattles—the polished
leaves clash stiffly together.

Is all this movement purely
decorative. Is a leaf
normally agitated,
or still; or is this movement
needful to the tree's workings.
Are the movements troubles. Or
merely the life of the tree—
neither necessary nor
irrelevant; its queenly
life—not indifferent,
its impartial experience....

Three times I had the same dream
about this tree, in boyhood.
But I must explain—the trunk
for all its harshness, its lack
of fine structure, mere rocky
crevices and ridges, still
was vulnerable, of course—
a fungus got into it
near the point where the branches
arch up—the bark turned spongy
and brown, a depression formed.

The affliction seemed to me
dangerous; I was distressed.
A fluid like clean water
seeped from the place. Yesterday

when I examined the trunk
I saw clearly, down one side,
the stain left by the fluid;
though the spongy depression
had largely healed some time since,
in one spot I found some wet
soft bark; it smelt like moist earth.

That is the site of the dream.
I approach and a cavern
slopes upward into the huge
interior of the tree.
At the threshold I look up
and see on the crest in light
(a regular, clear nimbus)
a great deer standing quietly;
in the cave's natural dark
the deer is wholly visible.
It looks at me; its eye shines.

I have no inclination
to approach any closer;
according to the dream's plan
I've had a look at my life
which is all I was to do—
that was the feeling at first;
then the sense of the dream changed—
the deer was merely life
itself, being presented
in repose for a moment,
so that I could look at it.

So the tree stirs readily
in my mind—stirred yesterday
when I saw some of its kind
being felled a mile westward,

the great sections of the trunks
and limbs like fallen big game
in Africa—great females
slain and strewn about—but what
is this but an incident
I drove past the summer day
they fell in a solid world.

Underneath the tree, grasses—
bluestem, wild rye. A kind of
sharp-edged grass bends evenly,
as if combed, over the bank
of the ditch, trailing its tips
in the brown water. Woodbine,
planted by a bird dropping,
doubtless, grows here—it would come
from an old vine in the yard,
set out by some grandparent.
It is flourishing in here.

A pretty place. The milkweed
is blooming—clusters of dull
or dead pink flowers, spikey
petals set on a flesh-like
protrusion, a hole
opening in the center
shaped like a five-pointed star;
the sweet odor's attracting
not only bees but ants—large
black ants with legs that raise them
high off the ground. On the road,

close, cars pass. In the grass lie
small branches shed by the tree;
the bark on some has loosened
and come off with the passage

of the seasons, and the wood
is bleached out. A few of these
look like antlers. As I turn
to examine one of them
a funeral procession
passes—black Cadillacs, then
a long line of every-day cars.

They bear the dead and mourning
to the new cemetery
put in just beyond this farm—
the mourners preoccupied
matter-of-factly. I feel
like waving to them, but check
the impulse. The tree stands on
this thirty foot strip of ground
between the road and the field;
beyond, now, is not only
the graveyard but new houses.

So the traffic is heavy
on a road which in my youth
was silent, usually—
three or four cars going by
during a morning, perhaps.
Coming across on this ground
from the road, through the bluestem,
to see the wild geraniums,
I came close to cutting my foot
on a beer bottle fragment.

Still it is a pleasant place.
I notice along the base
of the great trunk a blackened
area—from an old weed fire,
I suppose. There is a weed

whose name I don't know—dark green,
tall, it too is blooming now—
greenish-white little flowers
in closely set clusters like
clover-blossoms.—Sacred ground,
as our life is not; and ground

inevitably profaned;
maybe inexhaustible,
too, in its way.—Yesterday,
cutting into a seed pod,
prodding it with the knife point,
hunting for the small white seeds,
trying to find some pattern,
I saw a small white spider
emerge from the packed cotton
and, while I watched, go racing
away across the table.

IV

ELEGY: THE OLD MAN

Edging between the truck
and the wall I work back
to the far end, past the concrete,
onto the original dirt—
triangles of broken glass
shine among the old straw;
I make out a hame-ring,
yellowed and fly-specked; a mended
strap, cracked and with salt
from dried sweat still on it; high
on the wall, hung there
perhaps by my brother, to be visible
and out of the way,

an old 'silver'
harness buckle, a heart shape
set in the center, catching
the half-light where it bulges—
a bit of the bold old
finery of a set of harness.

I take it down. The heart is starred
with corrosion, dented on one side—
the whole buckle's bent awry,
across the concave underside
a spider has stretched a web:
in the quiet I can hear
the strain and give of the fabric
as I poke at it … nothing
underneath but a trace of fine
reddish dirt. I blow it out.

Regarding in the half-light
the heart's convexity, I consider
(in the heart's half-light)
taking the piece home with me.…

The buckle and such scraps
are like the notions surviving
in the gaunt, brittle, half-dark
interior of an old man
and the barn an old man
lasting into this other world
maybe in a subdivision
in California: he has come out
to live with one of his children,
and runs the power mower
once a week. He actually
cuts the grass, the barn
really shelters a truck;

the old man finds himself
wearing a sportshirt,
the barn is carrying
in its inner flank a stack
of grease-gun cartridges.
The barn still holds the smell
of harness leather, and manure,
and feed and the like—faint,
dry, distant, the fragrance
persists like the manner
of an earlier day in the speech
of the old man.

My sons may never know
how satisfactory a place
a barn is to take a leak in,
and this is a barn, since you can still
do so, in the brown half-light,
the comfortable seclusion
—as for the dead in here,
I think of them long since busy
at burying their own, as I make my way
back out, toward the day-glare.

V

THE SUMMER

The birds keep to their routines.
The big cottonwood glitters.
In the approaching heat
of the middle of the day
the elm makes little movements
now and then, like a dozing horse.

And on a distant county road
the sun bangs for an instant
on a windshield, flashing
like a signal; no reply.

A big butterfly, strongly
constructed, yellow with black
ribbing and trim, works the air
between the house and trees,
disappearing from time to time
around the corner of the house
or inside one of the trees,
reappearing abruptly.

I come out after breakfast
every day, and sit writing
in the morning shade. Clear hours!
Butterfly's in the foreground
frequently; tall dusty weeds
by the road; small house, trees, fields,
in the middle distance; then
the pale, vapory mountains.

If I look up from my page
the butterfly is often
the one moving thing in sight.
I watch him rise at the end
of a glide with a broken,
tottering movement, working
his way up to a high bough
then not alighting, but merely
poising in the air above it
and veering briskly off. Well,
he's not after anything.
A kind of extract of this
place, having worked free, he stays;

his apparently hesitant
turning this way and that is
just delighted watchfulness.

Afternoons he spends mainly
resting. And nights
on a weed stem, I suppose,
stiffening with the chill,
the stem knobbly with dew when
the morning sun first strikes it.

VI

UNATTENDED

Decrepit-looking, the elm
has come back every summer
for forty years I know of,
gradually filling up
with dead gray woodlike brush,
and its crooked, blackish boughs
have held out, so far,
this summer, too,
against the wind-storms,
its leaves scanty,
dark and strong-ribbed
as if independent
of the old structure
from which they plainly hang.

VII

THE 'PASTURE'

—what we called the strip of ground
eight or ten paces across
at the widest, in between

the road to town and the fields

the place and ditch. Pushing through dwarfish
wild geranium, spearmint,
snow-on-the-mountain, milkweed,
and rougher weeds, ironweed, red-
root, dock, and the various
grasses in here made the air
strong to breathe on a hot day.

What brooded in that silence
was a hen pheasant, on nine eggs,
and when I strayed too near her
she sprang up out of the weeds

a life with a cry, and a noisy
frantic rapid slamming
of her wings—their wings are short
and the body thick, heavy—
an explosion and a blur
right at my face; her warm eggs
on the bare ground looked demure.

Forcing a stand of high weeds
on another day, I met
the authoritative stench
of a cat dead for a week

a death or longer and it stopped me
like the palm of a big hand
rammed in my chest. I went
in for a look at him, too:
stiff and disintegrating,
his eyes shut tight, and his teeth
bared, set on edge by the death.

Up the pasture, to the west
a fourth of a mile beyond
the great cottonwood stands a
grove of hardwood trees, slim-trunked,

a fall   their boughs flat, in spaced layers;
maidens. One morning I fell
from the top of one of these
clear to the ground—gradually,
bumping and crashing from one
sunlit layer to the next,
landing dazzled, on the ditch bank.

And up the east side, one tree
only, a willow that leaned
over the big ditch, the roots
having less to grip on that side;
the reflection   her dainty foliage shadowed
in the brown water charmed me;
this tree blew down years ago;
parting the weeds I found
a piece of its trunk—a rough
quarter moon of the gray wood,
weedy ground held in its curve.

VIII

THE TROPHY

A globe of bright haze, made up
of fine silvery fibers
in hexagons that were braced against
each other

while each was supported by
a slim stalk extending
from a seed fixed in the crown
at the center.

It looked fragile, but had withstood
strong gusts, last week, and it flexed

and rolled intact when I dropped it
coming home.

A trophy of late summer
on the floor of the side porch,
stirring a bit now and then
in a breeze.

Afternoon cloud-quiet; then just
as I leaned to look once more,
a wind struck, I smelt the rain
on the way,

the globe scudded off, bouncing
down the stairs, and caved in, the whole
structure careening and breaking up
as it went,

dozens of the seeds lodged in things
at odd angles, the silken
hexagons wrecked by the drench
the wind brought in.

from *Between Matter and Principle*

(1963)

Be with me, powers
    of the tongue I love,

sources of clarity in
    the turns of life:

that the slow action of the
    understanding and the motions

of the rapid feelings
    breathe in unison—

health howsoever brief.

MOMENTS IN A GLADE

Abiding snake:
                At thirty-four
By unset spirit driven here
I watch the season. Warily
My private senses start to alter,
Emerging at no sign from me
In the stone colors of my matter.

You that I met in a dim path,
Exact responder with a wrath
Wise in conditions, long secure,
Settled expertly for the kill
You keep a dull exterior
Over quick fiber holding still …

Rocking a little, in a coarse
Glitter beneath fine, vacant space,
The hillside scrub oak interlocked
Where year by year, and unattended,

And by abrasive forcings raked
Against itself, it had ascended.

And yet below me sixty feet
A well of air stood dark and sweet
Over clean boulders and a spring.
And I descended through a ripple
Of upper leaves, till noticing
That a rock pattern had grown supple,

And whirred, I quietly backed off.
I have considered you enough.
The rattle stopped; the rigid coil,
Rustling, began to flow; the head,
Still watching me, swayed down to crawl,
Tilting dead leaves on either side.

You in the adventitious there,
Passion, but passion making sure,
Attending singly what it chose
And so condemned to lie in wait
Stilled in variety—to doze
Or wake as seasons fluctuate,

Eyes open always, the warm prey
At best but happening your way.
And I too slowly found a stone
To break your spine; and I have known
That what I will have surely spoken
Abides thus—may be yet thus broken.

ONE OF THE MANTISES

*Homer, who was a poet of war ... knew it was the
shield of such happiness as is possible on earth.*

— SANTAYANA

The trim three-cornered head,
the body brought to an elegance
of elongations, the spiked

and heavy forearm tipped with
a surgical hook for the distracted
or the inattentive—in sandalwood

and light green his parts are one
deadly sanctity, twig-like
among the overlapping leaves.

MY FRIEND THE MOTORCYCLIST

Like you I have shunned unrest
by moving, drawn up into
my matter, engrained and tough,
to force a future: my past
was that matter; blank air drew
over the blank, fearless stuff.

If I drove deep into fear
of blankness, what indifferent
principle stopped me, beside
the quiet road? Dry and clear
in the wind, some chance weeds spent
their pitted and wrinkled seed.

To be dislodged in minute
hard scatterings alien
to my hot intents, I found
was the principle, and brute
the miscellaneous man
dwindling down the road to town.

OUTSIDE THE HOUSE, UNDER MOONLIGHT

Surviving their own depths and bounds
The rooftops of the neighborhood
Seem to have suddenly drawn near—
Over the blanched and molten grounds
Where boulders and old peach trees stood
The shapes look papery. Up the air

The moon, clean cinder of a blast
Whose glare is neither day nor night,
Has entered, violent and still,
Driving the substance from a past—
My carnal mind goes like a bright
haze on chill surfaces. A chill

Sleep can acknowledge best the might
That set loose these dead essences
Of what by day came steadily on
Then hunched in evening's slackened light—
Sleep (till we enter, like old trees,
The fresh restrictedness of dawn).

THE ELEPHANTS: LECONTE DE LISLE

The red sand like a sea without an edge
Flares quietly, subsided on its bed,
Undulant, fixed, charging with copper fumes
The air where men live, past its farthest ridge.

No life and no sound. Now the lions sleep,
Full-bellied, in the backs of dens miles off,
And a giraffe is drinking from blue springs,
In the date-grove where each night panthers creep.

Not a bird whips a passage with his wing
Down the thick air a huge sun circles through;
From time to time some boa warmed in sleep
Will stir a little, dry scales glistening.

Touched off beneath clear skies, space is aglow.
But while all lies in a slack solitude
The wrinkled elephants, making for their home,
Advance across the deserts, rude and slow.

From the horizon, masses of dull brown,
They come, holding a straight course through the dunes,
Throwing the dust; under their broad sure feet
The far sand-crests successively break down.

An aged chieftain leads them single file.
His hide is hard and creviced like old bark,
His skull is like a boulder, and his spine
Bows up with his least effort. Powerful,

Neither retarding nor increasing speed
He guides his followers to the certain goal;
Turning a sandy furrow up behind,
The dusty pilgrim bulks accept his lead.

Trunks between tusks, fan ears held out, and eyes
Closed tight, they pass. Their bellies throb and reek,
Their sweat goes up the burning air in steam;
And each one paces in a whirr of flies.

But what do thirst and insects signify,
Or the sun that bakes their black and fissured backs?
They ponder, as they go, the land they left,
The stands of fig their race is sheltered by.

They'll see once more the stream a great peak feeds,
And, throwing forth their hulks, white in the moon,
While a soughing hippopotamus swims off
They will descend to drink through snapping reeds.

So, moving steadily by night and day
They draw off as a gray line through the sands;
And the hot wastes grow once more motionless,
The cumbrous voyagers having thinned away.

A CHERRY TREE

after a maxim by Joubert

I gave my blossoms and my fruit; grown old
I am this heavy wood that throws scant shade.
But lean in my shade, and listen, to be made
Sure of the hard ringed resonance I withhold.

A CEDAR

Look at me here. I stand
And grow still more the same
On this low hill of sand,
Compacted with my name.

This is my agony.
And blizzards cannot break
These boughs I build to be,
In weathering, awake.

Far down the August light,
Clouds form and shift at ease;
They're not free either, yet
Edge me in distances.

Come closer—touch my bark,
Smoke-silver and so thin
Your nail can shred it; dark,
The heartwood's just within.

Now you've begun, go on.
I am. I cannot mean,
Mere growth. Have me cut down,
Caught in a motive, seen

In, say, a little chest,
Rip-sawed, cross-cut, and planed
For a small good, to last,
Stopped, in a living end,

Disclosed by changeless lines,
Lampglow on my deep red;
Have among your designs
My minor fragrance freed.

SOCRATES ENTRANCED

Supper and wine; but where
Is their friend Socrates?
Out on the thoroughfare;

One of his ecstasies
Surprised the hale grotesque
While he passed through the dusk
Amongst the talkative
With whom he likes to live—

Who are like him, in bone,
Muscle, and busy veins
That feed their rootlets down
Into alert membranes
All eagerness to vary.
He finds them necessary.
Bent on the human noise
How excellent in poise

The grave Silenus head
Looks at the trampled ground,
For a time quieted.
And once more to have found
In the conception there
The one man in still air—
Once more, for the sake of thought,
Himself in passion, caught.

—And soon he will come in,
And with the wine and talk
The questioning begin;
Bewildered friends will balk,
Swerve, and perhaps agree,
Toward daybreak, sleepily;
With one exhausted friend
He'll go, time still to spend—

With them to his last day!
Near dusk he will have sent
The wailing women away,
And checked the friends' lament

So that they finally see
The citizen, as he
Adjusts to the city's will
A stiffening animal.

HAP

a picture postcard to my own boyhood

There is containment by small
brown mountains, by the Channel
waters that run in upon
the shores and sleek and litter
the sand; the pale firm islands
shut in the swarming lights and
cross-moves of the Pacific—

as if a topographic
ordering of the desires
lay ready; in season, low
clouds will form, and, thunderless,
come in changing rapidly,
set loose their spattering rains
and sweep off, torn by short winds—

the diversity of shore,
hill, and gorge is clarified
with stands of rough, bulbous oak,
a luminous sycamore
here and there, somberly thirst-
ing eucalyptus, mustard
washed yellow over the slopes—

nicely scaled for the human
eye, under a small soft sky
suggesting that, if you wished,

you might walk to what you see
anywhere here, observe it,
and make your way back during
the morning hours, through the trees.

Under the ordinary
bright gentle light of the place
I look in across a fence
at a bed of wild grasses
stippled with alyssum, with
a few native poppies—slight,
chill orange, snipped out finely.

A poppy is struggling
and the others barely shake;
one of its petals comes loose,
wavering down a kind of
creek of air. Son, you could choose
at such times to be happy,
yet free of your happiness,

knowing that its root is hap—
I'd have had you arriving
so as not to be bemused
in it; say, splashing ashore
as one of a colony
of Greeks fresh from disaster
who glance about expertly.

THE OPEN WORLD

I drive up on the headland
to the campus, to finish
some last chores—down through the gaps
between the big buildings a

wind's coming in, clear, heavy,
coursing the Channel from the
open seas to the northwest.

It is cold—and could have crossed,
a week since, the Aleutians
from waters far back over
on the curving of the world;
it looks to be intently
cleansing this place of used air
in corners, of particles

on walks and in shrubbery;
students—of the few still here—
crossing between library
and dorm are minor figures
blown bare and vivid in the
strong sparkle of the light, the
bleakness is energetic

as I enter South Hall. But
the main switch has been thrown, the
windows locked tight—the air's dead
that had been well divided
and held in bright dry spaces
as of the mind itself, for
some feat of our attention—

as if a mind, having been
closed down, left a bitterness
suspended here—a mind grave
and perhaps magnificent,
that had again been failed of,
and was again awaiting,
fatefully, some dominion.

So a term's done; I hurry
and finish my chores, leaving
as if I'd been driven out
so as to meet with this wind—
an unoccupied roaring
inside my ears. At the tip
of the headland the sea is

racing and the eye plunges
and ascends alertly; and
the bottom of the sea, some
intricate system, surely,
as of conceptions left un-
tended, bears those contorted
currents and lashed surfaces.

Santa Barbara, California,
August-September, 1962

from *The Sum*

(1958)

A WALK IN THE VOID

I could not see the life I live.
Wheeling to catch it as it was,
I found myself the fugitive;
There were my footprints, in reverse.
I could not praise them, could not curse.
Bare of their principle and cause,

They lay caught fast within that realm
No inquiry can justify,
No good or evil overwhelm.
To enter was to be interred
Where the gross lip absorbs the word.
It was what dead men occupy.

Or so it seemed. And yet I live.
Living I left my tracings there.
Driven historian, I arrive
Here where I blindly went, and see.
Dark walker through dubiety!—
Resuming you I grow aware,

Which is my life. O formless ground
Of quick experience, but not
Experience itself, I found
That I had walked upon your void
Saved by the blindness I employed
Till I stood blinking in my thought.

THE BABY COCKATRICE

I'd read of the vast reptiles, maybe seen
Some musty drawings of them, years ago.
The rumor that such creatures have once been
Will make a child fear, idly, *They are, now.*

Preoccupied and happy, I had fished
Well through a June day on Commotion Creek
And had my limit; now the water rushed
In shadow, mostly. Almost at the lake

I climbed the bank, tired, quiet. There he was.
He happened; total; there. He barely lay
A finger long—bone mouth and ruff and claws,
The plated body, and shock on shock, the eye.

And once I turned, all I had been stayed there
Whole in a gaze where no more could occur.

THE DAIMON'S ADVICE

So you of the slow-changing room
That each day you had wakened in
To be your own, provisional,
Slyly-known fellow, tried the sill,
Slipped out, renounced what you had been,
To tamper with this sourceless calm.

How long ago? you ask. But time,
The even circling round a center,
Has nothing here to circle through.
Where movement's neither false nor true,
To turn is not to leave, or enter,
But to stand, tenser yet, the same.

No, you must practice unconcern.
It will not do to glare, and call
Thunder to break from lightning-crack
That the world, at once, come densely back—
You'll owe to some stray, prose detail
Your unremarkable return.

THE DEATH OF A BUFFALO

out of Parkman

Heavily from the shadeless plain to the river
The bull slants down and bends his head to draw
Bright water in, that goes unbroken ever.
He pauses, water threading from his jaw,
Impenetrably as he is, and old.
And, while the harsh beard drips and shines, the shore
Beyond grows flashing grasses. Through the cold
Water he lifts a foreleg, as before,
Showing the naked spot the ball drives through.
A shiver. The coming hour, the windy grass
Under the suns beyond him, these he knew,
Knows and shall know. They make no shift to pass
    Through death. Death is the elsewhere, an unwit
    Of the great body down, this side of it.

VIATIC

J.G.S.
Colorado, 1885

for Edward Loomis and John Williams

I

I came in eighty-five, but not for gold.
My wife and child with friends, my goods all sold,
My farewells quickly said, I boarded ship,
We left the Thames and wallowed past the tip
Of Land's End, beat through winter seas to dock
At Boston; next, shut up in noise and shock,
I came by train to Kansas; and by horse
A week's ride westward, reining with the course
Of the Platte River till I reached my claim.

I plowed and sowed and cropped it, made it tame—
So the facts were; yet they were roundabout.
By fall I knew that I had come in doubt.

Five thousand miles away and eight months back,
Having become habitual and slack
In means and aim, I had thought out a place
Blown clean of thought—the clear winds would efface
Each scribbled trace of it; there I would drink
Purest perceptions down, and then would think,
While winds blew fresh each keen particular,
Exacter, suppler thought: no edge would blur.
I saw a plain, a sky. There I began.
I was to be an instantaneous man
Dark and exact against bright emptiness—
I think the nugget-diggers sought no less.

Indeed, I rode through such a place, five days
Out of Dodge City. Earth was a white blaze.
Lizards clung flat in it. Dissolved in light,
The distance jerked and rippled out of sight.
I was moving through a county of no name;
I watched my perfect shadow; flatly same,
It slid unflawed through scanty rigid grass
Vibrating in the wind. I could but pass
Each instant as the instant's functioning,
Yet could not quite, like the throbbing lizard, cling
So pure, taking each instant as eternal,
So helpless, physics of light my speechless journal.

II

My horse had quickened; it was noon. Ahead
The road dropped gently to a river-bed.
A cottonwood gave us a place to enter—
Of all that vacant flaring the dark center,
Scarred and historical, from root to tip

Controlled, a brute of balance. On that trip
It gave good shade to me.—I have since seen
My fenceline cottonwoods, in windy sheen,
Release bright drifts of seed, each speck of brown
Spun in a silken sprocket; field and town
Catch them in clots of fluff. When lucky air
Lodges one well, it builds its order there.

But generation's structuring of chance,
The fine dark interlockings in events—
The still interior of a thing, which is
Its history—how could I know of these?
I had been lifted in a silent blast—
That nameless blaze had nearly had me fast.
I rested for an hour, and then rode on.
As the lesser glow of the late afternoon
Cooled in the washes cut through sandy banks,
I gained the last long rise, and saw the flanks
Of fields beyond the Platte, harrowed for wheat
In trim square miles, held in the level light.

The whole land lay accomplished in one look.
Blue mountains backed the pastures, grazing stock,
Farm buildings, fences, fallow fields—complete.
A woman on her porch shook out a sheet;
A horseman harried cattle with faint cries;
The low light bronzed the air below the rise.
My mare, feeling the reins go slack, had slowed,
Then paused, looked round at me, then at the road;
She stamped a forehoof; dust as fine as smoke
Lifted and softly coiled; before I spoke,
She slanted down the hill. As the dark came
We reached the town; and the next day, my claim.

I hired a hand, a strong, methodical,
Quick-laughing man who worked for me till fall,
Then drew his pay and left as if his work

Had been a shrewd evasion, or a quirk—
A man external, transient, and adept.
We dug and roofed a cellar, where I slept,
Put up a livestock shed and a corral,
Sank, inch by inch, my windmill-driven well;
I went in debt for housegoods, seed-grain, tools,
A milk-cow and a span of vicious mules.
My nearest neighbor helped me plow and plant.
I worked and had no time for puzzlement.

After the wheat was in and showing green,
We turned to build the house. We plumbed each line,
Raised stud and rafter, fastened sill and brace.
The days were slow, and huge with sun and space.
We had the shingles on by late July.
The wheat flashed heavy-headed, hissing, dry.
I wrote my wife the news. In the late fall
She and our child would come. The year would fill.
—Yet I have said that I had come in doubt.
After the threshers left I found it out:
My wheat lay binned in silence; I would stare
And lean to hear the motion perished there.

My man had left. I learned the numbing pause,
The after-harvest, severed from its cause.
—That autumn on the eastern slope was dry.
Thundery cumulonimbus, white-domed, high,
Rose from the mountains every afternoon,
Dropped lightning on the foothills, met the sun
Above the plains, lost shape and spread away.
The sun set shining at the end of day.
The air was warm by ten. The mountains hung
Disjunct from the low hills they lay along,
Like neither sky nor earth; unbroken, still,
The blue illusion always visible.

Through noon my fields lay cold, fields that I sought
For stricter motive, suppler act and thought—
As I had worked them, they had fastened me
Into their workings, imperceptibly
Had edged me into their own silences.
I fled, made my own motion, furious.
Climbing the Platte along its southern arm,
I rode through foothills while a thunderstorm
Bellied from high bare scarps; quick lightning-joints,
Drawn by the lines of crest, struck veins and points,
Blind thunder banged the clefts and buttresses,
And then it passed; light filled the streaming trees.

—Passed, and let in the river-noise; all night,
Camped at the canyon's mouth, I felt its weight.
The water's complicated roaring pressed
Over me in continuous arrest
Till it included me at every sound,
And filled by sleep, commotion without ground,
Equal to silence, merely happening.
I woke and would have shouted anything,
But could not reach the first, in-breaking word.
It was as if nothing had quite occurred.
So deaf, I headed for the inner range
Through twisted, crumpled strata locked in change.

Then windy glacier meadows. To the west
The tundra jutted swiftly to a crest.
I tied my mare and angled up the face.
The summit was but rock, two-thirds in ice.
Beyond, below me, lay but further land.
An hour I stood there. If I touched an end,
Then upward (all space opened out) I won
My final terror of the instant sun.
The wind was cold. It steadied, like a wall.
Neighbors had mentioned that the first snowfall

Was due to pack the passes twelve feet deep
Within the month. So time and space would keep.

Yet, as I paused, it was as if I saw
My passage as the work of blinding law,
Law like a bright illimitable day
That lit no single spot where meaning lay.
Figures moved there—my own, others like mine—
And, secretive with distance, gave no sign.
And fifty winters since that hour passed
I see them still: they move and are held fast,
From time to timeless rising in recall
Like water dammed above its natural fall
Irresolutely rippling, and then stilled.
But I was no such image caught and held.

III

And knew it, too. Where year-old snowbanks leaked
In eastward trickles while the cold unlocked,
I eased myself off backward, had to watch
One at a time each foothold I could catch,
Every recalled detail of polished rock
Pulling my boot against it with a shock;
Then crossed the tundra to my horse, and wound
Through water-flashing pine-shade. Water sound
Joined water sound in fresh identities,
Broke downward through the valley-cramming trees,
Then gathered in the canyon, and the roar
Tremored the rocks I rode through as before—

Both old and new: I had turned back on the year
Before the year was done. Old waste, old fear
Remained its matter; and, since unconcluded,
They could not be accepted, or eluded,
Lest I should die before my life was done.

I paused above the farm. I had begun
A barbed wire fence around the stubble-field,
And had the posts aligned. The wire lay coiled
Where I had left it. Even as I glanced,
I knew the air it lay in had advanced
The thinnest shade toward a snowstorm gray;
Those flakes would lodge on what I knew today.

The flakes would tip and spin through the still air,
And I could see, jarring along the bare
Cold-hardened wagon tracks that led from town,
My wife and child and me (huddled and brown
In gray light closing in the gray landscape)
Assembled in a single, awkward shape,
The very motion of our ignorance
A jarring into actual events,
And therefore true, and therefore to be sought,
In our warm winter room, until the thought
Of what was true grew actual at last;
A mortal, late, might clamber from his past.

THE VANISHING ACT

for T.G.

After he concluded that
he did not wish to raise his
voice when he spoke of such mat-
ters as the collapse of the

Something Empire, or of things
the folk suffer from, he sim-
ply set in words such meanings
as were there, and then, when he

finished the final verse, van-
ished in the blank below it:
he'll reappear only on
the next page (not written yet).

SMALL SONG

"Turn on the hose," I say.
I kneel down on my lawn
To watch the water play.

At the depression where
The tree is set, it fills,
Transvisible as the air,

To level, tentative,
Then, trembling, overbreaks.
Its boundaries always give

Where the clear instants slow.
I stand, walk toward my house.
Shade slips. Place is aflow.

TWO PHOTOGRAPHS OF AN OLD POET

I.

Light and the features run together.
Though the dark eyes are clear
The rest of the face is neither one nor other.
Entry of flesh by atmosphere.

You can just make out what lines will come
As time confirms each feature;

But now it presses shadows with vague thumb
To make the handsome, mobile nature.

You see no further. In this picture
The face alone is there,
As if there were no need for other matter.
And the expression is severe.

2.

Deep in an ancient chair (behind,
A tall door stands ajar,
Before him burns a window with no blind,
No place for vagueness here)

He rests distinct. A massive cane
Gleams in his hand against
The shade of his dark sleeve; shrunk bone and vein
Sustain a grasp advanced

Through every long-past shift of air,
Ready for utter shock.
But the hand lags behind his candid glare.
Death and the eyes already lock.

"YOU NEED A CHANGE OF SCENE"

Sick of the slippery rot old oaks beget,
The spongy browns of a summer sunken, wet
Leafy destructions, all the heavy smell,
The heavy going of the trees to hell,
I thought of the desert—sand, merely, and air,
The white region of sun, brilliant, bare,
In all directions blank simplicity....
Good lack I sought, have I come close? I see

The wiry greasewood; scrub; pale trees whose trunks
Choke off in mistletoe; the riddled chunks
Of cactus snapped, or, leaning, hovering rife
With angry dying trapped in angrier life—
But nearer, now, the sun burns sure and bare,
Sure because bare. Let his stare be my stare.

White River Poems

(1976)

conversations, pronouncements, testimony,
recollections and meditations
on the subject of
the White River
Massacre
Sept. 29
1879

NOTE

In some respects the Nathan Meeker of this poem bears only a slight re-semblance to the historical Nathan Meeker, and the same is true of most of the other characters, though much of what he and others say here comes from records of what they actually said. As for the events surrounding the massacre itself, I have given these as I found them in the historical accounts and documents. How much I am obliged to my sources, in this and other important respects, I detail in the Acknowledgements. The poem is a composite made of pieces in various shapes and sizes—strictly documentary, autobiographical (i.e. *Going There*), quasi-documentary, completely imaginary.

A.S.

Book One

CONVERSATION WITH SHADES

From my researches, musings,
inquiries, trips to the scene,
I come forward, pause, feeling
not sure what I'm doing here,
head buzzing with my reading,
in silence, vagueness, poor light;
yet have no inclination
to leave; and begin pacing
back and forth, agitated.
A corpse appears in the air
above and to one side; stripped,
and blue as an alcohol
flame, with red-brown stains of blood
on mouth and neck; in the mouth
is rammed a piece of broken
barrel stave; around the neck
a length of chain has been wired.
As these details become clear
there rises above the corpse
the shade of the man Meeker—
a tall, angular, white-haired
musing man, hale as he might
have been had this not happened.
He stands looking at his corpse,
and the dimness behind him
rustles with wan presences
(like moths outside the windows,
on a still summer evening,
nuzzling the bright panes and screens,
and inside a man hears them

as he reads).—It is people
half ready to appear
with Meeker, now that he's here;
and behind them stands the dark
shape of a mountain barely
discernible, a scrap
of smoky red light in it
from a fire; and voices carry
through the pre-dawn air—the scene,
the White River high country,
is coming back, with all those
who lived in it at that time,
when another voice begins,
a calm dry official voice,
and the dimness around us
empties of life, and Meeker,
it is clear, is listening
though still looking at his corpse—

… troops were coming and the Indians knew that, for there is nothing
of any moment pertaining to themselves but what they understand; the
fact that the commissioner had recommended that Utes be sent to In-
dian territory was all understood by the wisest Indians, and they did not
want to go there, they wanted to remain at home, in Colorado; all these
causes, the failure to give them their supplies, their starving conditions
away back, Mr. Meeker's unfortunate appointment and administration—

and Meeker stirs, I notice

—awakened the old Indian frenzy; the soldiers were coming in just as it
had been said they should come; the Utes met the soldiers out there with
this fierce fight; one of the Indians who was in the fight starts for the
agency and carries the news there of this bloody fight, and then follows in
this wild excitement the massacre. This is about the story as I …

Meeker asks, 'And who was that?'
'His name is Fisk,' I tell him,
'former member of the Board
of Indian Commissioners;
now a banker.… Would you say
the man got the story straight?'
'Oh, yes.' But he says the words
dismissively, glancing down
at the piece of barrel stave.
And I say, 'I only meant
to ask for the truth.'—'The truth.
Everybody has the right
to say that certain misdeeds
in his life shall be left out,
—and those of the gravest sort,
simply left out of account.'
'You're speaking of forgiveness.'
But he brushes this aside.
'What a man does is mostly
not personal, since he is
a sort of clan of desires
coming from savage country
he does not know much about
for a long time—he's busy;
with most of them he is not
on close terms; then, some have died
in infancy; some falter
lifelong; some vie for the lead
and a few get it and have
their day; or fail; some get by
quietly, keeping their heads down—
and meanwhile the man's *busy*,
maintaining the whole outfit
even if they are deadlocked
with one another, or with
bad weather, or both, too much

of the time to claim from us
much interest. Necessity's
tedium racked me often,
and if they called me tactless—'
And I say, 'They use that word
in the official account
of you, in the D.A.B.—
"tall, awkward, slow of speech, and
tactless;" it was tactlessness,
they say, that got you murdered.'
He: 'In the nature of things …'
then pauses and considers.
As he does I realize
the shade of his wife, a small
and meagerly made woman,
is here, and listening
from a place on the far side
of Meeker's corpse. But Meeker
has not noticed her. He shrugs,
looking at the blue-lit corpse,
'Though what a ghost, left over,
has to do with the nature
of things is perhaps too slight
for discussion.' Then the sight
of his wife vivifies him,
though he looks at her without
surprise, as if she'd come in
from the next room of a house
where they still lived. A silence,
and she watches him mildly;
we all stand, as if waiting,
in what we soon realize
is simply emptiness; so
my voice sounds small when I say,
'In the cosmology of—
of the dead, what are you now?'
Arvilla says, 'You would guess

he comes here from a distance—'
He: 'Think of the stars this way:
steady burners in distance,
a housing for the small earth
absurdly vast; and the heart,
fashioning for itself room
too large for its future....' She:
'You spoke of them as barrens
of bright distance, I recall.'
—'That is how I think of it.
Mere unoccupied desire.'
But his attention has turned:
'You, though, are inseparable
from the places you lived in.'
And then an afterthought: 'We
are no longer important.'
Which seems not to interest her.
Again there comes a silence.
Then she: 'Do you get lonely?'
And Meeker replies promptly,
'I was not good with people.
I never lasted with them.
Though there were times when I'd see
myself with people—distinct,
each one himself completely,
all perfectly together
in their separate movements …
I had learned at the Fourier
Phalanx, long ago, how much
cooperation people
would bear, in less than a year …
I was at my best alone.'
And I say: 'Think of that time
you wrote the piece called "Lonely."'
He says, 'And I would call that
maybe the best thing I wrote—

"So the sun goes down over the mountains and one looks down the narrow valley, looks along the wagon road where only one track has been made this year, as if someone were coming, tired and ready for a warm supper, looks out through the gap in the range as if a four-horse team might be discovered in a hurry to make the five or six miles before dark, but not a soul is seen, nothing moves.

If there were neighbors five miles away, or ten or twenty, it would be quite cheerful and one could ride over for a visit once a month. But it is 65 miles to the nearest house where, by the way, no family is now living, the woman having gone East because it was so lonely. It is lonely, so lonely."'

As he stops the darkness pales,
light discloses an upland
valley in the early spring;
mountains edge it, and the light
of late afternoon pours through
a thunderstorm in progress
that blurs, in one place, the low
blue mountains on the far side;
the valley, smooth brown meadow
with a river winding through,
lies in sunlight. Meeker says,
'Yes, it's lovely; empty
loveliness, though, never much
caught my eye.' I recollect
the words of a visitor
to the Agency, not long
before the end, on Meeker:
'To look at him was to see
plows and harrows and fence wire.'
Meeker says, 'It was out there
we spent some of our best time.'
Then adds, 'Then came the bad part.'
She says: 'You don't remember
how bad,' while he is saying
with a restrained eagerness,

'We put the Agency where—'
and is leaning and pointing, when
Arvilla says, 'There, My God.'
Near the corpse-apparition,
which she has yet to bother
looking at, she and I see
Meeker and a wide-faced, tall,
heavy-bodied Indian
face to face in the office
of the Agency. The Ute,
rigid with fury, raises
his hands deliberately,
and, speaking some abrupt phrase
repeatedly, shoves Meeker—
shoves him away from the desk,
keeps shoving, Meeker flailing,
to keep his balance, the shock
tensing his jaw, as his eyes,
looking hard into the Ute's,
become uncertain—back, back,
lurching out the door, the Ute
giving him one last hard shove
against a low hitching rail;
and Meeker goes over it
backward, and lies in the dust
and horse-droppings, while the Ute
walks off and two white men
run to Meeker, help him up,
gingerly—for he's a man
now in the isolation
of the humiliated.
The scene fades, I look around,
the shade of Meeker is gone,
Arvilla is gone, the corpse
burns with an intenser blue
a moment, as I get out.

Book Two
What Happened: Questions and Answers

___

PROLOGUE

I

The town lights are glittering
in the sudden winter dark
far below—in the room, light
comes only from the fire—flame shapes
waver in the plate glass.
Much Pueblo pottery. Fine
Navajo rugs on the walls
and floors; Washington Matthews'
vast work on Navajo rites
lies half in quivering shadow,
where it dominates a sprawl
of papers, books, old pamphlets
on Southwest Indians; talk
has shifted from the ghetto
riots—it's 'sixty-seven—
to travel plans: how our friends
will go to Jemez Pueblo
for the Corn Festival dance,
and we? 'Weather permitting,
I'll go to Meeker,' I say:
the associational
blank around 'Meeker' contrasts
pitifully with Jemez
and its masked dancers moving
in the cold under starlight.
'Meeker ...?' and 'Where is Meeker?'
'Meeker's over the mountains,
I've not been there yet, just read

about it; a ranchers' town.
It lies among the broken
plateaus that run out to those
flat barrens of Utah, dead
as so much chemical waste
through which the Utes, who had lived
where the town is, were driven
to a new reservation.
Meeker's named after the man
they killed and mutilated;
there was no town then, only
an Indian Agency.
Meeker was the Agent there.'
'How'd you become interested
in all this?' (after a pause).

2

(MYSELF TO MYSELF)

Tell them the story.—Tell them
a story, you mean, because
that is what the story is
first and always—a story;
and then?—And then we shall see
emerging in silhouette
the shape of the tribe, the way
hills with their prosy detail,
their houses, fences, trash, roads,
when the sun drops behind them
turn one smooth shape of darkness
against the radiance.—Ha.
What radiance and what tribe?
—Why, our tribe; the radiance
that comes of finality;
I know all this is in doubt.
Tell your story. They're waiting.

3

Meeker founded my home town.
I found his story retold
in a Sunday Supplement,
with photographs, recently.
And I've done some more reading.
Meeker looked like Uncle Sam;
like Ralph Waldo Emerson.
He was a man of eager
feelings, the best intentions,
with a ranging, loose-jointed,
abrupt intelligence, and …
a nice man, as we should say—
at the hearings afterward
a witness called him 'a most
excellent gentleman,' though
'without the tact, and knowledge
of the Indian character,
which is required in Agents …'
The colony he'd founded
had prospered, but he himself
at sixty, after a life
of jolting change, and no slight
distinction, lost his money
and now, in debt, and tired out,
resolves to go out once more
in the wilderness, agent
for the Utes, who at this time
possess a third of the state
and find the whites crowding up
against them; the old story.
Meeker goes out with orders
(and the desire) to turn them
from their hunting, and make them
into farmers—as farmers

Utes will take up much less land,
though that's not Meeker's motive …
They resist, naturally,
naturally he presses them;
they resist, he presses more;
fear, threats, rage, and then one day
a Ute roughs Meeker up: now
exhausted and furious
he sends for troops. Utes meet them
and defeat them; a few Utes
return to the Agency,
shoot Meeker and the eight whites
in his employ, carry off
Meeker's wife and grown daughter
and one other white woman
with her two small children. They
rape the women, they burn
the Agency buildings, smash
and strew whatever won't burn
among the bodies; Meeker
they drag, stripped, behind a horse,
crush his skull, ram in his mouth
a piece of broken stave
from a flour barrel. Meanwhile
more troops are called in, the Utes
retreat into the mountains.
An emissary finds them,
there are parleys, the women
are released, there are hearings,
outrage, confusion, speeches
in Congress, editorials …
with the result that, within
a year, the Utes are driven
into Utah and the whites
move onto their land. Such is
the story as you'll find it

in the histories. Also
the story our conscience tells
and tells us how to hear. Well,
I'll even say it is true.
But it is not the truth. So
I'm going to Meeker. To see
what I can see. I'm going
over the mountain, like the bear.

PART I

GOING THERE

1

This is how it was. Alone
and liking it, off-season,
travelling in the late winter
the route that Meeker first took—
around, not through, the mountains,
north, then west over high prairie,
then south on the western slope.

2

I saw the clearness of things
clear of people, clear of all
the shapes of their purposes
and doings—use, and trouble,
and comfort—except the road,
and the fences, running straight
across the eventlessness.

3

How distantly beautiful,
I thought, this country is; how
in it I am far from it,
small to it and gigantic
and remote too, to myself—
being far from where I live,
And from Meeker. Seeing things.

4

—Saw mountains, rather the tips
of a range, like blue crystal
behind the brink of the dun
of the plain: for the young light,
the one kind of light that shines
in this country, seemed shining
less on them than into them.

5

—Saw the stillness of the plain
that, this time of year, after
the abrasions of winter,
looked like an old pelt, dimmed, worn,
dropped casually and lying
in folds that being natural
have an unemphatic grace—

6

with the cloud-filled, light-filled sky
always busy above it,
Meeker would have looked at it
now and then, though long settled
into his thoughts—left to them
by the long empty stretches
that show themselves at a glance.

7 & 8

Watched a storm sinking slowly-
quickly over Elk Mountain,
all a bluish mistiness
outside, while inside would be
the intimacy of snow
or rain entering the pines
and grasses in the quiet—

at last only the foothills
stood clear, under the storm's flank,
the low sun shining on them
across the plain. Later, saw
some antelope near the road,
seeming made of the buff light
in the grass they were grazing on.

9

Dropped into broken country—
bluffs and washes, dead gray, bare.
Right at the surface, deadness
of what was never alive,
deadness of the oldest rock,
deadest clay, scandal showing
what the alive have come from.

10 & 11

And late, lost on a back road,
storm warnings on the radio,
how large loomed up the first man
I spoke to after driving
for hours. He wears a red cap
with white polka dots on it.
Leaves the horses he's tending,

puts a slow horny finger
on the map, "Here we are"—looks
at me through rimless glasses
quietly, with pale blue eyes,
as I thank him. "You're sure
welcome," he says, his hand raised
slowly as I drive away.

12

What I was doing out there,
city clothes and red sports car,
and with a storm coming on,
was the politely withheld
topic in his manner; I
out of place, and Meeker gone
too far back into the place.

13

Enter the town of Meeker,
driving through a wet snowstorm.
The houses are small and old,
the stores, built along one side
of the main street, are all dark.
Down the street, a parked pickup.
My car is the one car here.

14 & 15

Sunday. Coming in through town
nearing the business section
I'd seen a white horse standing
at the back porch of a house,
eyes half shut against the snow
and a white goat on the steps
sheltering under his neck.

Also three small boys, playing
basketball in the snowswirl
in a front yard of bare dirt.
Also a young, pregnant woman
who watched me as I drove by
from the doorway of a worn
house trailer, her coat flapping.

16 & 17 & 18

That a man should die for such
may not be sweet and fitting.
In its unassuming way
the town seems the worthier,
though, when you think how common
to die for a town has been,
how the survivors come back,

to finish a lifetime's slow
and wobbly trajectory—
weathering a winter storm
along with white horse and goat …
if you were Utes, you came back
to lean-tos made of brush,
or skin tents for the winter …

—Is it so simple as that?
No, but it might as well be,
I tell myself, looking out
at a bleak old dry-goods store
through the wildly blowing snow,
and I sit watching awhile,
happy, as darkness comes on.

20 & 21

Next day, try the obvious,
go see at the museum
the plow that enraged the Utes
(Meeker ploughed up the pasture
they used for their pony races),
photos of Utes, of Meekers;
beaded buckskins, arrowheads,

old newspapers, a photo
of the tree where the captive
women were handed over
by the surrendering Utes.
Nice lady in charge tells me
the site of the massacre
is a rancher's hayfield, now.

22

No, you can't get right to it,
it's fenced ranchland, you see. No,
no trace of the Agency
remains, the only building
they didn't burn was later
carried away by the river.
Take this road, you'll see a sign....

There is the smooth meadow, the low
mountains and the White River
on the far side; Herefords graze
among snow patches; a ditch
with willow brush, and a fence,
barbed-wire, stop me. From somewhere
woodsmoke threads the cold, sweet air,

killdeer cries his skittery
alarm, blackbird goes *chirr—tring!*
wind whoos low and steady from
behind me, chilling the back
of my ears; *whoo*. Now and then
a snowflake. Look for a pole,
she had said, with a white ball

on it. "It's a quarter-mile
from the road, and hard to see.
But it marks the actual site
in that hayfield." I see white
in the glasses, but whether
it's the white ball or a bit
of the snow all the cattle

have trampled in the long grass,
I cannot make out from here.
Whoo, in the stillness. Some cows
come and shine their eyes at me,
the bear that reached the other
side of the mountain—and then
he couldn't see what he saw.

PART II

GOING AMONG THE DOCUMENTS

From the inquiries of Federal commission and Congressional committee

I

A QUARTET OF OFFICIALS

Hayt, Pitkin, Byers, Fisk—
at the start of the hearings,
in the clear prosaic light
of office and hearing-room,
each man is firmly outlined,
details of feature and dress
are plain. Each is translucent,
all the same, like certain shrimp,
and as the veins and organs
of the shrimp are visible,
inside these men can be seen
luminous panoramas
on a miniature scale:
now a plain, population
darkening it in places—
canals shine among the green
oblongs of fields; now a vast
army encampment. These men,
having public existence
only (at such occasions)
are only partially real—
although such reality
as they have is firm enough
in this conjoint appearance
of individual features
lacking intrinsic interest
(aside from such vague menace
and promise as may be seen

in every man in office),
and the vistas inside them
with human activity
that might interest us, were it
not featureless from distance....

~

The Hon. Edward A. Hayt
Commissioner of Indian Affairs
phrasing his Indian policy

... my attention was called early to the position
of these Indians. Here is a labyrinth
of 600 square miles where they are at home.
A war with the Utes would outlast the Seminole war
in time, and exceed it in cost. The whole body
of the Utes at war would take enormous sums
to overpower. In that country our troops
would be at the mercy of the Indians
at every point.—Q. Would you think it wise to place
those Indians in the Indian Territory?
—A. There is wide difference of opinion about that.
The reason I have favored it is this:
The Indian Territory has fertile land enough
to enable those Indians to settle comfortably.
Again, the country is not broken, ridged,
and labyrinthine; the Army could use artillery,
against which, the Indians know very well
it is useless for them to go on the warpath:
as a defensive measure, then, it would be wise
to take them out of their fastnesses, put them
where they are safe and can support themselves—
at no other point can they be fed so cheaply
as in the Indian Territory. Then, too,
there is a large mining population

pouring rapidly into Colorado
which must be fed principally from the soil
of that State, which has little arable land—
perhaps less than 10 per cent. That land is needed
to support this population of white people.
Of course I would not take these Indians
to Indian Territory till they had been paid
every dime owed them by the Government.
—Q. But looking to the interest of the Indians themselves
would our experience with the Nez Perces
teach us that that would be good policy?
—A. Possibly they would lose some lives; however,
as they became acclimated, in perhaps
two years, they would be healthy there. However,
my policy on the removal of these Indians
is flexible and general; my report
calls for their resettlement, but where
is a matter for discussion.
    By Mr. WADDILL:
                        This policy
of filling up that country with wild Indians—
how will it affect the neighboring states?
—A. My impression is, if you put the Indians there
with military posts along the borders
the Indians will be in a sense corralled
and the white settlers would then be secure.
    By Mr. POEHLER:
Do you think the Utes would consent to be removed
to Indian Territory?—A. I am glad you asked;
for I would not remove them without their consent
fairly obtained—unless they have been on the war-path,
and have forfeited their rights. Such Indians
would be removed at the government's discretion.

~

The Hon. Frederick W. Pitkin, Governor
of the State of Colorado
reporting a conversation
with Ute Jack; and an
opinion
Washington, January 30, 1880

The committee met at 10 a.m., Mr. Gunter in the chair.

Gov. Pitkin speaking—
… Jack said he had come to secure my aid
in having Agent Meeker removed.
I asked him for what reasons. He said
that Meeker tried to make them work,
and go to school; that he was plowing
and putting crops in, and wanted them
to go to work like other people.
He said, "Indian no work; Indian
hunt; Indian no want to work."
He pointed to me and said, "You no work."
He pointed to Mr. Byers and said,
"He no work." He drew himself up
and put his hand on his breast and said,
"I no work." I said, "Would you be
a governor or a postmaster?"
He said, "Yes." I then asked him
if the Indians would not work the mines,
on their land in the Elk Mountains,
dig for gold, get out money,
and get rich as white men did. He said,
"No, we will not mine at all."
I took him then to a large map
where the Reservation is defined,
pointed out the White River
and the Elk Mountains, and asked would they,
then, let white men go and dig the ore,

they being unwilling to do it themselves?
He talked with the chiefs for some time
and finally said they had no right
to consent to white men going in there.
—While speaking on the subject of work
he said that Indians would not work
but squaws would work a little; Indians
themselves, though, should not work at all.

~

—Q. Are relations between the whites and Utes
open and friendly on the whole?
—A. I don't think the people of the State
like an Indian.—Q. Are they afraid
of them?—A. I think the great mass of people
have a sort of chill run over them
when they encounter Indians. They are
a dangerous-looking people, in their style
of dress and their demeanor; also,
the fact that they do not talk much
makes white people afraid of an Indian.
I confess that has always been my feeling.
The people in sparsely settled places,
except the oldest settlers, always
are fearful when Indians come around.

~

Observations by Mr. William N. Byers, Newspaper editor,
Postmaster of City of Denver, and
owner of ranch lands near
the White River Reservation
Washington, Feb. 5, 1880

William N. Byers sworn and examined:

By the CHAIRMAN:
We are investigating the late Ute outbreak, and have sent for you to give us such information as you may have on the subject. If you know anything which will throw any light upon it please state it.
The WITNESS:
Do you desire that my statement should go back any considerable length of time?
The CHAIRMAN:
If you are satisfied that it will have any bearing on the subject we are investigating. We do not want any evidence which may or may not show that the Utes should or should not be driven from Colorado. What we want is anything which will throw light on the cause of the Ute outbreak, and you can carry that back a year or two.
The WITNESS:
 I came to know the Northern or White River
 band of the Utes about four years ago;
 in those days they were camping outside Denver
 and its attractions—they even called themselves
 the "Denver Utes" sometimes—and riding off
 at intervals to hunt in Middle Park,
 where I was ranching, or out onto the plains
 for buffalo.—They are part civilized,
 part wild, and really neither; what they are
 really, one could not say…. More to the point
 was how they hated their head chief, Ouray;
 Ouray collaborated with the whites,
 they said, and was no true Ute, but had defrauded
 their band of treaty-money. They would kill him,
 or drive him off, they said; make their head chief
 one of their own White River Utes. (The Utes,
 as I suppose you know, are several bands
 each with its chief, loosely confederated
 under a head chief.) Still more serious,
 they bitterly objected to the whites

settling the country north of their White River
Reservation—they did not recognize
the treaty ceding Middle and North Parks,
made by Ouray, but not with their consent—
they said this was Ute country.—Q. That accounts,
then, for the fact that they have driven out,
or tried to, miners and others from that country.
—A. Yes, sir. I have been ordered out myself,
a number of times. But then we made an agreement—
houses already built they would allow
to stand, but no more houses might be built,
for that was Ute land, they were saving it
for Ute deer and Ute antelope, they said.
They protested bitterly the bringing in
of cows, and fencing land and plowing it.
Horses they don't object to. Cows, however,
mean permanent settlers.
    by Mr. DEERING:
They regard the cow as leading the advance of civilization?
—A. Yes, sir. Last summer a group of Indians
ordered some miners near my lands to leave
within two days; and then before their eyes
began to fire the grass and timber. Partly
from fear, partly because of the dense smoke,
the miners left—and left their tools behind.
Colorow, who is the most characteristic,
perhaps, of any man among the Utes
of the White River band, led in these warnings—
up the Blue River valley, on the Swan River,
at Georgia Gulch and Buffalo Flats, we heard
of his entering houses and, if he found a woman
alone, taking her by the hair and making
the scalping motion, then telling her that she,
and her people, must leave within "two sleeps."
Last summer, camping with a hunting party
on the Bear River, we met Colorow,

and Jack, with a small band of followers,
camped up the river. They often were among us,
begging and trading and hanging around the camp.
Numerous fires were burning all about us—
I recall three up in the high timber
and two in the foothills. I asked Colorow
why they had kindled all these fires. He said
it was "to make heap grass next spring, for ponies."
But most of these fires, I told him, were burning high
in the mountains, where no grass grows. And he was silent.
I said they must be trying to destroy
the value of the country for the white man—
no fires were set inside the Reservation—
which Colorow did not deny.
     by Mr. DEERING:
                       —You mean
they were particular to burn the timber
on the lands north and east, but not within
the Reservation?—A. Yes, sir.—Q. They distinguished
between the two?—A. Yes, sir; and with exactness.

*The Byers testimony has spiralled in to the point where he is describing a visit to
the White River Reservation with a sheriff's party in search of some stolen horses.
The time is twelve months before the massacre:*

     During our talk that afternoon I saw
     the first signs of the Ute dissatisfaction
     with Agent Meeker. When Mr. Meeker spoke—
     and he was mostly silent—the Utes were quick
     to manifest displeasure. At the end
     of the parley, when we once again demanded
     that they return the horses, Meeker said, "Yes,
     they must be given up," and Colorow
     sprang to his feet and said, "Meeker, you
     no talk; we no want you talk. Let Pius [Byers] talk,"
     and Indians all around the room grunted

their approval. I spent that night in Meeker's house,
and while we were eating supper a Ute came in
unasked, and said he wished to talk with me.
Later, when I came out, he would say nothing,
but sat there, sullen. Mr. Meeker asked me
into his private office, and we talked
till late that night about his situation.
He said his task was thankless, that the Utes
looked upon him at best as a provider,
chiefly as an intruder, and somehow both
at the same time.
—Q. … but had not previous agents been attempting
to educate them, and show them how to farm?
—A. Yes, sir. But I can explain to you the secret
of Mr. Meeker's failure. Mr. Meeker
went there with great enthusiasm to make
his agency succeed, and was a most
conscientious and enthusiastic
gentleman in his ideas of reform.
Now, from the beginning he confined himself
strictly within the letter of the law
and his instructions; something seldom done
by Indian Agents. Thus he was instructed
to issue the Utes' rations every Wednesday;
and if the Utes did not appear on Wednesday
they did not draw their rations. This was a strictness
previous agents never had observed.
Their habit was to issue a month's rations
at a time, and even then wink at the absence
of certain Indians, allowing someone else
to represent them. But not Mr. Meeker.
He undertook to hold them to the rules.
This was to check their hunting and their roaming
beyond the Reservation.—Q. Were not the Utes
in part dependent upon game?—A. Less so
than upon trading and begging from white settlers.

They chiefly cared for roaming about the country.
—Q. You ascribe Mr. Meeker's trouble, then,
to his strict application of the rules?
—A. I think that was the groundwork of his trouble.
—Q. Did they object to Mr. Meeker's plowing?
—A. Yes, sir. Most bitterly. They said they needed
that ground for grass, for ponies.—Q. Do you know
of any intrusions by miners or stock raisers
into their Reservation?—A. I do not.
—Q. This Middle Park, where you have your property,
adjoins the Reservation?—A. That is correct.
It is a part of the purchase made by treaty
in 1868.
      by Mr. WADDILL:
From the Sioux?—A. No, sir.
The purchase was from the Utes.—Q. I thought the Utes never owned
that.—A. They claimed it, and we bought it.
      by Mr. POUND:
What are these regions you designate as parks?
—A. They are depressions in the mountain range,
like prairies ringed with mountains. The word "park"
is the old Spanish designation, "parc."

~

Former Indian Bureau Commissioner
A.D. Fisk, on earlier Ute
grievances:

    … and if you will permit me, I will read
    from the report for 1877
    by Agent Danforth, Meeker's predecessor
    at the White River Agency. He says:

"An unusual number of Indians have been off the reservation during
the past year, and they remained away for some time. There are several

reasons for this. The annuities and supplies furnished these Indians amount to not over one-half that required for their support. None of their annuity goods and but part of their supplies have reached this agency during the year. Goods purchased in August of last year have been lying in the railroad depot, 175 miles away, since November last, a period of over nine months. Flour purchased the first of June is still at Rawlins. No clothing, blankets, tents, implements, or utensils of any kind have been issued for nearly two years; no flour, except once fifteen pounds to a family, since last May. Now the only way all but a few of the Indians here know how to provide for themselves is by hunting. By department regulation the sale of arms and ammunition on the reservation is prohibited. At the same time the Indians have only to go off the reservation to obtain all the arms and ammunition they desire, a number of trading posts being accessible and no white man refusing to furnish these articles to the Indians; pretty good evidence that the people do not stand in any great fear of the Indians. Many settlers have made it their principal business to trade with the Indians this past year, and have offered every inducement to them to leave the reservation."

    That report reached Washington in early autumn.
The failure to distribute the supplies
continued through the winter and the spring;
the Utes themselves then made the trek to Rawlins,
where the goods were held pending the settlement
of a freight bill dispute. I corresponded
with Mr. Meeker about it in the summer,
on his arrival at White River, and he was
importunate in his pleas that ways be found
to relieve these people. Which at last was done.
—Q. Do you know what the Ute complaints are now,
and how they justify this outbreak?—A. Only
as I have been told about them by Ouray.
—Q. Then we would like to hear Ouray's complaints.
—A. They start with the treaty of 1868,
which, the Utes soon found, gave up much more
of their land than they had ever meant to cede,

and with signatures not properly obtained;
they go on to the failures to pay up
the monies owed them from that treaty; then
encroachments by miners on the lands
left to them by that treaty; then the failure
to give them their supplies; then the order
forbidding them to purchase ammunition
or arms within their reservation; then
Ouray's opinion (which is much the same
as mine) concerning Mr. Meeker's fitness.
—Q. And what is your opinion?—A. Mr. Meeker,
whom I had known for a great many years,
was about as unfit as a man could be
to go into that country and take hold
of the White River Utes and manage them;
a man of too many years, and unhappily
constituted in his mental organization
and temperament, for such a place as that.
—Q. Was Agent Meeker a Colorado man?
—A. Yes, sir; he lived at Greeley, Colorado.
—Q. A man acquainted with the Indian character?
—A. He was not. He had for years resided
in New York City; he was a journalist,
a columnist for the *New York Tribune*
over the initials N.C.M. He went out
to Colorado to found the town of Greeley,
sponsored by Horace Greeley; and he did so,
and the town has prospered. He could do
good service in a place like that, but not
as an Indian agent. A gentleman of high
character and of great intelligence
of a certain sort—what you would call a real
good man—was Agent Meeker, but not acquainted
with the Indian character. It was a most
unfortunate nomination, in my view.
—Q. Do you know why the money granted the Utes

by treaty was withheld?—A. I have asked that
a great many times. I went to the President,
once, with the Secretary of the Interior,
and we discussed that; the only reason given
was fear that the Utes would spend the funds on arms.
—Q. You have said you were opposed to the instructions
given the 1878 Commission?
—A. Well, the plan was to have the Utes removed
to Indian Territory. I opposed that.
I did not think any Indians should go there,
but that each community should keep its own
Indians and take care of them. We drove them
to the Pacific, and they were on their way
back, pushed here and there; and by and by
no matter how many we put in the Territory
someone would want them out of there also,
white people would want that land, or the railroads,
and the Indians would be compelled once more
to find some other resting place. I thought
with all the valuable farming land
in Colorado, the Utes, who owned that land,
should be left there, and be protected there.

2

THE UTE OFFICIAL

Ouray
A broad-faced, deep-chested man.
He was contemplative,
the historian Sprague remarks,
as well as tough and cunning.
Had lived the daily life
of both Indian and white.
Knew that the hate and delusion
which each saw in the other
were mainly the contraptions

of habit special to each
which each mistook for the world.
He tried to align the contraptions;
tried till the day before
he died (eleven months
after the massacre)—
his body flooded with pain
from Bright's disease, his mind clear.

~

Washington, D.C., March 17, 1880

—Q. Were your Uncompahgre Utes
in either the battle or the massacre?
—A. No. Some people in that trouble claimed
to be Uncompahgre Utes, but they were really
White River Utes.—Q. State as well as you can
from the reports you have received, what people
from the White River did take part in the massacre.
—A. I know nothing in regard to who was there.
They hide it from me, saying I am a friend
of the whites....
—Q. What excuse is given by the White River Utes
for committing the massacre?—A. I think that Meeker
wanted to make some row in order to get them
out of the land. That is how it seems to me....
—Q. Do you know anything about the fires
it is said the Utes have started?—A. I could not find
that they had burned up any forests. Last year
was a very dry year. Where there had been a camp
and a little fire was left, in the morning a wind
might scatter it, and the whole country burn
in that way. Everything was dry and dead.
I do not think anyone was to blame—
miners, campers, or anyone else. It was easy
for everything to catch fire.

~

Chipeta, wife of Ouray, supplies some facts:
    An early photograph
    shows a level-eyed, smooth-skinned,
    smooth-featured beauty.
    The face is intelligent
    and quite expressionless.
    Newspaper feature writers
    surrounded her with glamour
    of the Indian princess sort,
    and after her husband died
    she left his farm and his house
    with its brass beds and lace curtains
    for a wickiup and some sheep.
    For years she lived alone.
    She died at eighty-one
    having long since gone blind,
    and was buried in a nearby gulch
    where, some months afterwards,
    a ranch hand hunting a stray
    found her bones exposed on the sand.
    No one knows what she thought.
    Perhaps her intelligence
    went into a resolve
    not to have thoughts at all.

~

—Q. How far were you from the Agency
when the massacre took place.—A. Not knowing
the exact time of the massacre
I cannot tell you where I was.
—Q. Tell us whatever you may know
of the cause of the massacre.—A. I know
nothing about it.—Q. Were you at home

when the Meeker women were brought in?
If so, who brought them there, and what
was their condition?—A. I was at home
when they came there. General Adams
brought them. They seemed to be all right,
but did not talk with me.—Q. What reasons
did the Indians give for this massacre?
—A. I do not know what reasons they gave.
—Q. Do they say that Mr. Meeker was
a bad man?—A. I heard some of them
say that.—Q. In what way was he bad?
—A. They say he was always writing bad
of them, to Washington.—Q. Is that
why they killed him?—A. I do not know
why they did it. I know nothing
but what I have heard among the women.
—Q. Tell us all you have heard from them.
—A. I have already stated all I heard.

~

A Ute, unidentified,
speaking in the nineteen-twenties
to an anthropologist
about the old days:

Then the people moved camp
to a new site. Those camps
and that life are gone now.
Everything moves on
and is lost. That is why
the Utes say 'It is bad luck
to plan ahead.' For nothing
can stop, nothing is left
of those days but my story
and your words. Nothing
remains behind.

~

From the post-testimony
murk and untidy silence
I see the shade of Meeker
emerging. When he sees me
he begins talking at once—
'The lyric declaration
of that Ute makes a clear place
in this air. Not that his words
do not come out of feelings
anyone may sink into
(for instance, Heraclitus)
upon occasion; even
a government official,
perhaps.' Now he watches me
for a reaction. I say,
falling in with what appears
to be his contentious mood,
'Officials don't sound like that.'
And he, 'Not as officials,
true. But then do not take it
as expressing the Ute view
of the nature of things,
either.' I say, 'Well, a Ute
said it, it rang true to me.'
And he: 'Contradictory
proverbs can be discovered
among the Utes as quickly
as among the rest of us—'
—'Contradictory, of course,
but never incongruous.'
Meeker is continuing
without regard for my nice
distinction.—'At least the Utes
were no more resigned to change

than the rest of us have been
when it drove against the flesh
of their lives its strange hard shapes.'
—'There are contemporaries
of mine, and some of yours, too,
who would be quick to declare
that what you choose to call change
the Utes felt as destruction.
One of our philosophers—
I mean one who came along
a little after your time—
remarked, *The Latin language
did not progress when it passed
into Italian. It died.'*
Meeker: 'And the transition
I tried to bring the Utes through
was like that. No, it won't do.'
He speaks with unexpected
mildness. 'Grant that these people
are right, and the destruction
of the Ute life at my hands
was coming—its destruction
at the hands of other men,
with a far worse aftermath,
was the alternative; and
the alternative happened.'
He adds, in a quiet voice,
'Surely it is obvious
that a choice of agonies
was what the Utes had. I think
to some of them the choice was
too obvious to be borne.
But this smacks of the tedium
of argument. It bores me
to defend myself.' Gazing
into the murk, he goes on,

'I know what an argument
is worth, even a sound one.'
And after a little pause,
'It can seem a natural force,
set moving by conditions
of which it is no portion,
like the trunk of a big tree
shooting along in a flood.
It can lead a man to suppose
the truth will make—break him free.
But I had a life, and death,
that left me musing upon
events much longer than words,
though I took words for my trade
and was a happy tradesman....'
I remark, 'You mean events
are ultimate,' and Meeker
contemplates me with an air
of friendly speculation,
as if figuring a risk
(of embarrassing us both?)
if he should speak out freely
what has flamed up in his mind.
'Not even those where I am
see more of the ultimate
than that it's our source, and not
our aim; the truth's a blazing
mystery, from faith in which, men
move not toward an empyrean
but into their lives, and death.
It's not something we see, being
the radiance we see by....'
He hesitates, and then says,
'And seeing is believing ...'
and pauses again. I say,
'And all this murk?' Meeker laughs.

I say, 'The testimony
leaves questions hanging—' and he,
'Hanging over the usual
conflicts of too-familiar
attitudes.' 'No doubt,' I say,
'It seems I have heard it all
before, and in my own day.
It seems we make no progress
in opinion on all this.'
—'Doubtless there's but slow progress
(if it's not just the changes
that happen, but slow progress)
in the situation; then
opinion's even slower;
it likes impassioned stalemates.
There are people whose lives are
opinion.'—'The opinions
I hate habitually
are no more wearisome than
my own counter-opinions,'
I say. And he: 'This is not
the world of ideas, nor
of action. Hence the tedium.
In the world of opinion
where the public life goes on
and all's partial and shifting,
events and ideas lose
their clearness and their quickness,
nothing happens cleanly, and
that is just as well, doubtless,
considering all interests—
and yet, and yet. I picture
the movement of a dull mass
of near-deadlocked opinions
like a mud-slide on a town,
a population dying

by suffocation in mud,
only more slowly—a set
of contending motives, each
being all too obvious,
as those hearings just disclosed,
is uninteresting and is
important. It kills people.'
—'It kills people. And therefore
that testimony raises
questions. Byers—' And again
Meeker laughs. 'Ah. Byers—'
It is clear that for Meeker
this is a touchy subject.
'A man with the energy
of a nightmare, and the same
relentless, skew momentum
in the way he carried out
his designs—with which he was
so entirely occupied
he scarcely noticed others
except as they obstructed
his movement—when they became
merely inconveniences,
calling not for resentment
or malice, but a further
burst of effort. Hence, the Utes
were to Byers very much like
a tree downed across his road
by a windstorm. Which gave him
a wonderful clarity
in testifying; things appeared
sharp, unclouded to him,
you know; his conscience was clear,
since it was unoccupied.'
I say, 'Calling Colorow
the most characteristic

of the Utes clarified them
sharply for the committee
when he went on to describe
some of Colorow's antics
in settlers' kitchens.' Meeker:
'I wonder if Byers knew
that Colorow was in fact
a Comanche ... which did not
keep Colorow from charging
repeatedly that Ouray
was no true Ute; well, in fact,
Ouray was half-Apache,
half-Ute. And reared by Spaniards,
as a Roman Catholic....
You recall what Byers said
in a rare reflective mood:
what the Ute character was
(part wild, part civilized,
and really neither) was hard
to make out—a composite.
Like almost everything. Like
the causes of all those fires.
Sunlight came copper-colored
through the smoke, and I well knew
Utes never hesitated
to fire a forest, to drive
the game out—it was their harvest
method, so to speak—to them
timber was no more useful
than the boulders in a creek
they came to drink from.' He smiles,
'I'm growing circumstantial.'
A meditative silence
comes over him and I say,
'I saw, in the museum
at Meeker, under the glass

of a showcase, a letter
by Woodbury, your blacksmith.
He wrote it on the way home
to Greeley on vacation,
wrote it, perhaps, even as
(quite unknown to him, of course)
the massacre was happening,
some forty miles behind him.
I copied this, making out
the faded, firm words behind
the glare and the reflections:'

At Hayden I fell in with the mail carrier and accompanied him as far as
Hot Sulphur Springs. This country was full of smoke from the fires which
were burning in all directions; following the trail along the Bear River, a
few hundred feet above the river, the smoke was so dense that one could
barely see the water running below. The fires had been set by both the
Indians and the whites. I was told of several large fires being set by the
whites and lain to the Utes.

'His letter had been published
in the Greeley press, one day
before the massacre news
arrived; and was forgotten,
therefore it was not cited
at the hearings.' Meeker says,
'The letter out on display,
hard to read under the glass,
inconspicuous among
dozens of other items
indifferent enough, makes
a nice image of the truth.'
And then a bit wistfully,
'Riding along the river
going home after a year
with us, for a vacation,

and using his eyes and ears,
Woodbury has unawares
the matter-of-fact goodness
people can have when the fates
draw back from them a little.
Goodness may make us happy.
But happiness makes us good
more often, I think.'* I say,
'But then, our topic was facts
just now, because there remain
questions about that testimony—'
Meeker waits.—'For example,
I have wondered why Ouray
says what he does about you.
For he was an honest man,
and took the hard way—so Sprague
the historian argues—
of dealing as best he could
with the whites, instead of dying
in martyrdom's quick splendor
leading a hopeless battle,
leaving those who survived him
to be taken off to die
in Indian Territory
of homesickness and disease.
Why does he lie about you?'
—'Whether it's lie or error,'
Meeker says, 'at his distance
from the events he simply
transferred the government plan
for getting rid of the Utes
to the government's agent,
me. As usual, justice

*cf. Simonides: *καπι πλειοτου χριοτοι τους βεοι φιλωσιω.*

was even-handed, though, when
the guilt of those who killed us
immediately was spread
to cover all the Utes.
I will tell you a story.
Johnny Tab-biscuit, a Ute,
was shot on a mountain trail
by a white he'd quarreled with.
Now, Johnny Tab-biscuit's friends
that same day shot a rancher
they happened to come upon
chopping wood in his door-yard.
They'd never seen him before.
After the uproar died down
Byers one day questioned these friends,
privately, and they told him,
"One Ute killed, one white man killed,
all right, pretty good." Byers
told me, "I tried to show them
the injustice of their view.
They never would admit it.
When I'd gone over the ground
a dozen times, they persisted
in thinking their custom just."
Byers never raised objection,
I think, to the white custom
according to which the Utes
were expelled from their country.'
—'What about Fisk's policy,
that each white community
ought to take care of its own
Indians?' He hesitates,
and grins, 'If I answer that
I shall soon be defending
myself. And yet the answer
is ordinary enough:

Fisk assumes an ownership
in the phrase "its own" that Utes
would find hard to understand.
This is a benevolence
as crude as the malignant
designs of Hayt and Pitkin.
Both outlooks are unworldly.
When an unworldly outlook
is acted on, as Pitkin's,
alas, was, then the world gets
a rare clear-cut disaster.'
—'Fisk on your temperamental
shortcomings—' And Meeker smiles,
'Dr. Johnson says, *Perhaps,*
if we speak with rigorous
exactness, no human mind
is in its right state. Perhaps
if Fisk had explained to us
what "the Indian character"
is, and what temperament
is fitted to deal with it …
—Truth to say, the Utes and I
were rather too much alike
than the contrary; that is,
neither they nor I were—patient.'
I say, 'That philosopher
I've been reading said, *It takes*
patience to appreciate
domestic bliss: volatile
spirits prefer unhappiness.'
He says, 'Volatile spirits
will have a reply ready.
Still, I plead almost guilty.
I sometimes wonder whether
my going to White River
was one headlong wrong impulse,

or individual missteps
leading off—rather: I was
like a rider that has lost
a stirrup, his own movements
disintegrating, invaded
and replaced by the surges
and the joltings of his mount.'
And adds, with resignation,
'No matter how I appeared
to others in that bad time,
and no matter what I said
or did, that's what it felt like.'

3

WHAT HAPPENED: NATHAN MEEKER'S WORDS AS

RECOVERED FROM THE RECORDS

Meeker: 'The world of events
entangled in opinion
is what we're going to see.'
I say, 'One historian
says history is lived forwards
but written in retrospect,
so we know the end before
we consider the beginning,
and never can recapture,
wholly, what it was to know
the beginning only.'* He:
'And neither could I do so.
It's a man the story changed
who's left to tell his story;
then, telling a story is,
itself, another story,

*The historian is C.V. Wedgewood (as quoted by Dean Acheson in *Present at the
Creation*).

but of the present, and here,
always the thing we know is
the beginning—where we live.'
I say, 'It's complicated.'
He: 'It wouldn't be, were you
shot clear of events, to hang
in clear speculative fire,
so to speak. Clear and forceless.'

~

How it was, driving back to the Agency with a high-piled load
of supplies, and the Utes coming to meet him far up the road:

Ever so many handshakes, ever so many
jokes and laughs went around. And then we travelled
over Yellowjacket Pass and down Coal Creek
and, just as the sun went down,
entered the gate of the Agency enclosure.

He sends a double request to Washington: rescind
the rule forbidding the sale of weapons to the Utes,
and halt the illicit trading for them by permitting
the sale of weapons on the Reservation itself:

For not to allow them to purchase arms at all
is to prevent the Indians from pursuing
the one activity they now engage in
which yields them some few of their necessities.

Which request brings this reply from the Commissioner:

It is not our aim to encourage the Indians
to engage in these hunting expeditions ...

He reports to Commissioner Hayt on progress so far:

…Twenty acres of land are partly cleared.
Some thirty Indians have been at work,
but the average of steady workers is nearer twelve.
These are induced to work by their chief, Douglas,
and are as subject to him as they would be
if they were slaves. The remedy for this
is to provide each Indian with the land
wherewith to have his own home, and get clear
of the chief's domination; then this species
of feudalism will be broken up.

He portrays Johnson, one of the sub-chiefs, at harvest time:

When Johnson dug potatoes, he retained
fifteen or twenty women to do the work,
paying them half a bushel a day. He watched,
and helped to sack; and smoked, and now and then
got tired and slept, face down, upon the ground;
and then was up and busy again.
                              He wore
a bottle-green flannel shirt, and buckskin leggings,
and a blanket strapped around his waist, to form
a sort of kilt. His plug hat hung on the fence,
for he had work to do. His face was painted—
a streak of crimson blazed on his forehead, a band
of yellow starting at his left eyebrow
slanted across his eye and over his nose
to the right corner of his mouth. Each cheek
Johnson had marked with three short brilliant strips
of red, yellow, and blue.
                        Johnson, you see,
is one of those men who lead from the savage life
to the barbaric, on the way
to civilization. He is not as far advanced
as Cedric, the Saxon, master of Garth,
in Scott's Ivanhoe, but he is probably

equal to the best among the British chiefs
who tried to withstand the invasion of Julius Caesar.

He writes a long letter to Washington, after
ten months on the job, taking a deep breath,
so to speak, in mid-December, for the next year's effort,
and incidentally countering the threat
of the Army's taking over Indian affairs:

The Ute idea of the Agency
was simple: it was the place to get supplies.
No crops had ever been grown here, and only
shirt-tail sized gardens, watered out of pails.
Their understanding of what it is to farm
was vague, and they wished to leave it so.
Further, they were, and are, split into factions—
Douglas the chief's, and Jack's, who wants his place.
To ask that they agree on a policy
is as absurd as to ask that Democrats
and Republicans shall in like manner agree,
for government is run, when it runs at all,
by the party in power, and cannot be blocked
by the party out of power. Douglas proposed
that they should work, Jack and his party opposed,
and Douglas drew off. At last my threats (to write
to the Commissioner) brought Jack around.
Twenty-five Indians worked early and late
fully a month, till freezing weather came.
The ditch will water about 1,000 acres,
as so far finished; all we shall want next year.
The result is, many Indians want to farm.
I am embarrassed by their needs—they want
wagons and plows, and harness, and corrals,
and seed of all kinds; and there is no question
that they will work, and gladly, for they believe
they will have something and be better off.

True, these workers are of the party in power,
and take pride in this, especially in being
on the side of the government: but I have no doubt
but the other side will, in a year or so, come over.
And then some other subject will be found
to quarrel about.
               Naturally I think
of the result should the Army rule come in.
The West Point man knows mathematics, some
history, and many novels. He is a judge
of wine, perhaps, but he has no knowledge
of how much seed is sown to an acre, nor when
it is sown—or reaped: nor what a day's work is
in a field; he knows nothing of hot-beds,
nor of small-fruit culture; has not the remotest notion
of township organization, by which schools
and roads and fences are established, knows
nothing of the primary wants of families
as they advance from one state to the next.
Another thing: the Indians fear soldiers
more than can be told. Soldiers in charge
would halt all progress in farming and schooling
even among these peaceable Utes. I speak
from experience, and labor, and success
with the White River Indians, when I say
it would be a cruel and an unwise thing
to place soldiers in charge here, and break up
what seems so happily begun.

Early summer: he thinks of work and education:

… It seems to me that work
goes before education. Only a worker
can gain an idea of the use of schooling.
A savage can have no notion of the value
of knowing many things. The savage family

lacks discipline and its young are neither heirs
nor its successors. I can get the men
to work day after day on penalty
of withholding extra rations. This in fact
is a kind of "compulsory education." So
with plenty of coffee, sugar, and dried peaches—
and time, some time—why, I can lead them forward
to civilization.

Springtime: he recounts a talk with Jane, who as an orphan,
in the Uintah band, was made a slave in the lodge of the chief;
he sold her to one Judge Carter, whom she served as a maid
till he released her, on her wish to marry. Now
she is Arvilla's helper in and about the house:

N.M.—Jane, you will be planting your garden soon,
but last summer's style of gardening is played out.
Jane—Played out? How so?
N.M.—Well, after things are planted
it will not do for you to canter off
and leave the weeding and watering up to me.
You, or some of your family, must stay
three moons and work your crops. No one else will.
Jane—Three moons? What for? One hoeing is enough.
N.M.—No, you must hoe them three times, perhaps four,
and keep watch of them.
Jane—But we never done so before, and we had heaps.
N.M.—Anything you have this year, you must work for.
Jane—Why can't white men do the work
as before? They understand it. We don't.
N.M.—I worked your garden last year, carrying
hundreds of pails of water; but the new ditch
brings plenty of water now, and you yourselves
can raise your garden.
Jane—But Mr. Meeker, ain't you paid to work?
N.M.—Not to work for you.

Jane—Well, what are you paid money for,
if not to work for us?
N.M.—Ah, I shall put it this way;
I am being paid to show you how to work.
Jane—But the Utes have heaps of money, from the treaty.
What is the money for if it is not to have work done for us?
N.M.—It is to hire me,
and the rest of us here, to show you how to farm
and get an income, like white folks, by work.
Jane—Ain't all these cattle ours and all this land?
N.M.—The cattle, yes. Now listen to me, Jane:
the land will stay yours only if you use it.
To hold it you must work it like white men
or white men will come in and by and by
you will have nothing. Do you understand?
Jane—Yes. But Mr. Meeker, I can't tell you
how bad you make me feel.

July: he reflects on Ute ownership of horses:

All winter they had grazed over this valley
and when the snow began to disappear
they covered all the sunny slopes and gulches,
then the whole range within a half-day's ride
except where they had eaten it out. The fact is
a conflict exists between the horses and cattle
for the best part of the range; as in such conflicts
in all pastoral countries from the days
of Lot and Abraham, one or the other
has to give way.
          The greatest obstacle
to civilizing the Utes, I have concluded, is
their horses. For the only Utes who work
are those who have few horses or none. A Ute
with a band of horses gives them all his time.
A Ute is wealthy, and has standing, precisely

as he owns horses, and the only use
to which he puts them—that is, aside from riding—
is to run races. Horseracing, and gambling on it,
are the main pursuits for nine months in the year,
and the Ute who has no horse to run is nobody.
Last January a Ute named Johnson, friendly
to the agent, and wanting to be civilized,
requested us to break a pair of horses—
wanted a wagon, wanted more land, must have
a team to work with. So the men spent some time
breaking the horses, and he learning to drive;
and of course we kept the horses on hay and grain,
to put them in condition for the work.
Then I discovered Johnson had been racing
these horses in the afternoons, and clearly
his object had been to get them in good heart
so as to beat his brethren of the turf.

Mid-way through a summer that's turned all dust and sun-blaze:

    To the Commandant of Ft. Steele:
Numbers of Utes have left the reservation
for the valleys of the Snake and the Bear Rivers;
now recent gold discoveries have brought in
a great many miners to an area
(the best hunting grounds in America)
the Indians wish to occupy. Though I have asked for soldiers
to clear those valleys of the Utes, no action
has been taken, nor have my requests received
the courtesy of a reply. In many parts
of the Bear River valley, clear to its head
in Egeria Park, they have burnt the country over;
they are slaughtering game only to get the skins.
I would hereby request you to arrest
all White River Utes bound north, and either hold them
or send them back to the Reservation. They
deserve a lesson.

       N.M.—I am going home. Home to my house
in Greeley.
            I have a letter here
which complains of Indians setting fire to timber—
I have had others like it. Now something worse
has happened.
             I came out here to help your people
to teach them a good life; save them from trouble.
But it seems no use. This letter says two Utes
have burned down a white man's home on the Bear River.
Jack—Where dey burn dis house?
N.M.—On the Bear River.
Jack—We ride up dere tomorrow. You and me.
Better go see dese houses. You see dem?
N.M.—I am an Indian Agent, not a sheriff.
Jack—Somebody paper say Indian bad men.
You Indian Agent, you go see, maybe bad,
maybe not. Maybe paper lie. You see.
N.M.—I am going home. Let the government handle it.

~

Remarks by Mr. R.D. Coxe, posse-man,
on arriving at the Agency
August 22, 1879, in search
of the two Utes accused
of arson on Bear River:
(the massacre is now 5 weeks away)

Facing the Agency buildings, under fence,
was a fifty-acre field, with garden truck
and corn; around were signs of the practical farmer,
and under the sheds of the Agency, the latest
in agricultural implements. Thought I,

Here is the model; another generation
will find our dusky neighbors tilling fields,
and the blessing will rest on the head of N.C. Meeker.
But a herd of horses skirted the fenced field,
and it seemed to me they looked with a jealous eye
upon the growing crops.
All the Indians we met had a red smear
over their faces. They were very quiet.
I asked one buck if anyone were dead,
but he did not reply.
Mr. Meeker said he would do whatever he could
to bring the two Utes to account. Chief Douglas said
these Utes were not on the Reservation, hence
he could not give them up. Mr. Meeker said
they could not be far away, and Douglas said
he did not know about that. Mr. Meeker told him
it was his duty to send Utes with the Sheriff
to identify the culprits. Douglas was silent,
and with a reed he had, drew lines in the dirt.
Finally he looked up, and a thunder-cloud
was on his brow. He said decidedly
and emphatically that he would not do it. This
ended the council.
At nightfall of the day we left, we saw
a large fire start ten miles from the Agency,
we constantly saw the smoke of fires, one fire
was sweeping the forests on Gore Range, the air
was blue with smoke, and upon every hand
we heard complaints of fires set by the Utes.

~

September 8: Meeker, to the Commissioner:

When we commenced to plow last week, three Utes
objected, having put up tents and corrals
on ground I had told them would be plowed. Although
I offered Agency men to help them move,
they refused. This land is good, and being close
to the Agency, their horses are protected.
In short, they simply need the ground for their horses.
It was clear that, if I moved the Agency
a mile downstream, the Indians would claim
squatter's rights there as well, and I told them so;
to which they replied I had enough land plowed,
and the rest was for their horses.
                              If they could drive me
from one place, they could drive me from another,
and so I ordered the plows to run as planned.
Two Indians came out with guns, and ordered
the plowman off. This was reported to me,
and I directed the plowing to proceed.
When the plowman had made one round, he was fired on
from a clump of sagebrush, and the ball passed close
to his person. Of course I ordered the plowing stopped.
Douglas, the chief, would only repeat the demand
that the plowing stop. I sent for Jack, his rival,
who has the larger following. After much talk
the two men said we might go on and plow.
But either this was not understood, or not
assented to by the claimants, for the next day
when the plowing started they came out with guns.
I sent for Jack again, and another council,
that lasted hours in the heat and smoke, was held,
and finally it was agreed that I might do
what I had originally proposed to do.
Plowing will proceed, but whether unmolested
I cannot say. There were no more than three

of the Utes engaged in this outbreak. In fact,
it is one family and its relatives.

~

Telegram to the Bureau of Indian Affairs:
SEPTEMBER 10, 1879

I HAVE BEEN ASSAULTED BY A LEADING CHIEF,
JOHNSON, FORCED FROM MY HOUSE AND INJURED
BADLY, BUT RESCUED BY EMPLOYEES. IT WAS
JOHNSON WHO STARTED THE TROUBLE REPORTED
SEPT. 8. HIS SON SHOT AT THE PLOWMAN.
OPPOSITION TO PLOWING IS NOW WIDE. LIFE OF
SELF, FAMILY, AND EMPLOYEES NO LONGER SAFE.
PROTECTION NEEDED AT ONCE.

N.C. MEEKER

He writes on the same day in a letter to William Byers:
I think they will submit to nothing but force.
How many are rebellious I don't know,
but if only a few are, and the others laugh
at their outrages, as they do, then the whole lot
is implicated. I did not come here
to be kicked and hustled out of my own house
by a pack of savages.

~

—Not that I myself cannot
sympathize with your rage. Still ...
My contemporaries will be
wide-eyed with disapproval.
I can't think how I'd defend
language like that to them. *He:*
Language like—yes, you mean that
'pack of savages.' Well, I

am hardly contemplating,
now, with pleasure the fury
in which my mind went up, all
timbers crashing and flames, smoke....

~

Message to Major Thornburgh, September 27:

    Sir:
        Understanding that you are on your way
with troops, I send a messenger, Mr. Eskridge,
and two Utes, Henry Jim, interpreter,
and John, to inform you that the Indians
are greatly excited, and wish you to halt your men,
at a convenient camping place, and thence
come with five soldiers to the Agency,
that a council may be held. This I agreed to;
it seems for the best, though I do not presume
to order your movements, of course. The Utes regard
your troops' approach as a declaration of war.
In this I am laboring to undeceive them,
at the same time attempting to convince them
they cannot do whatever they please. Just now
the prime objective is to allay their fears.
                     Respectfully,
                     N.C. Meeker

~

Sept. 28, the night before
the massacre. Frank Dresser,
young Agency employee,
writes in a letter home:

It is now half past ten, and I must close.
I have to stand guard. Meeker is afraid
the Utes will fire the hay. As regards danger,
don't fret. We are as safe, and sleep as sound,
as if in your quiet town of Greeley. Tomorrow
the soldiers will come, and the plowing will go on,
for Meeker must carry out orders or resign.

~

Meeker, the next day, leaving his office with the key
to lock the gunroom—his daughter remembered this—
asks if she knows this day is an anniversary.
She doesn't, though since her father has been reading Pepys
in the new Bright edition he takes such pleasure in,
she supposes the answer relates to that. Then Meeker says—

Why, on this day in the year ten sixty-six
William the Conqueror invaded England.

He returns from having locked the gun room and writes a letter.
There are about two hours of life remaining to him.

White River Agency
Sept. 29, 1879—1:00 P.M.

Major T.T. Thornburgh
White River Expedition, in the Field
Dear Sir:

I shall leave with Douglas in the morning to meet you. Things are peaceful. We have been on guard not because there is danger but because there might be. I like your last programme. It is based on true military principles.

Most truly yours,
N.C. Meeker, Indian Agent

~

Meeker, with a minimum
smile, 'What a lot of reasons
I had at that time … It's clear
when God said Let there be light
and there was light, he set up
a dangerous model for us.
Then I've asked myself, if all
had gone well at White River,
would all have gone well for me,
when I felt myself prolonged
into the prose of running,
day by day, that Agency?
Succeeding, I'd have ended
like a mountain stream in sand
one day vanishing somewhere
out in an empty sage flat.'

4

WHAT HAPPENED THEN: GENERAL ADAMS, THE EMISSARY WHO
LATER EFFECTED THE RELEASE OF THE CAPTIVES

Q.—Then Major Thornburgh, moving his troops forward
to the Reservation border, sends a party
to find a camping place; they meet some Utes
who he supposes may be hostile. So,
he deploys his line, the Utes deploy their line,
and the question of which side fired the opening shot
has never been answered?
         A.—No, sir. The inquiry
was expert and painstaking, for General Hatch
is a man of some experience in such matters.
It could not be determined who fired first.
Q.—And after this the Indians killed the Agent
and others, and took these captives?

A.—A Ute runner
went back to the Agency with news of the fight
and the Utes there attacked the Agency people.

5

HOW THE REPORT WENT IN THE PRESS

The Denver Daily News, Oct. 13, 1879

A SCENE OF SLAUGHTER

ARRIVAL OF TROOPS AT
WHITE RIVER AGENCY
The Horrible Scene that Met
the Gaze of Merritt's
Command
*Discovering the Bodies of Agent
Meeker and His Men*

Rawlins, Oct. 13 (Special to the *News*)—I have just interviewed Mr.
Webber, a courier who has just arrived from the White River Agency.
General Merritt

REACHED THE AGENCY

on the 11th inst., when a scene of horror and desolation met
his view.

All the Agency buildings except one unfinished house were
burned to the ground.

The remains of Agent Meeker and all his employees were
found and buried.

A chain was found around

AGENT MEEKER'S NECK

his head smashed, a piece of barrel stave sticking in his
mouth and his hand badly burned.

The women & children, families of the agent and employees,
have all either been murdered and put out of sight, or else
have been taken away as prisoners.

Eaton and Frank Wells, two of the employees, were found

BURNED TO A CRISP

Sheppard was found naked, with a lot of paper sacks in his
arms, his face eaten more or less by wolves, body partially
burned, and
                  A BULLET HOLE
in his left breast.
    Mr. W.H. Post
            AGENT MEEKER'S SECRETARY
was found one hundred yards from the Agency house, toward
the river. He was shot through the left ear and one shot below
the ear. He was also stripped naked.
    Frank Dresser's body was found twelve miles this side of
the Agency, in a coal mine. He had evidently crawled
in there after being wounded,
                AND THERE DIED
Dresser had been sent from the Agency to the command with a
dispatch. The letter found on his person was from Meeker to Thornburgh,
asking Thornburgh if he had had any trouble coming through the
canyon, and stating there was no sign of trouble at the Agency.

                        6

        Governor Pitkin Makes a Statement to the Press
                (Meeker—'But it's less the speech
                        of an individual
                    than a sort of muscle twitch
                    in the body politic....'):

        I have thought for weeks there was a likelihood
        of the Utes making trouble at White River,
        and have so informed General Pope in letters;
        now, I think this affair will bring an end,
        at last, to depredations in this state.
        It will be impossible for Indians
        and whites to live in peace, after this outrage.
        The whites now understand they can be attacked
        in any part of the state where Indians

are in sufficient force.
                        My idea is
that unless removed by the federal government
the Indians must be exterminated.
This State is willing to settle the Indian trouble
at its own expense—the advantages accruing
from opening twelve million acres of land
to miners and settlers, would more than compensate
for the expenses of the operation.

                         7

Statement to the Press by the Famous Indian Fighter
        General Pemberton, Conqueror of the Modocs,
          the Jicarilla Apaches, the Arapahos, the
            Chiracahua Apaches, the Bannocks …
             (of whom it is written in the D.A.B.,
              'He thoroughly understood the Indian
                character. Realizing their hopeless
                struggle to hold their lands against
              white encroachment, he was more prone
                   to pardon than to punish.'):

              Most of the Indian troubles
              are caused by Indian Agents—
              mismanagement of supplies
              or the like—or broken faith
              on the part of the Government.
              Indians should be placed,
              now, under the control
              of the War Department.—*What
              would be its policy
              toward their disposal?* Why,
              train them to support
              themselves; there is no reason
              why they should not. They are willing
              to do so, all they want

is proper facilities,
and proper instruction.
Of course, you have got to use
a little force. I have spent
twenty-six years among
the Indians; have lived among
tribes whose language I spoke,
and know them intimately,
in their private relationships.
When we give these Indians
small farms, survey and fence them,
and let them have their own
horses and cows and sheep,
we will have done away
with the Indian tribal bonds
of which so much is made;
once a man sees that his food
is secure, he does not care
what his chief may tell him.
Nor should we go to looking
after the spiritual good
of the Indians, before
securing their physical.
Of course, that is a thing
to come after a while.

~

Meeker is grinning. I ask,
'Is he stupid?'—'Oh, I think
for all his experience,
it's his inexperience,
which is hard to be aware of
for a man of action. Then,
I suppose the General,
who speaks from too far away,
could be expected no more

than I, who was much too close,
to notice that for the Utes
to have submitted to such
reforming regulations,
they would first have had to be
reformed. No, he's not stupid.'

8

THE MAN WHO WENT THERE: GENERAL ADAMS REPORTS

General—one of many
in the Colorado militia—
Adams, but christened Schwanbeck,
Karl Schwanbeck, in Anklam,
Pomerania; student in classics
in '48; rioted
against the King; fled
for his life, to this country;
soldier; scout; agent
to the White River Utes
some ten years earlier;
friend of Ouray; later
U.S. Minister
to Bolivia; Inspector
for the U.S. Postal Service;
commander of a unit
of deputies at Cripple Creek
against striking miners;
dead at fifty from the explosion
of a hotel steam boiler;
a self-possessed man, his career
as much a miscellaneous
composite as Colorow's,
Nathan Meeker's, or Ouray's....

~

Without the least personal emphasis
Adams is speaking of his ten days' mission:
once he had ridden, by daylight and by moonlight,
up little-used mountain trails to reach the Utes,
he found them ready to shoot him, as likewise
the soldiers when he met them, each side being eager
to think he was betraying it to the other;
he parleyed coolly, successfully, with both.

… I concluded, then, the matter could be settled
by the surrender of those Indians
actually guilty; for the tribe was anxious
to make peace, even the women and children
gathering around me crying and begging me
to keep the soldiers away. When I met the soldiers
I found that they had set out from Fort Russell
in a great hurry, and very ill-provided,
with only the clothes they were wearing and one
blanket apiece, and hardly in a fit condition
to follow the Utes: their animals were weak
from lack of feed, and the whole country barren,
just dotted with sagebrush, in between the point
that they had reached on the White River, and
the Ute forces a hundred miles away.
I had an Indian pony and he nearly
broke down from want of forage when I rode
back to the Indians' camp across that country.

~

What the Utes told General Adams
at the end of their parley with him:

They said: "We don't want
to have anything more to do
with the government. All we want

is that the soldiers shall not pursue us
in our own country. We can live on game
as we have lived before. We do not desire to have
anything to do with the government, but we give these women
to you, and if you can do anything for us afterwards, all right."

9

SONG FOR THE CAPTIVE WOMEN

They are of those
who are without "power"
who live among events

necessarily,
to whom the events are as real
as they are themselves

they are of those
who have times of being perfectly clear-eyed
over the years, watching the willful—

one may as well observe,
here one is (no prompting
to self-importances or big ideas)

they are of those
on whom events can leave
a clear imprint

fine white sand lapped by ripples
at a stream's edge where a coyote
came and drank, here are impressions

of the five pads, grainy-surfaced, petal-shaped, on each paw,
of each smooth blunt toenail, one of them split at the tip,
and see, of the sparse, thick hairs growing between the pads.

10

WHAT HAPPENED

Testimony of the Women at the Hearings

Arvilla's words
'She is entirely passive,'
Meeker once complained;
he never became aware
of her matter-of-course respect
for how things happen thus *and not otherwise.*

one

Douglas came in at dinner time
(just after we had finished up)
with several others, and we gave them
some victuals, thinking nothing of it.
We always have a kitchen-full
of Indians, more or less, and squaws,
and children underfoot at meals.
Mrs. Price and I were looking out
at the window, when we saw a Ute
coming on the dead run. She said,
    "Just see that Indian run.
    It must be he has news."

two

We were running and had reached the sagebrush
when the ball struck me, and I dropped
so as to be less of a mark;
I then saw that my wound was slight.
As I lay there I saw them capture
Josie and Mrs. Price, and then
they saw me; the one who came for me
thought I was hurt as I lay there.

As he came up he said, "I am heap sorry,
I am heap much sorry." He was a young,
smart, good-looking Indian.
He said, "Can you get up?" I said,
"Yes." He said, "Will you go with me?"
And I said, "Yes, sir," and he gave me
his arm, as nice as anybody,
        and took me off to see Douglas.

three

When Douglas said I must go back
and get my medicine book, the house
was burning, and this Ute with me,
not liking to go in, kept saying,
"Hurry up, hurry up, got to go
a long ways tonight." I found
the Pilgrim's Progress; the medical book
I gave to the Indian, and I guess
he left it there. He found and lifted
the medicine chest, and said, "No carry."
I got my shawl, blankets, and hat,
and thought of other things to take,
        but knew it would not do.

four

When we were going back, I saw
Mr. Meeker lying stretched on the ground.
He had been shot in the forehead.
Blood was running from his mouth.
His head was leaning back, his hands
were at his sides, the fingers straight;
and he was lying very straight.
        I was a little ways from him
the moment I saw a dead man there

and went a little nearer, thinking
it might be Mr. Meeker; I went
right up to his head. The Indian
was in front of me, and as I stooped
to kiss Mr. Meeker's face, the Indian
turned around and looked at me. I thought
it would not do, and started on.
I didn't say a word to him;
        nor did he speak to me.

            five

Douglas would ask me where the Agent
was now, and laugh. He said, "Agent
no understand about the fight
Indians make." He and the others
had bottles of whiskey, which they held up
between their eyes and the moon, to see
how much was left before they drank.
Douglas as he rode along
sang what seemed to be an obscene
song to a pretty melody
in slow measure. When he finished
he asked me how I liked it. My limb
ached terribly, and Douglas held it
awhile, then made a sling for it.
A villainous looking Indian
rode up and slapped me on the shoulder
and asked if I would like to be
his squaw. Douglas listened and laughed—
this Indian was an Arapaho,
he said: I might one day kill Utes
        if I should marry him.

six

Douglas I had connection with
once and no more. His children told me
I had to be a Ute squaw that night;
I expect Douglas wanted all
to be ready for him. I would be killed
if I did not submit, they said.
Douglas himself made up my bed.
Then the men sat and talked till midnight,
and then as soon as they had gone
Douglas came in to where I lay.
One great advantage of it was,
he was protection for me later
when others asked me to sit down
in their tents; I would tell them, No
for I was Douglas's squaw, and that
        kept them away from me.

What Josie said
Behind her ingenuous and sober
rigidity for the official occasion
her fire glimpsed once or twice.

one

Q.—In your opinion, the main
cause of this outbreak was,
on the one hand, the effort
of the government, through its Agent,
to civilize the Utes,
and on the other hand
the resistance of the Utes
to any such effort? A.—Yes, sir.

two

The Uncompaghre Utes
had given us much trouble;
they'd visit the Agency,
gather our Utes together
and insist that having them work
was a sort of whim of the Agent's,
it was not the government's wish
that they should work—indeed,
it was counter to regulations,
they said, for Utes to work.

three

On Sunday night a war-dance
was held at Douglas's camp.
It lasted most of the night;
and they were keeping a watch
over the Agency.
The Indians at first
had been much frightened; then
as the soldiers delayed their coming
we could see that the Indians
were growing more and more angry,
and they were all well-armed.
Father had thought to take us,
and the hired help, and go out
to the troops, then come in with them.
But he knew now he couldn't,
for the Agency and all
the goods placed in his keeping
would be destroyed, and he
would be held responsible
for everything there. Therefore
he decided to remain.

four

We suddenly heard firing.
I ran to the window and saw
the employees running off
in various directions,
and the Utes firing at them.
We gathered up the children
and went into the milk-house,
which was built against the kitchen,
bolted the outside door
and sat down on the floor.
We sat there all afternoon.
At intervals all would be quiet,
then firing would break out,
perhaps a dozen shots
or a half dozen. We saw
they were busy looting the goods,
and whenever they found a man
belonging to the Agency
they would shoot him. This kept up
till about five, when we found
that they had fired the house.

five

They called to us to stop
and Pah-sone called to me
and said, "You come to me;
no shoot you," and I said,
"You'd better not." I saw
that one had Mrs. Price,
and one had hold of mother.
They took us toward the river,
where each one had his loot
stacked up, and Pah-sone placed me
on some blankets he had stolen.

six

Pah-sone packed his things
on a government mule, and I
was put on a horse with May,
Flora Price's little girl,
behind me in a blanket.
An Uncompaghre Ute
whom we had not seen before
took Flora. Just at dark
we started across the river.

seven

Pah-sone unpacked the blankets
and spread them for my bed
and made some for a pillow.
Two squaws danced at the foot
of the bed after I got in.
At a certain point in the song
all the men laughed. Pah-sone
sent them away with blankets.
Of course they were drunk. That night,
Pah-sone took me for his squaw.
    We did not dare refuse them
to any great extent.
Several times I pushed him off,
and made a fuss; Pah-sone
did not threaten me,
but once when I asked him
if he wanted to kill me,
he replied, "Yes." I said
"Get up and shoot me then,
and let me alone." He turned over
and did not say anything more
that night.
        It was done while his own

squaws were there in the tent,
and one of them told me
I must not make a fuss about it,
it was pretty good. I think
that she felt sorry for me
but that she did not dare
do anything for me.

Jane
What she of the garden-
discussion with Nathan Meeker
explained to Josie:

Well, I cannot help it
if these Utes want to take you.
We will give you enough to eat.
You will not starve with us.
If Pah-sone wants to protect you
I cannot help it.

Flora Price
Flora's the wife
of Shadrach the plowman;
she is sixteen
and mother of May
and the baby, Johnnie.
—A girl, as Josie
and Arvilla are women.

one

The bullets whizzed by my head.

two

A squaw came up and took
my little boy from the horse
and cried over him like a child.

three

They spread some blankets for me
but I could not sleep.
The moon shone very bright
and everything looked ghastly.

four

I want to have those Utes
taken and killed, and I want
the privilege of killing Johnson
and that Uncompaghre Ute
        myself.

PART III

LEAVE-TAKING

~

U.S. Congress: House Miscellaneous Document 38
"Testimony in Relation to Ute Outbreak,
Taken by Committee on Indian Affairs
Washington, 1880"
Docs. Sec., Ser. Set. 0925

~

From the dark of the stacks
and a half century
with other ones waiting
with their names on their backs
behind a locked grating—
fetched out for me

by an old lady
with a lively gray eye
and a fine-featured face
(the muse of the place),
its binding gives way
each time it's opened,
a dried-out tendon
in the spine snapping,
or the old glue cracking
and a dead scent flowing
from the thing (it lingers
in leather so dry
it sheds crumbs and flakes
that cling to my fingers)
and the cardboard showing
at the corner breaks,
and a yellowy brown
damp-stain sunken down
through the brittle pages—
it gave me my Meekers
in the words they say,
gave me Hayt, Pitkin, Byers,
Chipeta, Ouray,
my sometimes truth-speakers,
my whole- and half-liars
(and each one sincere)—
and these others I'll mention
who were bound in together
and share their detention
with my people by chance
and, in that same year's weather,
were occupied elsewhere
and far otherwise,
so that the events
in far off White River
would have shared their attention
with many another:

~

Here is the Pittsburgh Chamber of Commerce
petitioning for Federal aid
in "improving the Ohio River."

And here, against the Commissioners
of the District of Columbia,
are set forth charges of malfeasance
involving forged certificates.

And one Henry Voelter applies
for an extension of his patent
for reducing wood to paper pulp
(diagrams of his machinery;
testimony, for and against).

Here is the settlement of a claim
of Beales, Nobles, and Garrison
against the government of Venezuela.
It concludes: "I therefore reduce
the indemnity to be awarded
in favor of the above-named claimants,
to two hundred and fifty thousand
hard dollars; and so I decide it."

Here are some of the goings on
in the corporate intelligence
of the National Academy of Sciences:
H. Draper, "On Photographing
Spectra of the Stars." J. Dalton,
"Some Observations on the Structure
of the Human Brain." J. Newberry,
"On Some Interesting Deposits
of Gold and Silver in Utah."
S. Alexander, "On a Direct
and Simple Method of Ascertaining

the Ellipticity of the Terrestrial
Spheroid." O. Rood, "Our Memory
for Color and Luminosity."
A. Guyot, "Some Remarks on a New Map
of the Catskill Mountains." T. LeConte,
"Mean Pressure of the Atmosphere
over the United States, at Different
Seasons in 1879."

~

—Which makes my people
seem distant and small,
left as much to themselves
in their life agonies
as they are on the shelves,
once more put away
from the day's light and air
with others in there
from other done ages....

Book Three
About the Destruction of Souls and Selves

... Then flush the world in earnest. Let yoursel' gang,
Scour't to the bones, and mak' its marrow holes
Toom as a whistle as they used to be
In days I mind o' ere men fidged wi' souls,
But naething had forgotten you as yet,
   Nor you forgotten it.

                —HUGH MACDIARMID,
                  PRAYER FOR A SECOND FLOOD *

PIAH

I

Is a self
so precious, Piah? I think sometimes
a self is an unnecessary growth, a kind

of wart, at best
harmless, not too unsightly—irritated
it will grow troublesome, at last maybe malignant.

Or sometimes it is
an instrument, to be rightly proud of,
that works well, is even perhaps attractive and amusing—

or even an article
of some elegance and beauty; to be
dismantled or discarded, though, if it becomes

**Toom is empty, fidged is moved.*

in 'this world of fleeting
trials and choices,'* out of place
or out of date, a piece of outsize bric-a-brac—I know selves

that should be, like some great
and now elaborately ugly Nootka woodcarving,
propped in the ethnic room of a dusty provincial museum....

But commonly a self
is a more modest thing, something improvised
by the spirit, over a stretch of some years, for daily use—

use that's no easier
on it than on any other implement;
scratches, corrosion, dented and mended places in time

may give it its pathos
and dignity—some old carpenter's tool, handle
broken and taped, blade nicked but smooth and bright still.

All this says nothing of
the temporary selves made for special
occasions, and sound and true for their purposes,

or of that self of selves
which is like those marine creatures
made up of different animals, no one kind

able to survive apart,
each kind providing in its own way
for all the others—a Portuguese man-of-war of a Self!...

*The quoted phrase is Churchill's.

—'The Utes
with the pious Piah at their head,'
wrote William Byers in his Denver paper

'held a scalp dance
last evening near Sloane's Lake,
over three bloody Cheyenne topknots,

which dangled
from three poles. (It was
disgusting to notice among the spectators

ladies prominent
in church and society circles
straining for a sight of the reeking scalps.)'

How it was
to be Piah: head of a minor band
never settling on what to call yourselves—

sometimes
you were White River Utes,
Uncompaghres sometimes, Denver Utes for that summer

(lured there
along with other sub-chiefs, by officials
busy at weakening Ouray's hold on the Utes)

knocked this way and that
in Ute and Ute-White politics
it was no part of your purposes to understand—

'Me great warrior,'
you tell the Governor, 'warriors no plow.
Me go to Washington and see John Grant.

He no work.
He no build White House. He
warrior like me. Tell you what, McCook.

You ask John Grant
to come here. We fight Arapahos,
and kill plenty braves and catch plenty squaws'—

pure innocence
(unlike Jack's 'Indian no work' rhetoric, used
on white officials to get him where he wanted to go next week),

it makes me think of Yeats
writing wistfully from the height
of the magisterial self he made, 'I now can but share with a friend

my thoughts and my emotions
and there is a continual discovery
of difference, but in those days, before I had found myself,

we could share adventures.'
So: to share adventures would be
enough, and as for the self, let that be sheer

decoration! with the serious
exuberance of regalia, shapely
as flames and authoritative as the flashing

of light from Hector's helmet! And
we find you, mentioned in passing,
a secondary figure at conferences and commissions;

lined up with others
beside your constant enemy
Ouray, for the official government photographer;

halted and turned back
by soldiers patrolling Middle Park
from the hot springs you had always visited;

in the scrape that followed
your damaging some ranch equipment,
disarmed by a posse, one of your band shot;

pinched off, blocked,
maneuvered (seated there with Ouray,
your eyes averted, feelings divided, thinning out),

and yet blazing back
(glimpsed in one chronicle as you threaten
with a buggy whip a member of the Treaty Commission of 1880),

and then this: 'It was
a favorite Indian campground,'
says the rancher, 'and I had not much more

than got settled with my cattle
when Piah and his band paid me a visit.
The squaws would come to the house and ask for sugar.

My trail led through their camp
when I would come back from town after dark;
the dogs would bark, but the Utes paid no heed to my passing.

They usually were chanting
in the teepees, and when I would dismount and go in,
they would quit, and then resume activities when I left.

Sometimes they would chant
till nearly midnight, and we could hear them
distinctly at the ranch house. One time I slipped down,

and got where I could see
into a lodge, and I saw one buck Indian
crawling in a circle, with bucks and squaws around him,

and another Indian
was chanting a weird, wild song. I took it
to be some sort of ceremony, but did not understand its meaning.

As time passed and the Utes
gave no sign of breaking camp, and the grass
was getting short because of the large herds of horses they had,

I asked Piah to move camp.
Piah said, "This old Indian campground,
for long, long, time. You move." I said, "Indian ponies

eat all the grass. You move
over on Willow Gulch. Good grass there."
Piah said, "No. You go Willow Gulch. This old Ute campground."

I told him I would write
the Indian agent if he did not leave.
"All right, you write." Piah said. In a few days

I had the Agent's letter,
telling Piah to move. "He say that?"
Piah says. "Yes. Here is the letter." "All right, Ute go."

And in a jiffy
they had broken camp and gone,
trailing their teepee poles behind their horses, as is their custom.

A year or two later,
no more Agency permits were granted,
and no more Utes troubled any ranchman on the plains.'

Then this, in a paragraph
on the aftermath of the massacre,
a historian detailing the fates of some sub-chiefs:

'… Kaneache was killed
by lightning. Shavano was shot in '86
by a friend. Piah committed suicide in '88.'*

Toward the end, Piah,
going to nothing, wonderingly feeling yourself go
vaporous, at first a little along the edges, Piah, warrior:

not for you
to dwell in a kind of cyst
in somebody else's body politic,

all occasion
for action having vanished
and what's left to you mere activity.…

At the end, old self, not
to have grown venerable, not to be an old
implement of the spirit, homely, shiny with use, in a bygone style:

but going to nothing,
Piah, pure Indian, warrior to vapor! Gone! And
the regalia of the self, discarded, torn, broken, scattered

some piece of it
lodged rotting by a stream in the alder roots,
some stained feather stuck among the rubbish after the thaw. Piah.

Who could have said
with a poet I have just read
I too am flame, ablaze on the hills of Being.**

*The historian is Sprague.
**The poet is Patrick Kavanaugh.

JACK

In photographs the light flashes
    Off his big cheekbones
Which are as definite as fists
    While his eyes flash
With their different light, looking out
    At the quick, hard
Movements of his own world.
    He is not a sufferer.

Sure of himself, for the reason
    That he has thought out
And made for himself—made by hand
    You could say—a weapon of a self,
A self for hard use. He named
    Himself—Nicaagat,
Who appeared from out of the desert westward
    One spring, and joined the Utes.

Some say he had White blood, some
    That he was part Mexican
Or Paiute or Apache. Sold as a boy
    By the Ute chief Walkara
(The one who castrated the boys he sold
    To Navajos for placid herdsmen)
To a Mormon family. They raise him—take him
    To church, send him to school.

Get him a job: six months
    Driving an ice wagon
In Salt Lake City and he vanishes
    To reappear the Ute
He remained to the end. Such a man
    And the world are brothers wrestling.
He does not forget which of the two of them
    Is the elder and will win.

Be a Ute for all you're worth.
      Marry a Ute wife,
Take your people each year into the mountains
      For the hunting, summer and fall;
Trading and (no purist) rations in winter;
      Fight the Sioux (with Crook—
'Jack's callous ferocity startled
      Even Crook's veterans');

Dance the Bear Dance, dance
      The war dance and sing
Its one word song the tribe name
      tsiuta all night long,
Slow the Whites down with words:
      You come see about dis.
Why all dese soldiers want to see too?
      Ain' no trouble dere.

You come. I show you Meeker
      Ain' beat up. Lot of soldier
Come to Agency, women get scared,
      Children get scared,
Young men maybe dey want to fight.
      Old ones say No fight,
But maybe young men don't hear
      Old men—then trouble.

When the troops come on anyway
      Slow them down with bullets.
And when more troops come on
      Use words once more, gain a month,
Gain half a year.… When the tribe
      Is driven out at last
From its country, when the Ute self's broken,
      Not to break along with it.

No, be separate again, be one Ute,
    If that is possible—a teamster
Once again. Then some soldiers, questions
    And a sudden argument
About a horse theft and 'Jack was wounded
    As he ducked into a teepee.
When the soldiers pulled down the teepee
    Jack ran into another.'

I remember him by what it took to kill him.
    'He was protected from our bullets
By bales of robes and rawhides.
    He fired his carbine and killed
Sergeant Casey. I then caused a shell
    From a mountain howitzer
To be fired into the teepee in which Ute Jack
    Was barricaded, killing him.'

A BUNDLE OF COLOROW'S THINGS

HIS PIPE

It lies in a glass case,
the bowl cut from red stone
rubbed smooth, the stem
carved of some pale wood.
on the stem's upper surface
a tortoise, a deer's head,
two ears of corn
laid side by side, and
the head of a mountain goat,
all in a row, spaced evenly
in high relief, each detail
clear-edged. From the dead
air of the case the pipe
calls up in its workmanship
a carver hunched with his knife

on a sunny winter morning
in a quiet so intent
he does not know he is happy.

HIS PICTURE

A huge face. Wide heavy cheekbones
and big hacked-out looking nose,
tired intelligent glittery eyes—
glittery as black grease. A sharp-cut
straight wide sulking mouth.
Beneath the lower lip and the cheekbones
emphatic black shadow, counterpart
of the light aglare against his forehead.
A willful face, an eager face.

~

DIGRESSION: A PICTURE NEXT TO HIS

A young Ute wrapped to his eyes
In a new blanket,
A fresh feather shooting forward
From his glossy black hair,
The whole person under that feather
Held in absolute stillness. Inscription,
In an elegant lady's hand, with ink
Gone gray with age: A Good Ute.

~

COLOROW IN *THE DENVER POST*

In '88, the year before he died:
'The Whites have asked for Colorow's removal
And the latter persists in staying on the ground.
He is by nature ugly and mean-tempered

And cannot be scared off or bluffed away.
This, coupled with his notion that he owns
The land, which has become a passion with him,
Has made it very unpleasant, and at times
Dangerous for the settlers.'

HIS SMALL JOKE IN A UTE COUNCIL

…The old man said to the whites:
All right, we give you some land
For your presents, only
You must take it away with you.
We do not want your land
Lying around over our country.

HIS ANCESTRY

His father was
a Comanche, his mother
a Jicarilla Apache.

WHAT SOME SAID HAPPENED TO HIM ONE DAY

Carl Adams, the man
who was born Karl Schwanbeck,
kicked Colorow downstairs
for waving a revolver
and calling the Governor
liar, damn liar, goddamn liar.

WHAT HE DID AT MILK CREEK

When the soldiers crossed over
the Reservation line, the Utes
met their advance and stopped it.
And then Colorow, the clown

with the enormous belly,
showed the Utes the way to hold
the soldiers inside the pits
they had dug when caught in the open—
hold them there breathing the stench
of their own dead horses,
and no water, tasting their own sweat
in the glare of the hot sand-flat.

MR. WOLF LONDONER'S COLOROW STORY

When I kept store in California Gulch
Colorow used to come in for some trading,
And I'd ask him to dinner, being afraid
If I didn't he might take our scalps. One time
He came with five squaws, and they ate and ate.
Colorow'd take a spoonful of soup, and spit.
Spit alongside the table, a villainous thing,
But I durst not say a word. When they were finished
Colorow mumbled something in Indian
And one of the squaws gave a buckskin to my wife.
She hardly knew what it was or what to do with it.
I was in the office later when Colorow
Came back. He was a terribly big Ute—
Blocked out the light and darkened the whole front.
He stood there holding his stomach with both hands.
I was a little afraid, about the dinner.
He said, 'Heap sick.' I said, 'Been drinking whiskey?'
'No, eat too much. Want doctor.'—'Doctor's gone,'
I told him. He said, 'You give me medicine.'
Now I was kind of scared. I did not know
But what he would go for me. I thought the best
I could do would be to give him some Epsom salts.
I knew it wouldn't kill him. I got a cup
And filled it, nearly, and he had a hard time
To get it down, and had to take a great deal

Of water with it. Then he went away.
Next morning, going down to the gulch
For a pail of water, I met my friend coming up.
He must have weighed 275, usually,
But now he looked like an umbrella cover.
We stopped, I thought I had better face the music.
'No good. White man heap bad.'—'Why, Colorow,
What is the matter?'—'Pretty near die. Want doctor.'
I helped him up to the store. Then I fetched the doctor,
And when I told him what the trouble was,
He said, 'How much did you give him, for _____ sake?'
'I gave him a tin cup full,' I said. He said,
'Why that was enough to kill an elephant.'
'Well,' said I, 'it hain't killed Colorow.'

~

    … Everybody's Indian,
    Even the Indians',
    Old many-souls!
    How many times
    Defeated (and the soul—
    That temporary product
    Of an obstructed spirit—
    Discharged like a breath, and the mind
    Gone oddly quiet, as in
    The aftermath of a burst of rage),
    Only to turn up elsewhere
    Unexpectedly
    In full force
    To the end, with the old
    Abrupt talent
    For getting into action!

    To die of old age
    In your own lodge,
    And on the White River

(Oh, far downstream, in Utah)—
Of the many souls
This last one, so light,
Like a puff of smoke!
Going up in stillness
Out of the hacked-out
Huge old self, that had been
So much photographed
For the papers;
That had supplied them,
And the Utes, also,
With the materials
For so many stories;
And that was a good, workable
Ute self, now
Lying still for once,
And solid, heavy; yes,
As if it had been fashioned
With chisel and hand axe
From a tree trunk.

NATHAN MEEKER

You again.—I again, though
This time I've come to listen.
—To be here for the hanging
of your picture beside those
of your old Indian friends.
—Hanging, you say.—I'll get on
with it, since I think you were
the pure White man as Piah
was the pure Ute.—And naive
as Piah, no doubt.—But that's
a compliment. It's naive
to care for life as you did,
both of you.—For doing things,

is what you mean.—Toward the end,
when you had all those reasons …
—Say they were decorations
like Piah's feathers.—You know
they were not. Piah's feathers
he wore to catch in headlong
action the play of the light,
or, to be solemn, the Light;
but you were …—Oh, I was balked.
We were overloaded souls
toward the end, Utes and I both …
it's your light soul that will last
a lifetime, that can no more
be hurt than a fly in flight
struck at with a board. Lucky
the man who can get along
without one altogether.
As I think Arvilla did,
by the way. She got along
with a neatly finished self
in which burned a steady fire
of a spirit. As for us—
we heavy souls *need* killing,
almost you could say, going
so out of balance with things …
and then, a soul's dignity
is brief, the world outlasts it.…
—I put this in my notebook:
"From his seventeenth year," says
the D.A.B., "Meeker was
a wanderer, changing homes
and vocations so often
that even his wife could not
remember, after his death,
when and why all the changes
had taken place. Ute agent,

lecturer on Fourier
and economic justice,
farmer, columnist, teacher,
founder of a colony,
Utopian novelist …"*
—Many-souls, like Colorow.
—I had that ready for you …
—Very well. And each one richer
than the force that baffled it.
—But not necessarily
richer than what lies behind
that force.—Well, that force alone,
blank-faced, is what the soul meets.
—The spirit, like love, is blind;
I question that the soul needs …
—Another matter. The world
itself is not *needed.* No,
the naivete you ascribe
to Piah and me goes well
with the hang of things. Desire's
the only thing worth having—
against the hard composite
of interlocking habits
the world would be without it.
Hang my picture among Jack's
and Piah's and Colorow's.

~

I suddenly remember
Meeker's reputation here
in Meeker, the town: for him
it's friendless territory.

*The title of Meeker's novel was *The Adventures of Captain Armstrong.*

The museum lady: 'Oh,
we reenact the massacre
every Fourth of July,'
with cheerful pride. 'Well, you see'
an old man told me, 'he lived
when Longfellow and them fellows
was writing, they were *idealists*,
he tried to turn these Indians
into farmers in a year,
about, and here it's taken
years, and they still aren't …' his voice
trailing off. And the lady:
'Mr. Meeker's grand-nephew
visited here (he's living
in Florida) and he said
Mr. Meeker's brothers thought
he might come to a bad end.
He was stubborn. Thought he knew
all the questions and all
the answers. So he said they
wasn't surprised when he was
murdered by the Indians.'

OURAY

A clear mind
and a liking for action.

When the brother of his wife Chipeta
tried to kill Ouray with a knife, for giving up

Ute land in a treaty,
Ouray broke the man's wrist and threw him in a ditch.

~

There being Whites
by the hundreds of thousands out here

and Utes
by the hundreds, to place the obvious

first, each time
he thinks, is his solitary distinction, and

crushing a Ute,
compromising with a White

impartially,
in honor of that first thought,

telling lies
to White commissioners, without hesitation

expelling the old chief
his adoptive father, when the old man would not

deal with the Whites—
what are these but tesserae in his mosaic

integrity
whom it suited Ute and White to call corrupt.

He had for company
Chipeta and his own accurate thinking.

~

In group photographs
it's always Ouray that sits, hands on knees, front and center,

fully there, solid,
alert, his gaze direct and ready to meet

with full attention
the attention of anyone looking at him here

as of—right now:
it is an expression that doesn't yield *anything*.

THE DEPARTURES FROM WHITE RIVER

EASTWARD

Eastward goes, by wagon
jolting over Yellowjacket Pass
and along Milk Creek, and winding
into the uplands to cross
the sage flats to Rawlins, then by train
over the high plains,
the smashed self
Nathan Meeker;
through the huge
matter-of-fact silence
of that country,
and no crowds
awaiting him along the way,
borne eastward home
or what will have to do
uninterestingly
for home, Greeley
and an official tombstone.

WESTWARD

Said the lieutenant,
The next morning,
shortly after sunrise,

we saw a thrilling
and pitiful sight.
The whole Ute nation
on horseback and on foot
was streaming by.
As they passed our troops,
their gait changed
to a run. Sheep
were abandoned, blankets
and personal possessions
strewn along the road,
women and children
were loudly wailing....

~

Some Ute
a long time after:

So you can turn
into a philosopher
for your own sake,
a derelict (your condition
cause for the formation
of many a commission—
so, for their sake, an occupation),
a political orator,
or all or some of these, me
wanting to be none of them,
nor an ethnic exhibit,
nor in a movie.
What it is
to come to
among the debris
and U.S. Government pre-fabs.
To dismantle your mind
as you walk away

rebuilding as you go
from pieces heaped up
so to speak
in your cupped hand. Sometimes
you find yourself being
intelligent. Maybe
a piece of knowledge
forms slowly.
What to do with it.
Sometimes there is
you connected with God
by emptiness. Ai!
This God does not breathe
and he is alive.
You are afraid.
You breathe in
a bleak freshness.

Book Four

____

A GATHERING OF SHADES

Once again silence, vagueness, a darkish atmosphere; in which after a few moments we hear jostling movements. Then voices grow audible, some heads and shoulders can be made out, becoming just darker than the dark they occupy, men distinguishable from women mainly by their hats. Meeker says, 'Ah. The successors.' Among them are the people who had been ready to reappear, in the predawn dark at the beginning, once Meeker himself had come forward, and who were displaced by the voice of an official. All official voices have long since lapsed back into the records and documents, and Meeker himself, it would seem, has pretty well had his say; not that he doesn't still seem willing to offer a comment on occasion, there being a certain eagerness about his continuing presence as he contemplates these who came after, into the country in which he died. Old, they are engaged in remembering, without nostalgia, and, as we listen, their remembering has something of that clearness, separateness, and belongingness in the dark, which the sound of crickets has on summer nights.

One of the old men speaking

—There shines in their
words that talent
for experience
one finds in
those who live
to tell such tales,
I say to Meeker.

… next morning we could look down
from Rogers mesa to the lower country.
One could not help thinking of the story
of the Promised Land. But we had no Moses
     along;
however, he only saw the promised land,
you will remember, and did not enter it.

He: Both tale
and experience
come by the way,
I think, to those
for whom life
is events. They
are participants.

But we all did. Near the Smith Fork
we found camps where Indians had been
a few days previous, their teepee poles
still standing, and little piles of rocks
in circular form as if children
had been playing there, and I fancy they had.

I say—A minor
but clear instance
of what is called
cultural assimilation and
differentiation.

Meeker—Well, well,
in any case,
all honor to Mr. Charley Grimes

An old woman remembers
we wore rubber boots to school
which we took off in the schoolroom
and put on moccasins made of buckskin.
One time we found an Indian mummy
tied in a tree. We brought it to the schoolhouse
but our teacher, Mr. Charley Grimes,
made us put it back in the tree.

And another
The summer of 1881, I remember,
we had good weather; beautiful days.
Then the fall and winter of that year
was long and cold. The snow was very deep.
Sometimes the wind blew all day from the
     north range.
We could see the beauty of the peaks
and we also knew what they could do.

I—Not an idea
in sight and every-
where the changing
lights and darks of
the truth—the
quiet remark
about the peaks,

the matter-of-fact
fear in their
admiration of them,

and her last remark
with its beauty
quite unplanned-for.

There was no tallow for candles.
None to be had. We lived by the light
the pitch wood made in the fireplace.
The evenings were so long and lonesome.
My brother George begged father
to play the fiddle all the time.
If father stopped to rest, the next thing
would be, 'Pa, I want to dance.'
We both danced to father's music.

An old man
… well, he put us to work,
me to skinning mules,
Duncan to a-whacking bulls,
and Smith to cooking.
We had to travel slow,
because they was bull teams, mule teams,
and horses, and all of us to go, you know.

—A life
as roaming
and loosely
articulated

(hear
its music)

as any Ute's.
Or as your own,
I say to Meeker.

He smiles
resignedly.

The voice fades, then drifts back
There was no road up White River,
we had a time getting up there.
Then we fellows throwed the wood in the river
and started driving it down.
I worked 48 days in that river,
wading. By the time we had all got down there
the boys had to quit. They got rheumatism,
the river knocked them out,
all but J.A. Duncan and myself.
Then the night we camped down there
it looked rainy and bad
and we made our bed under the wagon.
Duncan took nightmares in the night
and went to jump up
and cut a big gash in his head.

Fades, and drifts back again
… and we branded up 3,300 head of Lo7 cattle.
That is what gave Lo7 Mountain its name.
We turned cattle loose on that mountain.

—Sometimes,
I say to him,
it seems one sees
a difference:
The women give
how it was—

He says, To sense
as some of them do,
that a life comes out
in detail, and
attendant detail
in compositions
unforeseen,
makes for
a quick eye,
that's all.

And an old woman
We broke a wheel, made camp,
and stayed two days,
made a new wheel,
and I washed and ironed
and had quite a housekeeping time.
How about making a wheel
in the heart of the Rockies,
no tools and hard wood.
We camped in a little park
with plenty of water and grass
and such lovely pine trees.

*—and the men give
the bare structure*

of what they did

and inferred,

a skeleton of

events and gaunt

conclusions.

*I say, Earlier
I heard her declare,
'I was pretty nearly
scared to death—
I was always
a coward.' And
as one listens
one sees how
fearfulness can be
a form of
vivacity.*

And another old man
    Next day I climbed a hill
To look around, then I came back
And said: 'Boys, I can smell smoke.
    They're having a fight up north.'

    It doesn't sound reasonable
That you could smell powder fifteen
Miles away, but I did. Joe Rankin
    Has told me about the fight.

    Two weeks later,
On the way to White River we camped
One night on the battleground. The dead
    Were not buried very deep …

    … I sold my ranch on Collum Creek
To Gossard, the corset man,
So I could spend my winters
With my daughter in California.
This isn't an old man's country.

*Toward the rear, a woman has been speaking
somewhat more animatedly than the others*
… I was afraid, and I would start to cry,
and my brother would tell me to hush,
that he wasn't afraid—but I was!…

In late summer the grass on the landscape
turned yellow like a field of grain.
It looked beautiful to me—and it was.
There was a natural meadow there
but it was close up under
the Flat Top Mountains,
and the winters were frightful,

the snow would drift so deep.
We built a new house in a place
that the wind used to sweep bare,
right on the brow of the hill.
Say, did the wind blow there!

She pauses briefly, and another woman begins
speaking in a plain, definite manner, but the
first speaker, evidently not hearing her, has
resumed, and the other gives way

… Papa was an insurance agent,
civil engineer, had studied law,
and had studied some medicine.
He surveyed all the first roads,
ditches, and ranch boundary lines
all through that country.
He was also Justice of the Peace.
When anybody was sick in that country
they sent for him, there were no doctors.
His medical supplies were kept in a box
eighteen inches long, twelve inches wide,
and six inches deep. It was partitioned
for vials of certain basic medicines.
He had aconite, and belladonna,
and other medicines. He would put a few drops
in half a glass of water, and give it
a teaspoon at a time, every half hour.
If the patient was real sick, he stayed
till they began to get better,
sometimes all night, or maybe longer.
My father delivered many a baby
in that country. I remember once
they sent for him to come over
on Red Dirt, somewhere. The snow
was deep, and he had to snow-shoe
ten miles to get there. He was gone

all night, and when he came home
he was snow-blind, had burned his eyes
and was in awful shape. As Justice of the Peace
Papa had to settle a good many quarrels.
Whenever anyone had a legal question
they brought it to him. For one lawsuit
involving some horses and cattle
they imported a lawyer from Red Cliff,
and Papa was judge. There was no jury.
I wanted to hear what was going on.
The stovepipe in the spare bedroom
had been changed, and a hole left,
so I laid on the floor upstairs
and listened to the trial going on.
I remember one day coming home
and a bunch of men who broke the game laws
had been brought before Papa. One man
talked a long time and almost cried.
They fined him and then suspended his sentence.
In those days people came in here
and shot any game they wanted.
They took it out or left it,
just as they pleased. Lots of deer and elk
were killed just for the head and horns.
So they began to have game laws.
Papa was on the election board,
and they had the elections at our house
before the school house was …

Though she continues, her voice gradually
recedes, the voice of the woman who had
earlier begun to speak emerges
I was going to tell you about the time
Chief McCook made a search for Ouray's bones—

I asked him, 'Did you find them?'
He said, 'Too many snows.'
'Do you think you found the place
where he was buried?' I asked,
'And how do you know for *sure?*'
He said, 'Indian boys *so high*'
and he put his hand just above his waist.
'Boys cut horses and crows in the rock.
Now crows and horses very high.
Ground wash away.' Again
he used his hands to show me.
I said, 'You found no grave.'
'Oh, too many snows. Too much
agua. No, grave gone.
Maybe so coyote get arm bones,
and bear get head. All vamoose.'

Book Five

WE LOOK IN ON THE LIVING

The fit of remembering
has spent itself, the old ones
have gone back into their dark,
the night smells of meadows drift
in the pre-dawn air currents,
we can hear cattle stirring.
We are standing near a sign
at the edge of the valley,
a bend of the White River
shines gray in the black meadows
and the few stars, far apart,
look small now, and inactive;
and it is Nathan Meeker
who is remembering now—
rather, coming to the end
of remembering. He says,
'What a slight thing the end is
or rather the after-end.
One visits the stone, maybe
there's a little clear vapor
of a presence standing up
in the consciousness, over
the incised name.—Small boulders,
for Ouray, in a loose heap.
And the end itself—for me,
when the Ute bullet entered
my forehead it was a burst
of light, soundless, and then
immensely high, separate,
silent.

The sound of the shot
arrived after I was dead,
so I only speak of it
as a certainty, and not
from experience, which is—'
(and here he glances at me)
'something I no longer have,
though I can understand it.'
—'But isn't that sufficient?
After all, to understand
is what we are put here for;
high authorities say so—
Plotinus declares that earth
is strife of opposites, *while
in the condition of fire*
(which is where, as I gather,
the bullet transported you)
is all music and all rest.'
And he: 'For the exhausted
and distraught. However, when
composed and rested … lacking
one's circumstances, not least
belly to feed and bare hide
to find coat and britches for
and hands to grip with—reduced
to being at most a mere
spirited argument, still
one would like to be present
for what is going to happen.
I'd like to have heard that shot.'
—'Though the end is a slight thing,'
I remind him. And he says,
in a remote, subdued way
that's new to me: 'Life itself,
you know I am well aware,
can look to be a slight thing,

pathetic, to its desires
about itself; by itself,
though, it fills the view, there is
nothing else, eh? *Do not talk*
soothingly of death to me
in this gloom, says the great shade
in Hades to the live man,
in your gleaming gear. Sooner
work for a destitute serf
than rule all the used-up dead.'
'It's getting light,' I remark.
'Light of three kinds,' Meeker says,
as he takes a look around,
'past, present, and future light:
a few stars still left over,
that ranch house light that came on
while I was quoting Homer,
and the east light—' 'We can see
what's lettered on the sign, now,'
I say. He reads, '*CROSS L RANCH*'
then spells: '*S - I - U - O - L*
Corporation of Meeker,
Colorado.' 'Well, we know
who owns it now—rather, what.'
I say, 'It's a sort of ghost,
a corporation being
incorporeal.' Meeker
shrugs and says, 'People have lived
enclosed in such ghost-creatures
wherever they have lived.' 'Well,'
I say, 'the name of this one
can't even be pronounced.' He:
'Oh, a pronunciation
will have been worked out somehow,
by the people needing one.'
The sun is about to rise.

The cattle have scattered out,
grazing in the flats. The light
in the ranch house is as pale
as the last of the stars were.
'I'm getting hungry,' I say.
'I'm ready to go to town
for breakfast.' He says, 'Yes, that….'

~

The Meeker Cafe is old,
high-ceilinged, roomy, and clean,
and busy now—the talk flows
quietly and easily,
without distinctions among
waitresses, customers, cook.
The atmosphere's of that prosy
habitual enjoyment
which those involved don't notice.
And many in here are men
in their fifties and sixties
who appear to have attained
a sort of charmed condition:
permanently unhurried,
and solid and affable
(though not unwary) they eat,
and light up pipes and cigars,
and talk, and listen, timeless
and thriving just as they are;
so unlike what Meeker was
with all his agitation
of ideas and projects.
A lean, brown old man comes in,
sits down briskly. The waitress:
'Well, have you got any news?'
He, as if to a question

completely unreasonable:
'No! I got no news at all.'
She declares, 'The only news
anybody has got is on
their selves, so no news gets out.'
And he: 'By God, only news
I have is on my own self.
And I ain't letting it out.'
Other talk in the background
of a gas leak in a house,
then a young woman standing
at the end of the counter,
a baby on her hip: '*He*
didn't care. He was thinkin'
about what other people
would think. I said, after I
got a few under my belt,
"What do I care?"' She says this
serenely, the baby sleeps,
and the motherly waitress
she talks to smiles musingly.
Meanwhile, I notice, Meeker
has never been so weakly
present as he is in here.
He looks dim and recessive,
not at all inclined to speak.

And that night at the cafe
while I eat at the counter
he watches the wet spring snow
that came on with the darkness,
falling outside the windows,
in wide, shaggy flakes. They stick
and slide down the glass; and I
watching them during a lull
in the talk, can hear them rap

on the window as a gust
drives against it; never mind
the snows of the past, this one
will do, that arrives melting,
the dry washes even now
run sorrel-red—including
that where Ouray's bones, maybe,
get turned up and rearranged,
tumbled smooth in the gritty
flow and re-buried yearly
further along in the sand.
A battered-up old cowboy
two places down stares at me—
he can't place me. Some ranch boys
in a booth raise a clamor
of barnyard noises, mooing
howling cackling oinking,
all embarrassed energy
in self-parody. No one
speaks of them but the waitress,
who says, 'My *goodness*.' Meeker
is taking in all the scene.
He turns and watches the old
cowboy get up and go out
head bent sidewise to the storm,
stiff-legged, slow, agonized,
and to-himself dignified,
all of him moving at once
(like the old man that Wordsworth
compared to a cloud moving)
his shape disintegrating
in the slant and swirl of snow.
A young rancher and his wife
at a table toward the rear
are feeding their two babies.
'Those two would have been the cream

of their high school crop,' I say,
and Meeker contemplates them
and nods. The pair seem poignant
somehow, she with her fine eyes
that innocently flash, he
absorbed, his movements crisp
and sure. I say, 'They don't know
what's hit 'em,' playing the seer
as only a spectator
can. I turn from watching them
to make a further comment
and see that Meeker's not here.
I sense the finality
in the air—he won't be back.
So. He's gone. I take a breath.
Well, goodbye, old companion.
I look around the cafe,
people eating and talking,
the wet snow spinning idly,
now, outside the windows, and
finish my meal and go out.

~

I sit writing letters
in the lobby of the broken-down
Meeker Hotel. The talk
of a bent old woman
and two old men,
desultory when I came in,
stopped some time back.
The buzz of a light fixture,
a sniff, a cough,
another cough. The TV set
stands gray and still.
More coughs. Silence.

Mounted heads of bear, deer,
elk, moose, occupy every
available space on the walls
above me, antlers decorate
the pillars and lintels,
against one pillar is an arm-chair
made entirely of antlers,
looking like some
instrument of torture. Below
the heads are mounted
photographs of still more game,
copies of early newspapers,
photographs of early-day
Meeker scenes—streams,
plateaus, mountains,
valleys—the whole
White River country
crowded into this one
stale room. Near the entrance
photographs of the Meekers,
of Ouray and Chipeta,
Colorow, Johnson, Jack;
on the wall opposite, hung
above the dead TV
a painting of the massacre
by a local hand. Meeker
lies front and center, outstretched
in the dirt. His naked
torso looks painfully white.
Later the talk starts up
led by the desk-lady—
chiefly of flying saucers
(she is a firm believer).
Talk lapses when a derelict
woman they know comes in
and tries, as they watch in silence,

to make a phone call,
fails to make her connection,
and then, not having so much as glanced
at any of us, re-enters
the snowy dark. They talk
of her marriages and divorces,
her several religious conversions
(which the desk-lady deplores),
her wanderings. Then one of the old men
declares, 'And she was once
a real good looker.' The other
after a long pause
looks out the window and says,
'I believe it's lettin' up....' And the first,
'Damn but she was a looker.'

~

When I finish my last letter
they have all long since retired.
I have the place to myself.
I step outside a moment.
The snow has stopped, the town
lies in the same stillness
as the low hills around it.
The cafe is closed and dark,
the streets are empty,
the buildings look small,
contracted hard
in the clear cold, under
the open starry sky.
I stay a moment longer,
feeling the cold
bite in, and watch the stars,
a great scattering,
variously flash and dim
over the country.

The poem owes a great debt to the two most recent studies of the White River uprising which I have consulted—the histories by Marshall Sprague (*Massacre: The Tragedy at White River*, Little, Brown and Co., 1957) and by Robert Emmitt (*The Last War Trail*, University of Oklahoma Press, 1954)—for many details and suggestions for understanding the events, as well as for the events themselves.

My acknowledgement of, and tribute to, my main source for the material in Book Two appears in the form of a lyric that begins on page 375.

Two passages in Book Three, and the monologues in Book Four, are adapted from passages in certain of the often quite wonderful recollections and memoirs printed over the years in *The Colorado Magazine*, official publication of the State Historical Society of Colorado. Specifically:

The rancher who speaks in 'Piah' in Book Three is A.K. Clarke; his memoir, "The Utes Visit My Ranch on the Plains," is in *The Colorado Magazine*, August 1928, 144;

Wolf Londoner's Colorow story in Book Three is adapted from his "Colorow Dines Out," *The Colorado Magazine*, May 1931, 93–94;

In Book Four, the first monologue is adapted from "Early Days at Paonia," by Ezra G. Wade, *The Colorado Magazine*, March 1927, 66;

the second, from "Childhood Memories of Kittie Hall Fairfield," as told to Margaret Isaac, *The Colorado Magazine*, October 1959, 293;

the third, from "Pioneering on the St. Vrain," by Zerelda Carter Gilmore, *The Colorado Magazine*, July 1961, 214;

the fourth, from E.P. Wilbur's "Reminiscences of the Meeker Country," *The Colorado Magazine*, September 1946, 200;

the fifth, from "Pioneer Life," by Mrs. Daniel Witter, *The Colorado Magazine*, August 1928, 144;

the sixth, from "Experiences in the Bear River Country in the Seventies," by Joseph S. Collum, *The Colorado Magazine*, July 1934, 153;

the seventh, from "We Move to Egeria Park," by Mary Adella King Wilson, from recollections which Mrs. Wilson recorded on tape and which were transcribed by her daughter, Mrs. Hazel W. Hanson; this article appeared in *The Colorado Magazine*, April 1963, 121;

the eighth, from "Our Ute Indians," by Mrs. W.G. King, *The Colorado Magazine*, April 1960, 128.

I have sometimes transferred to the White River country experiences that took place elsewhere in the region but could very well have happened there. Regarding Mrs. King's account of the whereabouts of Ouray's bones, I suppose I should add that, for all its definiteness, this version is, alas, only one of several in a controversy that went on for some time.

The lyric by the anonymous Ute on page 334 ('*A Ute, unidentified*') is made out of a prose statement by an unnamed Ute quoted on page 119 of "The Southern Ute of Colorado," by Marvin K. Opler, in *Acculturation in Seven American Indian Tribes*, Ralph Linton, editor, D. Appleton-Century Co., 1940. Meeker's subsequent reference to Heraclitus was suggested by one of Opler's comments on the statement by the Ute.

The lines which serve as the epigraph to Book Three form the fourth stanza of Hugh MacDiarmid's 'Prayer for a Second Flood,' in *A Lap of Honour*, published by The Swallow Press.

Certain further acknowledgments—of sources for particular passages or phrases—are made in footnotes at appropriate points in the text itself.

Book One and the Prologue to Book Two appeared first in a considerably different version in *The Denver Quarterly*, Summer 1971.

A selection from 'A Bundle of Colorow's Things' appeared in *Spectrum*, Spring 1975.

A NOTE ON PIAH

Piah in his regalia is a man of action, and not to be associated with esthetes like those young men of a tribe near the center of the Sudan who, E.H. Gombrich reports, 'spend a good deal of their time decorating their own and each other's bodies with colored earth, renewing or changing the elaborate designs as soon as they get smudged. Here as elsewhere it is the women who do the work....' (Gombrich quotes a solemn and sinister Marxist opinion of the young men's occupation: 'It is probably not in the national interest of new socialist states that art traditions such as these survive.')

Index of First Lines

About the Author

Alan Stephens was born December 19, 1925, in Greeley, Colorado. He grew up on the family farm there, and served in the U.S. Army Air Corps. Thanks to the G.I. Bill, he attended Colorado State Teacher's College (now the University of Northern Colorado), the University of Colorado at Boulder, the University of Denver, and the University of Missouri. He received bachelor's and master's degrees from DU, and a Ph.D. from Missouri.

Stephens taught English at Arizona State University from 1954 to 1960, with a year at Stanford on a fellowship (1956–1957). He joined the faculty at the University of California, Santa Barbara, in 1960 and remained there until his retirement in 1989, except for a year at DU (1967–1968). He was a founding faculty member of the College of Creative Studies at UCSB.

He was married for 60 years to Frances Stephens. They raised three sons. He died July 21, 2009, at home in Santa Barbara. He may be found in his verses.

Editor's Note

This collection includes all the poems published after the early 1960s, and selections from Stephens's first two books, *The Sum* (1958) and *Between Matter and Principle* (1963). The selections are taken mostly from his own choices for republication in *In Plain Air* (1982), and from an unpublished manuscript he compiled in the late 1990's, titled *Late in the Day*.

The epigraph at the front of this book is taken from "Anniversary Sequence," a poem in *The Sum*.

The books are presented in reverse chronological order, for the most part. The major exception is *White River Poems* (1976), which appears last; its long narrative form sets it apart. Also, because Part I of *Goodbye Matilija* (1992) is made up of poems that appeared in *Water Among the Stones* (1987), the *Water* poems come first, followed by Part II of *Goodbye*, then the *Stubble Burning* poems that were published in the interim (1988).

Other changes in sequence were necessary to avoid duplication. The poem "Three Studies from Two Days" in *Away from the Road* (1998) was originally "Four Studies," including "An early spring day ..." from *The White Boat* (1995). The *Stubble Burning* chapbook included the Sophocles lines in *Away from the Road*, a number of poems in *The White Boat* ("Martial of Bilbilis," "Old Man Afraid," "The Clubman," "The Morning of Glenn Gould's Funeral," "So-and-so Reassesses Yeats," "Professor Bath's Talk on Shakespeare's Sonnets," "Geron the Heron"), and "To My Matilija" in *Water Among the Stones*. *In Plain Air* included selections from *Tree Meditation and Others* (1970), *Between Matter and Principle*, and *The Sum*. And *Tree Meditation* included versions of *The Heat Lightning* poems (1967), except for "Second Evening" and "Unattended."

Stephens revised some of the poems that reappeared in later books and in the *Late in the Day* manuscript. His revisions were always slight, except for omissions from *The Heat Lightning*, a very limited edition, when selections were republished in *Tree Meditation*. From all the variants, I have chosen what seemed to me the best versions, favoring the originals when in doubt. In some poems, I accepted certain revisions but not others.

There are some changes in punctuation, spelling, and italicization, but I have preserved Stephens's idiosyncratic use of single quotation marks. In a few poems I revised phrasing a little, or deleted a word or a short passage. These revisions were based on an early manuscript (the sonnets "The Other Runner" and "50 continued"), on revisions Stephens penciled into his copy of *Goodbye Matilija* ("Dream Vision," "After-words"), or on my judgment of what he would have welcomed ("The Open World," "The Summer," "Elegy: The Old Man," "Tree Meditation," "Third Deposition," "And the Fat One …," "After-words," "Study of Wild Oats #2," "The Clubman," "The White Boat," "Under Cricket Music"). In making that difficult judgment, and in other respects, I was glad to have the counsel of John Wilson, John Ridland, Tim Stephens, Robyn Bell, Bob Blaisdell, and Jace Turner.

I thank Dan Stephens as well, for his brotherly support.

A.A.S.

www.ingramcontent.com/pod-product-compliance
Lightning Source LLC
Chambersburg PA
CBHW021220060726
47590CB00005B/1574

9780985781200